Reading and *Writing*
GENRE
with **Purpose**
in K–8 Classrooms

Nell K. Duke

Samantha Caughlan

Mary M. Juzwik
Michigan State University

Nicole M. Martin
*University of North Carolina
at Greensboro*

Reading and Writing GENRE

with Purpose

in K–8 Classrooms

HEINEMANN
Portsmouth, NH

Heinemann
361 Hanover Street
Portsmouth, NH 03801–3912
www.heinemann.com

Offices and agents throughout the world

The authors and publisher wish to thank those who have generously given permission to reprint borrowed material:

Figures 1.1 and 1.2: From *Language Stories and Literacy Lessons* by Jerome C. Harste, Virginia A. Woodward, and Carolyn L. Burke. Copyright © 1984 by Jerome C. Harste, Virginia A. Woodward, and Carolyn L. Burke. Published by Heinemann, Portsmouth, NH. Reprinted by permission of the authors.

Figure 1.3: FIBERONE® is a registered trademark of General Mills, Inc. and is used with permission.

Figure 1.3: Goldfish coupon courtesy of Fish Doctors, Canton, MI.

(credits continue on page x)

Library of Congress Cataloging-in-Publication Data
Reading and writing genre with purpose in K–8 classrooms / Nell K. Duke . . . [et al.].
    p. cm.
  Includes bibliographical references and index.
  ISBN-13: 978-0-325-03734-9
  ISBN-10: 0-325-03734-5
  1. English language—Composition and exercises—Study and teaching. 2. Literary form—Study and teaching. 3. Language arts. I. Duke, Nell K.

  LB1576.R412 2011
  372.6'044—dc23   2011025128

Acquisition editor: Wendy Murray
Developmental editor: Margaret LaRaia
Production: Lynne Costa
Cover and text designs: Lisa Anne Fowler
Typesetter: Gina Poirier Design
Manufacturing: Steve Bernier

Printed in the United States of America on acid-free paper
15 14 13 12 11   PAH   1 2 3 4 5

Dedication

To my mentors, especially Vicki Purcell-Gates and P. David Pearson, with unending gratitude—*NKD*

To Jerry and Kate Caughlan, my models for engagement with the world —*SC*

For Julia Maudemarie Ferkany—*MMJ*

To all the teachers in my life, including most importantly my parents and my mentors, Nell Duke, Mary Juzwik, Sam Caughlan, Carol Sue Englert, Doug Hartman, and Pat Edwards—*NMM*

Contents

Acknowledgments

First and foremost, we thank the educators and students whose work is featured in this book. Their intellectual rigor, creativity, engagement in their work, and willingness to take risks allow theory and research to come alive.

We thank as well the many administrators who have supported these educators in their work, even when, perhaps especially when, it was outside the box. A special thanks to Kathy Peasley of the Grand Ledge School District, whose leadership was invaluable to this book.

The original inspiration for this book came from a conversation during a meeting of the Principal Investigators of the Literacy Achievement Research Center. We thank the Center and the Michigan State University Research Excellence Funds that have supported it.

We are grateful to editor Wendy Murray for her work on the early stages of this book—for having faith in us and the possibilities of a new book on genre. We thank editor Margaret LaRaia for seeing us through the later stages of the book's development—for her vision and skillful balance of push and patience. Thanks are also due to Alan Huisman, who often helped us to say in four words what we had said clumsily in fourteen. And Kate Montgomery deserves thanks for ensuring that we were always well taken care of. We have been blessed to work with such a powerhouse team of editors.

This book has many and varied graphical elements. We are so appreciative of the talent and care that Lisa Fowler has put to the task of designing the book. We are also grateful to the production team, led by Lynne Costa, for seeing our manuscript through to publication.

We thank marketing, now and in advance, for helping us sell the book on our terms.

Finally, we thank our families. Nell thanks Julia and Cooper for their inspiration and Dave for his understanding. Sam thanks Steve for keeping us on an even keel through yet another rewrite. Mary thanks Maudemarie for offering wondrous opportunities to witness narrative language development in action and Matt for forgiving her worsening housekeeping. Nicole thanks Jeff for his enthusiasm, willingness to listen, and tolerance for late meals and nights.

Nell   Samantha

Mary   Nicole

Reading and Writing in a World of Varied Texts

After a couple of months in my writing workshop, I'm bored and my students are too.

I spend a whole marking period on each genre, but even then my students don't seem to get it.

I teach genre features, but then all my students' writing sounds the same. They're just following a formula. Sometimes what they write doesn't even make sense.

I spend the whole year teaching the seven comprehension strategies. It's not working. Students know the strategies—they can name them, they can explain them—but they don't use them.

Our informational reading scores on our state test are low every year. I've tried everything. I'm out of ideas.

These are the kinds of comments we hear from teachers about their reading and writing instruction. Teachers and students alike grow bored in a writing workshop that leaves what students write largely up to them without specifying a purpose, genre, or audience. Teachers who do teach genre in the writing workshop often report it either doesn't stick or sticks so well that students' writing becomes flat, formulaic, and uninspired. Teachers complain that their reading workshop doesn't engage the very students who most need help, or that they teach reading strategies—sometimes the same strategies students were taught the grade before—but find students don't apply these strategies during most of the reading they do. These problems can be addressed by approaching genre differently—with purpose.

Teaching Genre with Purpose

Above all, *teaching genre with purpose* means creating compelling, real-world purposes for students to use genres and then providing instruction in genre features and strategies to serve those purposes. Teaching students to write persuasive genres with purpose does not mean asking them to "pretend" that their school is considering requiring uniforms and then to write an "essay" about whether the school should or should not and why. Rather, teachers find a real issue facing the school (e.g., school funding), the community (e.g., a controversial development project), or the world (e.g., habitat destruction) on which students could write in a real persuasive genre (e.g., an online news-site editorial) to convince a real audience (e.g., readers of that news-site editorial page). Teachers teach characteristics of effective editorials to help students be more convincing for this specific purpose and audience in the short term. But students learn these characteristics better in the long term as well because they are using them to convince real readers.

The root cause of many of the problems reflected in the comments at the beginning of this chapter is that too many U.S. classrooms lack a colorful, compelling context for reading and writing. A pressurized atmosphere surrounding standards and testing has led teachers to feel they don't have time to plant their reading and writing instruction in a rich bed of purpose. Too often, students read a text because they are assigned to do so, not because they want, or even understand, what that text has to offer. Students write in a genre because it is assigned, not because they want to accomplish what that genre is well suited to do. Yet theory, research, and professional wisdom—indeed a long history of work by scholars and educators such as John Dewey, James Britton, Dorothy Heathcote, James Moffett, and Harold Rosen—all suggest that students learn better and more deeply when their learning is contextualized and genuinely motivated. The experience of teaching is also improved when the context of our teaching is more interesting and our students are more engaged. Teaching genre with purpose reinvigorates teaching.

Teaching genre with purpose is about replacing weaker practices with better ones. You'll still teach students to write how-to text and comprehend informational text, but you'll do so differently and more effectively. In this approach, you apply five basic principles to any genre you teach:

1. Design compelling, communicatively meaningful environments.

2. Provide exposure and experience.

3. Explicitly teach genre features.

4. Explicitly teach genre-specific or genre-sensitive strategies.

5. Offer ongoing coaching and feedback.

This book shows how these principles come to life in reading and writing projects (often using several genres simultaneously) in a diverse group of K–8 classrooms. Some we have led ourselves, others we have helped develop, still others teachers have created on their own. Some are elaborate, others require little time and effort. All of them place top priority on reading, writing, speaking, or listening to many genres for real purposes; with this goal in place, all else follows.

How Teachers Teach Genre with Purpose: A Glimpse into Some of the Projects We Share in This Book

- *Hattie Dornbush and her kindergartners created testimonials to convince preschoolers that they would love kindergarten (Chapter 6).*

- *Kate Roberts led the K–2 boys enrolled in a summer school program in writing animal guides for the local zoo (Chapter 4).*

- *Dawn Kennaugh and her fourth graders put on two plays to entertain their school (Chapter 5).*

- *Sheila Bell and her fifth graders created procedural texts to teach younger students how to keep their messy desks clean (Chapter 3).*

- *Carmela Rademacher and her K–8 English language learners created quilts and museum exhibits to share their family histories with others (Chapter 2).*

Why Teach Genre with Purpose?

There are many reasons to teach genre with purpose. We focus here on three.

Our Natural Predisposition to Learn and Use Genres

Human beings are innately capable of, even predisposed to, learning genres. An infant learns how to play peekaboo long before she can say a single word. A toddler pretending to be Mommy sounds like Mommy. The three-year-old who scribble-wrote the two texts in Figure 1.1 identified the first as a shopping list, the second as a story! The four texts in Figure 1.2—a birthday list, a letter, a map, and a story

Figure 1.1 Hannah, age 3, writes a shopping list and a story (Harste et al., 1984).

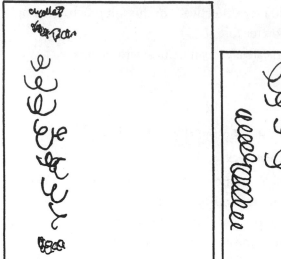

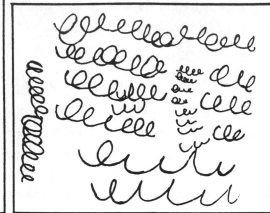

Figure 1.2 Four texts by a child about to enter first grade (Harste et al., 1984)

BIRTHDAY LIST
Melisa
Laura Guests
Tic-Tac-Toe
(Game to be played)
White Cake
Balloons

Mdllssa
Lauy
QA□x
WOAeT
BLAN

LETTER
Dear Mom
I
hope you
come back
Love
Steph
(Note:
Stephanie
decorated her
paper to look
like stationery.)

DARMOM
I
HOYOD
CemBA
LOVE
ste
ph

MAP FOR
BIRTHDAY
GUESTS TO
GET TO HER
BEDROOM
My Bedroom
Hallway
Door to
come in

mi BeDRm

DoRtol
CM^   HW^

STORY PAGE
My dad and me
was swinging
(Note: Quite
different
functions for
art in story
as opposed to
letter and
map.)

Mi DaD A Me
WAS SWee

page—were created by a child just before she entered first grade. Look at all she knows about genre! She knows that lists help us remember and group, that they are typically columns of short, topically related entries. She understands that a letter is a means of communication from one person to another and often begins with a greeting, such as "Dear Mom," followed by personal sentiments and then a closing. (She has even created stationery.) She understands that a map helps people locate or navigate. She has integrated the text and graphics of her map (typical for maps) but keeps the text and graphics on her "story page" largely separate (typical for stories).

Embedded in the practices of their culture, children readily observe patterns or regularities in language (or any symbol system). Educators need to capitalize on this predisposition and on students' own cultural know-how by exposing even young children to a broad array of genres and making genre a driving force in our teaching.

Advances in Genre Research and Theory

Research and theory from groundbreaking scholars such as M. A. K. Halliday and Ruqaiya Hasan (1985), Mikhail Bakhtin (1986), and William Hanks (1996) have led us to many insights about genre.

Genres serve purposes.

Every text is meant to do something for someone—an advertisement to convince us to buy something, a nutrition label to tell us what a food product contains. Largely gone are the days when the term *genre* was associated with identifying the forms of text, particularly literary forms—for example, the cinquain compared with the sonnet compared with the elegy (Dubrow 1982; Freedman & Medway 1994). Today many scholars see genres primarily as defined by their purposes, not by their forms or characteristics—which follow from the purpose (Paré & Smart 1994). We readily identify both facsimiles in Figure 1.3 as coupons because they share the same purpose, yet they have very few features in common.

Figure 1.3 Coupons

Genres are part of larger social conversations.

Language, broadly defined, is inherently social. Genres develop and function to enable social interaction (Cole 1996). As such, they are *dialogic*—they arise from some past communications and are used to anticipate future responses (Bakhtin 1981). For example, teacher storytelling is a common genre in classroom talk. Stories teachers tell often respond to previous student comments and anticipate student responses. But they can also serve the broader purpose of socializing students to "the moral of the story." And often that moral is tied to broader cultural values and beliefs (Juzwik 2009).

Genres comprise all texts.

Those who study genres closely now think of genres as not only literary texts but also texts we encounter at the grocery store, at the community center, in the science classroom, anywhere.

Genres can be oral or visual.

Speech genres (Bakhtin 1986) include such recurrent events as "show and tell," the toast at a wedding, and the university lecture. Visual genres include graffiti symbols marking gang territory, find-the-hidden-whatever picture books (e.g., Where's Waldo or the I Spy books), and sudoku puzzles. Today alphabetic print does not have a monopoly on genre.

Genres evolve within cultures.

Genres are continuously changing, and new genres are constantly emerging (Berkenkotter & Huckin 1995; Juzwik 2004; Martin, Christie & Rothery 1987). You may remember when cable news channels featured a talking head, with little or no text on the television screen. Viewers now expect news channels to present a running feed of breaking news stories along the bottom of the screen, include the time and weather in a set location, and display key points of the current news story to the left or right of the speaker. The print on cable news channels is even being parodied, as by *The Colbert Report*'s segment "The Word." The genre has evolved right before our eyes.

Defining Genre

We define a genre as a recurring and recognizable communication with particular communicative purposes and particular features to accomplish those purposes.

Reading and writing are genre specific.

The traditional instructional premise is that teaching reading is, well, teaching reading. We may say it's about teaching phonics, fluency, comprehension, but we don't tease it out much beyond that. Similarly, teaching writing is viewed as teaching a process of composition that applies to any type of text. But research is now showing us that it is more accurate and true to these processes to slice and dice them more finely in our practice and in our curriculum. We need to think specifically about how to teach reading and writing procedural or how-to text, for example, and recognize that this is going to be different in many important ways from how we teach reading and writing of personal narratives. It's not just "comprehension" or "composition" anymore. It's comprehension *of what for what* and composition *of what for what*. We need to differentiate the teaching of reading and writing according to genre because:

- *Readers and writers engage in different processes to different degrees when reading different kinds of text.* (See Duke & Roberts 2010 for a review of the research.) To take a simple example, although we read most narrative text from beginning to end in order, we often read informational text selectively and nonlinearly, turning to the index first, for example, and then just to the one part of the text that addresses our question or meets our need. So when teaching students to read narrative text, we need to teach students to read linearly; when teaching students to read informational text, we need to teach students strategies to help them read nonlinearly.

- *The same student can be much better at comprehending or composing one type of text than another.* For example, many U.S. students show a stronger ability to comprehend various kinds of literary texts than informational texts, though this pattern is reversed in some other countries, and there is parity in still others (Park 2008). And different factors predict students' ability to read different genres—for example, world knowledge seems to be a stronger predictor of informational comprehension than of narrative comprehension (Best, Floyd & McNamara 2004). So we need to differentiate our instruction by genre. We may need to focus more energy or attention on particular genres for particular students and do different kinds of things to lay the groundwork for success in one genre versus another.

■ *Different genres have different features.* Researchers who study written language have identified many differences in the features of different genres. When these features are the subject of instruction, instruction needs to be genre specific. For example, although the pronunciation guide is an important feature for understanding informational genres (see Chapter 4), it rarely comes up in narrative genres. In contrast, there is a range of temporal transitions we want students to comprehend and use when writing narratives (e.g., *no sooner had*, *suddenly*, and *the next day*; see Chapter 2) that rarely come up in informational genres.

■ *Some effective approaches to reading and writing are tailored to specific genres.* For example, the "theme scheme" (see Chapter 2), which helps students identify the theme of a story, has been shown to improve narrative comprehension substantially. However, this approach is certainly not appropriate for improving comprehension of informational texts. Rather "collaborative strategic reading" (see Chapter 4) specifically improves comprehension of informational texts.

Given the genre-specific nature of communication, we should think of moving our instruction from generic to genre-rich.

Generic ⟶ Gener-rich ⟶ Genre-rich

The Release of the Common Core State Standards

As this book goes to press, the Common Core State Standards (CCSS) have been adopted by forty-three states, the District of Columbia, and the U.S. Virgin Islands. The standards are "designed to be robust and relevant to the real world, reflecting the knowledge and skills that our young people need for success in college and careers" (CCSS Initiative 2010b). They will inform or replace state standards, guide curricula, and drive test development for years to come. Genre is all over these standards.

Regarding reading, the document states, "To build a foundation for college and career readiness, students must read widely and deeply from among a broad range of high-quality, increasingly challenging literary and informational texts (CCSS Initiative 2010a, 10)." Specific text types and genres (*text type* is sometimes used as a broader term than *genre*, sometimes the two are used synonymously) are named for grades K–5 and for grades 6–12 reading:

Range of Text Types for K–5

Students in K–5 apply the Reading standards to the following range of text types, with texts selected from a broad range of cultures and periods.

	Literature		Informational Text
Stories	**Dramas**	**Poetry**	**Literary Nonfiction and Historical, Scientific, and Technical Texts**
Includes children's adventure stories, folktales, legends, fables, fantasy, realistic fiction, and myth	Includes staged dialogue and brief familiar scenes	Includes nursery rhymes and the subgenres of the narrative poem, limerick, and free verse poem	Includes biographies and autobiographies; books about history, social studies, and the arts; technical texts, including directions, forms, and information displayed in graphs, charts, or maps; and digital sources on a range of topics

Range of Text Types for 6–12

Students in grades 6–12 apply the Reading standards to the following range of text types, with texts selected from a broad range of cultures and periods.

	Literature		Informational Text
Stories	**Dramas**	**Poetry**	**Literary Nonfiction and Historical, Scientific, and Technical Texts**
Includes the subgenres of adventure stories, historical fiction, mysteries, myths, science fiction, realistic fiction, allegories, parodies, satire, and graphic novels	Includes one-act and multi-act plays, both in written form and on film	Includes nursery rhymes and the subgenres of the narrative poem, limerick, and free verse poem	Includes the subgenres of exposition, argument, and functional text in the form of personal essays, speeches, opinion pieces, essays about art or literature, biographies, memoirs, journalism, and historical scientific, technical, or economic accounts (including digital sources) written for a broad audience

In the area of writing, three of the ten college-and-career-readiness anchor standards focus specifically on genre:

1. Write arguments to support claims in an analysis of substantive topics or texts, using valid reasoning and relevant and sufficient evidence.

2. Write informative/explanatory texts to examine and convey complex ideas and information clearly and accurately through the effective selection, organization, and analysis of content.

3. Write narratives to develop real or imagined experiences or events using effective technique, well-chosen details, and well-structured event sequences. (CCSS Initiative 2010a, p. 18)

A note adds: "These broad types of writing include many subgenres." Two other writing anchor standards explicitly mention purpose and audience (which, as we explained earlier, is at the heart of modern views of genre). Referring to the entire set of anchor standards for writing, the Common Core State Standards contend that students must

> learn to appreciate that a key purpose of writing is to communicate clearly to an external, sometimes unfamiliar audience, and . . . begin to adapt the form and content of their writing to accomplish a particular task and purpose. (2010a, p. 18)

This book is all about teaching students to do just that.

Seven Ways Teaching Genre with Purpose Will Change Your Teaching

① You'll move away from stock assignments that don't work.

A genre-with-purpose perspective reveals critical problems with many assignments routinely used in schools. In Chapter 2 we take on the "summer vacation" assignment; in Chapter 3, the infamous "how to make a peanut butter and jelly sandwich" activity. Here, let's address "fifty-states reports." As this assignment often goes, each student in the class is assigned to write a "report" on one of the fifty states. Sometimes students get to choose their state; sometimes they draw a name out of a hat or the like. The student then "researches" the state—from a number of perfectly good, already-published books on that state—and writes a report on the state to turn in to the teacher for a grade. In some cases, the report is also placed in the classroom library—along with the same books that informed the report in the first place—or taken home to share with parents whose interest in North Dakota is probably questionable at best.

Seen through a genre lens, this assignment is rife with problems. First, although it is meant to prompt students to write informational text, it is not based on the purpose of informational text, which is to convey information about the natural and social world (normally from one presumed to be more knowledgeable on the subject) to someone who wants or needs that information (Duke 2000; Purcell-Gates, Duke & Martineau 2007). The teacher has already read many years' worth of reports on North Dakota, and there are already several good books on North Dakota sitting right there in the classroom, so there is little real need for the text the student is writing. Second, the label *report* is confusing at best. We would not call a trade book on North Dakota we found in our local library or bookstore a "report" on North Dakota. Calling the product a *report* signals that this situation and the text are different from those in the world at large (reports outside school are something quite different).

When you teach genre with purpose, you assign better projects than "fifty-states reports" (the projects described in Chapters 3 and 4 are compelling examples). Teaching genre with purpose, you create a situation in which your students have a purpose—beyond satisfying you—for conveying information on a specific topic to an audience for whom they genuinely want to explain or clarify the topic, and compared to whom they are more expert, using a genre—such as an informational magazine article—that exists in the real world, not just the classroom.

② You'll move beyond the constraints of "genre study."

Some teachers, recognizing the importance of genre, have students spend a month studying a specific genre—myths or how-to texts, for example. Perhaps you are one of them. But if you are reading this book, something about this kind of teaching isn't sitting right with you. Your instincts are right on. There are a number of dangers in approaching genre in this way:

- *Studying a genre a month, you tend to focus too much on form and features, not enough on purpose.* Just as we learn a foreign language best by using it, studying specific features as they help us communicate more effectively, we learn genres best when using them, studying specific features as they help us achieve our purposes. Genres have developed as a means to accomplish specific purposes and are best learned when they are being used to accomplish those purposes rather than simply being held up for "study."

- *Studying a genre a month may not motivate and engage students.* Studying a particular genre feels, to many students, very "school-y." Some students are sure to announce they "don't like" whatever genre the class happens to be studying at the time. If, instead, students are working on projects that happen to use one or more of the genres for some larger appropriate purpose—as in the examples in this book—you'll see greater levels of motivation and engagement.

- *Studying a genre a month may lead you to focus on too large a category.* It can be useful to group genres into larger categories defined by general purposes, such as to inform, to persuade, and so on (and many textbooks do). In this way of thinking, a newspaper article, a medical website, and a social studies textbook are all "informative texts," and a newspaper editorial, a commercial website, and a book for teachers that recommends integrating controversy when teaching social studies are "persuasive texts." However, defining genre this broadly erases important differences among various texts and their contexts. On the one hand, these subsets of texts do share the same general purpose (to inform or to persuade), but on the other hand, there may be important differences among their specific purposes (e.g., to inform a medical decision—the medical website—versus to inform students' knowledge of their country—the social studies textbook), features, and contexts. The chapters in this book are named for these broader categories but the projects described in each chapter use more specific genres within the broader category, depending on the project's purpose. This is very much linked to the genre-with-purpose perspective. In real life, we rarely say, "Hmm, I think I want to narrate this month," or "I feel compelled to write a persuasive text." But we might well be inspired to write an *editorial* about a particularly frustrating stand taken by a local politician.

- *A single point in the year may not be time enough to learn deeply about the genre.* Teachers often complain that students enter their classroom without having previously learned to write informative or persuasive texts, but the students' former teachers testify they've taught the persuasive essay or informative report. So maybe once a year is not enough. And once-a-year scheduling does not allow teachers and students to develop their knowledge of a genre *during* the year. Students may be better off, for example, learning how to write how-to genres at several points in the year as they grow and develop as writers. Or they may—especially in the early grades—learn more about myths by reading a myth related to each science concept they study (pourquoi tales, a type of myth, are stories developed to explain natural phenomena) rather than by reading many myths at one time disconnected from a larger curricular context.

- *Focusing on a single genre at a time may prevent students from understanding that genres often act within systems or genre sets* (Bazerman 2004; DeVitt 1991; Prior 2009). People rarely use isolated genres in everyday life but typically conduct activities within, or through, or with the mediation of systems or sets of genres. For example, in campaigning for a change in our property tax assessment to lower our property taxes, we might read a chart of current assessed and taxable values of all properties on our block on the assessor's website. We then use data from the chart as evidence as we craft a *persuasive letter* to the city assessor stating why our assessed value is too high relative to those of other properties. Finally, while talking with a friend we might tell the *story* of what a headache it was to change the taxable value of our home. Each of these specific genres is marshaled for the larger purpose of lowering our property taxes or sharing that experience. Each has particular features that serve the purpose of each particular communication. In real life, we combine genres to suit our purposes, moving from one to another as needed. We want students to see how genres can work together to accomplish larger purposes. Studying a genre a month too often has a myopic focus that crowds out other genres and their relationships to one another.

Genre is still front and center in this book but is learned not through genre study or genre-of-the-month but through projects, large and small, that employ one or more genres for real purposes.

③ You'll motivate and engage students.

When you teach genre with purpose, many—sometimes all—students become wrapped up in that purpose. They can't wait to send off the first printing of their text to purchasers around the community and country (Chapter 2), sell their book at the local home store (Chapter 3), offer zoogoers their animal guide (Chapter 4), perform a comedy for parents and fellow students (Chapter 5), or persuade the preschoolers that kindergarten is safe and fun (Chapter 6).

It's amazing how students' motivation and engagement vary from one classroom to another, even when teachers are addressing essentially the same content. Ms. Edwards'[1] second graders were studying a unit on "pond life." As many teachers before her have done, she took her students to a popular nature center regularly visited by many other school groups. Although having many strengths, this center had relatively few materials available for students. At Ms. Edwards' suggestion, a nature center guide wrote the students a letter (quoted in Duke, Purcell-Gates, Hall & Tower 2006/2007, 344):

Dear Boys and Girls,

I hope you enjoyed your visit to our pond. I enjoyed answering your many good questions about what lives in ponds. After you left, I thought about all of the other children who visit us and who also have many of the same questions. I thought it might be a good idea to have a brochure for them with answers to some of their questions. I am writing to ask if you would prepare a brochure like this. It could be called something like "Questions and Answers About Pond Life." You could include some of your questions that you had before you visited us. If you write this, I will have many copies printed that we can put in the main office. That way, people can pick one up when they come or as they are leaving. I hope you can do this for us.

Sincerely,

Mr. Hernandez[1]

Students eagerly agreed to oblige. They did considerable research, both hands-on and in books, about life in ponds like that at the nature center. Then, using brochures from museums and other sites as models, they wrote a pond-life brochure, which was reproduced and made available for other students who visited the nature center.

Ms. Edwards designed a context in which students read and wrote informational genres for reasons authentic to this genre, and the students in this classroom looked different from those in many other classrooms studying pond life. They were more on task, surrounded themselves with more reading and writing materials, looked more interested in what they were doing, and appeared to be working harder. Students seem highly motivated in these kinds of reading and writing projects (Guthrie, McRae & Klauda 2007).

④ You'll empower students with reasons to read and write better.

In previous research, Victoria Purcell-Gates and her colleagues (2007) found that second and third graders whose teachers conducted more activities like the one described above—with reading and writing purposes and texts similar to the

---

1. Ms. Edwards and Mr. Hernandez are pseudonyms.

purposes and texts for which those genres are read and written in the world out-side school—better understood what they read and were better writers. Part of this probably stems from the context in which the learning took place—language is best learned as it is being used. But students also had a *reason* to write and read better. Students work harder to understand a text that they are going to explain to younger students, not simply assigned to read for themselves. Students are more concerned about the mechanics of their writing when they know it will be read by consumers or people in positions of power in a community rather than by just their teacher and classmates (who may already have entrenched notions that a student is a "bad speller" or the like). Lessons on strategies and genre features that traditionally end up as inert knowledge can be applied, deeply, when students have a compelling reason and context in which to do so.

⑤ You'll move students away from cookie-cutter texts.

When teaching genre with purpose, you won't ask students to follow lockstep formulas, such as specific text structures. You'll rarely ask students to write a traditional five-paragraph theme; when you do, you'll frame it as a genre to use strategically in high-stakes testing situations. Instead, you'll encourage writers to borrow or "remix" features in unexpected and inventive ways, just as great professional writers do. You'll encourage textual innovation because you recognize that genres are not mere formulas to be followed but rather resources to be drawn on, adapted, and sometimes reinvented for particular purposes and audiences.

Figure 3.5 (page 57) is a how-to text written by a group of fifth graders. Notice the many traditional features of how-to text, such as a section on materials needed and a set of numbered steps, but also observe the innovations these students developed in response to their audience (younger students in the school with messy desks), such as a "before-and-after" look at a desk (page 5 of Figure 3.5). Or consider the example in Chapter 2 of a narrative text in which student Julia Skinner writes, "Ah, the mall. A landmark that will forever stand in the hearts and wallets of Boulder County citizens." Into a guide for tourists, Julia has injected the celebratory tone public officials take during ribbon-cutting ceremonies. This kind of textual innovation is not a genre violation but an innovation worth celebrating—a hallmark of good writing.

⑥ You'll balance the genres you teach and ask your students to use.

Teaching genre with purpose, you'll become sensitive to which genres you are (or are not) privileging in your curriculum.

Genres That Aren't Getting Enough Attention

You might notice that your curriculum doesn't include genres important in students' worlds outside school—such as hypermedia informational text or game manuals—or in the adult world (e.g., proposals, plays). Or you might notice that texts you were categorizing as one genre really don't fit the purposes typical of that genre.

Genres That Are Getting Too Much Attention

You may also find that some genres are getting too much attention—genres that exist only in school, such as essays, textbooks, worksheets, and spelling sentences. Or you might notice that some of the texts you have students write are hard to place in any genre—responses, meant only for you, to prompts such as "What would you do if you had a million dollars?" or "What is your favorite day of the week?"

What about the high-stakes-test essay? Shouldn't I teach the compare/contrast essay when I know it is going to be on the state test in my grade?

If you are integrating writing into your curriculum using a genre framework, you can also teach the genre of the test essay and how to approach it: Analyze the prompt, quickly plan a response, signal by using topic sentences and transitions, use evidence and elaboration in the ways valued by the test-makers (Gere, Christenbury & Sassi's Writing on Demand *[2005] and Janet Angelillo's* Writing to the Prompt *[2005] are both good guides). Teach your students to ace the test, but then go back to writing for more compelling purposes.*

Genres That Are Especially Appealing

A genre lens might help you pick up on student preferences. For example, you might notice the popularity of self-help books, such as *A Smart Girl's Guide to Money: How to Make It, Save It, and Spend It* (Holyoke 2006) or *How to Do Homework Without Throwing Up* (Romain 1997). Or you might notice that students love the opportunity to write procedural texts (students, so often the receivers of directions, love to be in the position of giving them).

⑦ You'll help students use genres for their own purposes.

When children start school, getting "school" right and pleasing the teacher are highly motivating. As children mature, their interests and purposes turn ever more outside the classroom, and motivation becomes a bigger issue. School as a social and cultural space aligns in some ways with the purposes and practices of the outside world; in other ways it does not. For some students, school's purposes no longer feel like their purposes. In current educational literature this is most often raised as an issue in teaching historically marginalized students (e.g., Delpit 1995;

Hicks 2001; Mahiri 1998), boys (e.g., Smith & Wilhelm 2002), and cyberteens (e.g., Arafeh & Levin 2003; Stone 2007). Fortunately, school's purposes and students' purposes can be aligned. Students' desire to be a part of many worlds beyond school can be harnessed in developing their skills in academic and adult uses of reading and writing once this stops being defined as reading school textbooks and writing the five-paragraph essay—genres almost never seen outside schoolrooms. Students are engaged when they are writing stories that appeal to their peers, sharing information on topics on which they are experts, writing editorials about issues they care about, writing instructions for their favorite games, or organizing and participating in a poetry slam. Taking on the role of creative writer, dramatist, scientist, computer programmer, journalist, historian, or citizen gives students a glimpse of an adult world they are motivated to join. The purposes of the various genres and the features that enable them to be achieved become valued tools.

A classroom in which the purposes for activities, assignments, and projects are the students' as well as the teacher's and the school's is a powerful place. Examples include: in science, keeping track of the actions required to keep a particular kind of plant alive; in social studies, interviewing grandparents to produce a record of what the fifties were really like; in language arts, directing one-act plays to perform in the lower grades; in health, researching the best snacks to put in the school vending machines—all these projects involve learning and mastering communicative genres that are important both in school and in real disciplinary and social settings outside school.

Here's an example of one project in which students read and/or wrote at least ten different genres (listed in bold type) for their own purposes.

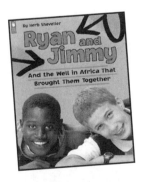

Figure 1.4 *Ryan and Jimmy and the Well in Africa That Brought Them Together,* by H. Shoveller is used by permission of Kids Can Press Ltd., Toronto. Cover © Bill Grimshaw.

One day teacher Jeff Svehla read aloud Herb Shoveller's **true story**, *Ryan and Jimmy, and the Well in Africa That Brought Them Together* (2005) (see Figure 1.4) to his fourth and fifth graders in El-Hajj Malik El-Shabazz Academy. The students were mesmerized. They immediately started talking about ways they had helped others and discussed how other students had practiced advocacy. They read and discussed **biographies** of famous Americans who had worked to improve others' lives. When Chantal worried that they didn't have the power to make the kind of change Jimmy had made, Jeff asked what kinds of immediate differences the class could make. Michael suggested they could help their school and mentioned the "good deeds" they had already done that year. So the class decided to conduct **surveys** to learn how they might improve life at their school. Then they made two **lists**: Things We Can Change Right Now and Things to Think About Later. An area in need of improvement was, perhaps ironically, the reading and writing skills of students in the school. During a subsequent discussion about ways to accomplish this goal, Jeff introduced a project he'd read about online called One School, One Book, in which an entire school reads one particular book as a way of building community and an interest in books.

Students were immediately excited about the idea and read excerpts from **an informational website** about the project in small groups. They sent an **email** asking questions about the project. They planned the two essential tasks that had to be completed before they could bring the project to their school. First, they had to find

Figure 1.5 Cover of *14 Cows for America,* by C. A. Deedy, with W. K. Naiyomah, illustrated by T. Gonzalez

a book that supported the mission of their school—building awareness about and pride in the accomplishment of our nation's citizens, especially African Americans. Over the next several weeks, Jeff and his students read a number of biographies and pieces of **historical fiction** focused on African Americans, developed **rubrics** for judging the books, wrote **reviews** to share with the class, and passionately discussed the merits of the various texts until they reached a consensus: Carmen Agra Deedy's *14 Cows for America* (2009) (see Figure 1.5). As they worked, Jeff embedded district- and state-required instruction lessons about the text structure and features of historical fiction, for example. Second, the class wrote a proposal to the administration. Jeff taught a series of lessons on how to use writing to convince, and students took these lessons to heart as, in small groups, they developed sections of the **proposal** (a clear and compelling statement of the problem, for example). For several days, they planned and practiced their **oral presentation** to the administration. Then Jeff printed out copies of the written proposal and set up an appointment for the class to present their ideas to the principal and curriculum director. The last piece needed to bring the One School, One Book project to his school was in place.

A project like this prompts students to read, write, speak, and listen to genres for purposes that go well beyond "doing school," satisfying the teacher, or performing well on a test. In this context, students learn so much more about genre than they do in more traditional curricula and thus improve their reading and writing skills. And they learn what genres can do for them and for the world around them. Seeing the social power of texts they have designed is nothing short of transformative.

Five Principles for Teaching Genre with Purpose

Drawing from the theory and practice of teaching genre, we have identified five guiding principles. Each principle is explained briefly below. They are revisited and elaborated on in Chapters 2 through 6, which describe how teachers have enacted these principles in real lessons and projects within their classrooms.

PRINCIPLE ① Design compelling, communicatively meaningful environments.

Genres come from and are defined by specific rhetorical situations (Miller 1984). We teach genre best when we create those situations in our classrooms. Communicatively meaningful environments include audiences students really want to connect with and tasks that involve issues or topics they care about. When writing in compelling, communicatively meaningful environments, students:

- work harder
- read and write better

- learn more about the genre

- are more inclined to apply what they are learning

- see more clearly the power of that genre, and literacy in general

PRINCIPLE ② Provide exposure and experience.

Reading and writing are largely genre specific. Being exposed to one genre for all the time in the world will not ensure that students are able to read or write a different genre well. They must be exposed to and have experience reading and writing each of the genres we want them to learn (Kamberelis 1999). Exposure and experience can be provided through:

- the classroom library

- classroom walls and other surfaces

- websites

- classroom experiences

- outside-of-school-time/space experiences

Model texts are powerful tools in developing speaking and writing (Dean 2008; Hillocks 2006). A study of the narrative writing of fifth graders shows that the higher quality the model, the greater the effect (Dressel 1990). Similarly, modeling comprehension processes through think-alouds appears to be a powerful tool for developing comprehension (Kucan & Beck 1997). Each chapter recommends specific texts to use with students and describes how teachers have used these texts to model specific reading and/or writing processes and strategies.

PRINCIPLE ③ Explicitly teach genre features.

It often helps to teach genre features explicitly. For example, it is beneficial to teach lower-elementary students about specific story elements (Baumann & Bergeron 1993; Gersten, Fuchs, Williams & Baker 2001) and upper-elementary students about the features of informational text that help you find information (e.g., index, headings; Symons, MacLatchy-Gaudet, Stone & Reynolds 2001). More broadly, teaching genre features explicitly can also help develop students' ability to think about text as text—what some call *authors' craft* or *metatextuality*. When students are metatextual, they can think not just about the content of the text but about how the author or speaker is conveying his message: "The author really grabs your attention with that lead," or "The picture helps show what a big problem it is," or "The author should have told what that means." We have heard these kinds of craft-based or metatextual comments even from young children. At the same time, it is easy to overrely on identifying and reproducing text features as an approach to genres, so we also discuss potential pitfalls.

PRINCIPLE ④ Explicitly teach genre-specific or genre-sensitive strategies.

The reading comprehension and writing instruction in many classrooms is too general. Comprehension and writing strategies are often taught as though they apply equally to all texts or all strategies work equally well for most texts, but this is not the case. For example, although we do make predictions while reading both narrative and informational text, the process is quite different. With narrative text we typically predict what is going to happen next; with informational text we most likely predict what the author is going to teach or tell us about next. Similarly, for an expert writer, writing a personal narrative about a recent experience will most likely be fundamentally different from writing about a specific scientific topic. Yet we teach students "the" writing process, and often do not share the ways in which this process and the strategies used within it might differ by genre.

PRINCIPLE ⑤ Offer ongoing coaching and feedback.

Time and again research demonstrates that more effective teachers spend more time coaching students, often in small groups—more time as the "guide on the side," less time as the "sage on the stage" (e.g., Fleischer & Andrew-Vaughan 2009; Langer 2001; Taylor, Pearson, Clark & Walpole 2000). The remaining chapters in this book show how teachers provide ongoing coaching and feedback, even within the constraints of their busy classrooms and school days.

☰ *Making Teaching Genre with Purpose Work in Your Context*

You may be worried about how you can make this kind of teaching work within the constraints of your particular situation. The concrete classroom examples, tools, and tips provided throughout the book will help a lot. But we'll address a few issues to allay your initial concerns.

With so many programs and district mandates, I feel pressed for time as it is. How can I fit in this kind of teaching?

Many of the teachers featured in this book teach in schools with mandated curricula. They fit teaching genre with purpose in between other official requirements, looking for parts of their school day in which they have more freedom. Moreover, mandated curriculum can serve as a valuable resource. For example, Niki McGuire used the district's mandated science unit on body systems to give her students the content knowledge required to write their books (see Chapter 4). By asking students to mine mandated materials for background information, you can meet requirements without sacrificing this teaching approach. It's also a good idea to plan a short, smaller-scale project first, document students' responses, and use this information to justify a larger, longer project. Backward mapping state standards and curricular goals may be especially important: Documenting that these standards and goals have been thoroughly met through alternative approaches can help you build a case for the value of this approach within the overall curriculum. As Regie Routman (2008) tells us, "Plan with the end in mind. Embed skills as a means to a worthwhile end" (53).

I'm overwhelmed at the prospect of planning projects like these. How can I manage the workload?

Many of the teachers whose projects we describe in this book initially felt overwhelmed. They mentioned that keeping track of the many details, trying things outside their comfort zone, and learning about genre were difficult, but they also said that the high levels of motivation and academic growth they saw in their students made it worth it. One teacher reminded us that like all her previous experiences learning new teaching techniques, the first project was challenging, but having walked through it, she felt much more knowledgeable and had several ideas about how to optimize her teaching during the second project. Here are several helpful ideas about managing genre-with-purpose instruction:

- *Use the planning sheets in this book.*

- *Work with a colleague.*

- *Get your feet wet by starting with a small, short-term project.*

- *Begin by selecting your target audience and genre focus. Use these two central decisions to envision the final products and drive the rest of your planning.*

- *Cluster your planning activities. Work on establishing the outlet (e.g., asking the hardware store to sell students' books, securing the fifth-grade teachers' permission to present in their classrooms) and scheduling a tentative "distribution" date. Then gather examples of the final products and study them to get a sense of what students will need to learn and do. Sketch out a rough sequence of activities and use it as a continual revised blueprint for planning formal lessons. Finally, gather the resources that will be needed.*

- *Take it day by day, and feel free to go back and reteach something that didn't go well or that needed additional attention.*

- *Listen to the students. They may offer new ideas about how to accomplish your instructional goal. Some students may even offer the same idea that you were hoping to advance anyway. The rest of the class will probably be more motivated by ideas from their peers, and you won't have to do all the planning yourself.*

- *Save your lesson plans and in-process notes, so recreating the project (or a similar one) will be easier next year.*

The teachers in my school are very committed to a traditional writing workshop. Most of them believe that students should be able to write whatever they want. I don't think any of them are going to like the idea that all the students will be writing about the same topic for one specific purpose and audience.

We too are committed to process writing; however, research clearly supports structuring that process for students, especially struggling writers (Applebee 1986; Graham & Perin 2007; Hillocks 2006; Roberts & Wibbens 2010). We are less enthusiastic about the write-whatever-and-however-you-want-to approach seen in many classrooms, what Hillocks (1986) calls the "natural process" approach. Happily, it is possible to allow choice while still having students write for specific purposes and audiences. For example, in the zoo-animal guide project, students chose the animal they wrote about.

In a relevant study (Duke 2008), Nell and colleagues randomly assigned five pairs of similar first-grade teachers either to continue their traditional write-anything-you-want writing workshop or to implement project-based writing of informational text for specific purposes and audiences (much as described in Chapter 4)—not every day, but three days a week for four months. They collected prompted informational writing from the students at the end of this time and scored the writing without knowing whether it was from an experimental or a control classroom. Students in the project-based writing classrooms had better informational writing overall in terms of vocabulary, organization, text features, and voice, though their scores on writing mechanics were lower than the control group's scores (the projects did not involve lessons in mechanics but the regular writing workshops' often did). These results suggest there are many benefits to moving away from the write-anything-you-want-to-write model, at least some of the time.

How to Read the Rest of This Book

The next five chapters each focus on a compelling communicative purpose and a category of genres that meet this purpose:

Chapter 2: Sharing and Making Meaning of Experience: Narrative Genres

Chapter 3: Learning How and Teaching Others: Procedural Genres

Chapter 4: Developing and Communicating Expertise: Informational Genres

Chapter 5: Exploring Meaning Through Performance: Dramatic Genres

Chapter 6: Effecting Change: Persuasive Genres

Each chapter revisits our five principles, bringing them to life in real class-rooms and projects. Each chapter describes several projects in which students read, write, speak, and/or listen in order to achieve these purposes. As in the One School, One Book project described earlier in this chapter—and as in life—these projects often involve a number of genres. The notion that different genres can be used together with powerful results is a theme of this book. That said, we foreground one overarching category of genres in each chapter, discussing a number of specific genres within that broader category. We end this book with an invitation. After reading this book, we hope that you're inspired to create projects that incorporate multiple genres in substantial ways and we invite you to share those projects with us.

You Too Can Teach Genre with Purpose

The teachers whose work is featured in this book would be the first to tell you that they are not superhuman. They don't have endless time or boundless energy. They have many, many demands on their time outside school, as so many of us do, and they are subject to demanding state standards, as so many teachers are. But in the face of all this, they have made teaching genre with purpose work for them. Their students have had the opportunity to experience reading and writing instruction that exemplifies our five core principles and leads, we believe, to greater growth in knowledge, skill, and engagement. We describe these opportunities and recommend practices aligned with the five principles in hopes that you find a model of how to make your teaching of genre more effective, joyful, and purposeful.

2

Sharing and Making Meaning of Experience: Narrative Genres

What Genre with Purpose Looks Like: The Family History Project, Grades K–8

English as a second language (ESL) specialist Carmela Rademacher's classroom at Delta Center Elementary School is transformed into an Around-the-World Quilt Museum. The English language learners she teaches are displaying quilts and accompanying stories, placards, and family trees they have made to share their family experiences with others. Parents, classmates, and teachers are visiting the museum today as students stand proudly beside their quilts and accompanying texts. Because it is a special day designated to celebrate family heritage, some children wear traditional outfits (e.g., see Nivedhya's ghagra choli; Figure 2.1). Admiration and recognition echo through visitors' snatches of conversation as they make connections and share their own experiences. One child is excited to learn his classmate is from India. Others exclaim at the languages of the wall placards (Srijith's wall placard in Hindi appears in Figure 2.2). Another child recognizes a quilt made by a sixth-grade book buddy. In the corner of the

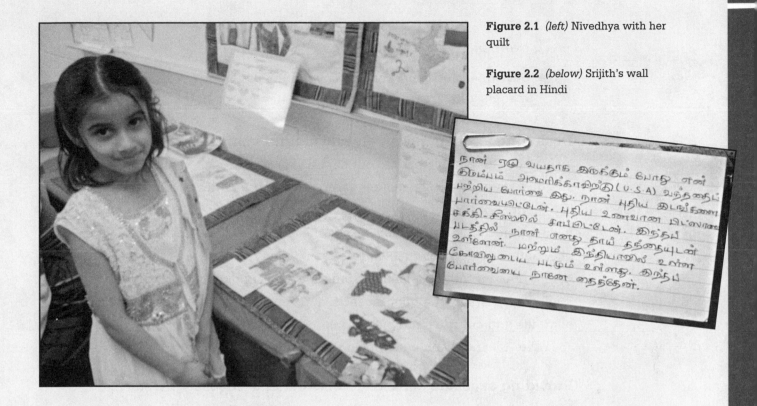

Figure 2.1 *(left)* Nivedhya with her quilt

Figure 2.2 *(below)* Srijith's wall placard in Hindi

room, right behind Carmela's desk, a valentine hangs on the chalkboard. A pink heart with ribbon threading through it bears the message, "Mrs. Rademacher / The fabric / that binds us." On the desk sits a vase full of roses from the fifth-grade teachers, along with a card of appreciation. As on the opening day of an art exhibit, visitors express enthusiasm and admiration for all Carmela and her students have accomplished.

Inspired by African American and Hmong story quilt traditions, Carmela invited her multi-age (K–8) students to thread their personal and family experiences together in a meaningful way—literally, in the quilts, but also figuratively, as they stitched together a range of genres and texts. The genres they read, listened to, and created included fictional stories, written and oral nonfiction narratives, family trees, and wall placards; all were vital links in setting up the quilt museum. Carmela had created a rich and motivating environment in which to develop her students' reading, writing, speaking, and listening skills. They:

- *learned and reflected on the meaning of personal, family, or community experiences and places*

- *practiced important social skills as they shared experiences with others and listened to and learned about others' experiences*

- *invited others into—and themselves stepped into—unfamiliar experiences, places, and events*

- *developed key genre conceptions that helped them become better readers and writers of narrative texts*

Designing a communicatively meaningful environment   Carmela, an avid quilter herself, decked out her ESL classroom with beautiful quilts she had sewn and collected over the years. She had her students study the quilts, observe the patterns, notice similarities and differences, and make connections among them. In sharing the stories of some of her quilts, she communicated her infectious passion for quilt making. She then asked her students if they would like to create their very own quilts about their families to display in a quilt museum and thus communicate their family histories and cultures to their classmates, their classmates' parents, and the other teachers and students in the school.

Providing exposure and experience   Carmela introduced her students to a number of genres to prepare them for writing their family story (the culminating genre, which would accompany the quilt). They read literary stories, like *The Keeping Quilt* (Polacco 1988), a fictional text about how a quilt is passed down by and holds deep significance for a Jewish family that immigrated to the United States. The story triggered a conversation about heirlooms and how they can sometimes help preserve family memories across the years and the generations. The students also read *The Whispering Cloth* (Shea 1996) and made a virtual (online) visit to the National Quilt Museum.

To scaffold the children's writing Carmela, with her daughter's help, videotaped oral-history interviews with students' parents. The interviews focused on the circumstances of the family's immigration to the United States and other experiences important to the family culture and became texts that the children reviewed and used in planning their quilts. The quilts featured cultural symbols both from the United States and from nations of origin, pictures of beloved family members, and national flags (see Katarina's, Vijeta's, and others' quilts in Figures 2.3, 2.4, and 2.5).

Explicitly teaching genre features and genre strategies   Carmela used model texts to explicitly teach features of narrative, such as plot development, characterization, and setting. She also reviewed the format and purpose of wall placards using models from real and virtual museums. While

Figure 2.3 Katarina's quilt

Figure 2.4 Vijeta stands with her quilt

Figure 2.5 Quilts, stories, wall placards, and family trees exhibited in the Around the World Quilt Museum

paying attention to genre features, students also pursued literacy strategies such as researching, planning, and using visual texts (their quilts) and oral texts (the parent interviews) as the basis for their narrative writing.

Offering ongoing coaching and feedback Thus equipped, the children enthusiastically began writing, working through multiple drafts until they—and Carmela—thought the piece was ready for exhibition (see Ravneet's family story, Figure 2.6). Then they moved on to the wall placards. They wrote the placard in English (and if they were able to, in their family language as well). Some students recruited their parents to write their placards in their family language (see Ravneet's placard, Figure 2.7).

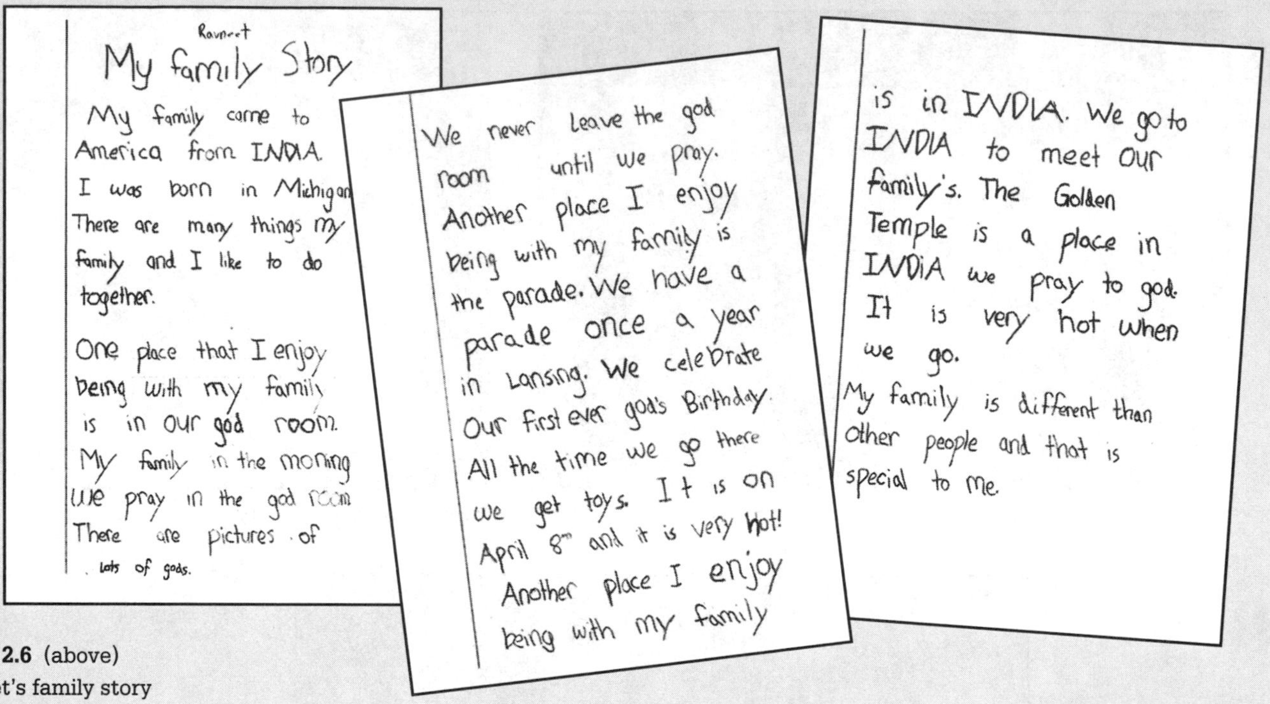
Ravneet

My family Story

My family came to America from INDIA. I was born in Michigan There are many things my family and I like to do together.

One place that I enjoy being with my family is in our god room. My family in the morning we pray in the god room There are pictures of lots of gods.

We never leave the god room until we pray. Another place I enjoy being with my family is the parade. We have a parade once a year in Lansing. We celebrate Our first ever god's Birthday. All the time we go there we get toys. It is on April 8th and it is very hot! Another place I enjoy being with my family

is in INDIA. We go to INDIA to meet our family's. The Golden Temple is a place in INDIA we pray to god. It is very hot when we go. My family is different than other people and that is special to me.

Figure 2.6 (above) Ravneet's family story and placard

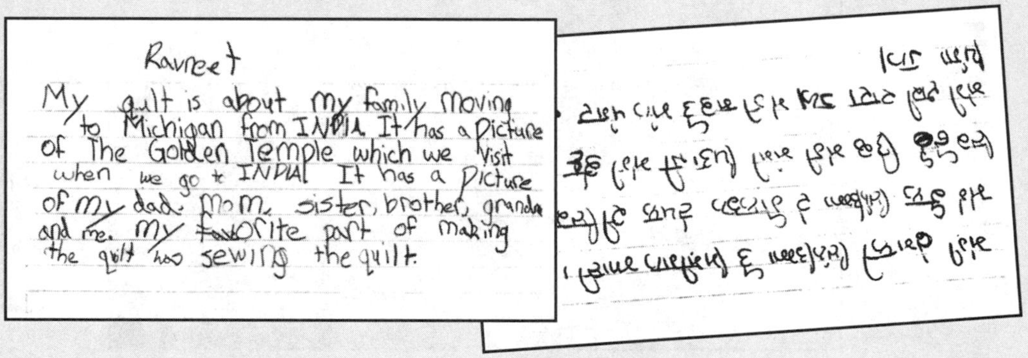
Ravneet

My quilt is about my family moving to Michigan from INDIA. It has a picture of The Golden Temple which we visit when we go to INDIA. It has a picture of my dad, mom, sister, brother, granda and me. My favorite part of making the quilt was sewing the quilt.

Figure 2.7 (right) The wall placards accompanying Ravneet's quilt, in Punjabi and in English

The Value of Oral Storytelling

The kinship between oral and written narratives is often overlooked in the complex process of working with narrative genres in the classroom. Some children and parents who struggle with narrative writing can be gifted storytellers in their native language (and in English as well). Keep this relationship between written and oral narrative in mind and use more familiar oral narrative practices as scaffolds for written narrative practices. David Poveda (2003) spotlights a culturally sensitive teacher who helped her students, many of whom were capable oral storytellers and listeners, to build on these strengths as they learned to read and respond to fictional narratives.

Figure 2.8 The summer vacation essay: A cartoon

"*I hope you realize that I'm the one who has to write about this stupid vacation next fall.*"

Rethinking Popular Narrative Assignments: Beyond "My Summer Vacation"

A common approach to teaching narrative—taken by Mary early in her career—is to assign the "my summer vacation" personal narrative in early September. These stories about summer vacations can inspire cynicism, even dread—as the cartoon in Figure 2.8 well shows! Unlike Carmela's project, the assignment lacks a broader purpose that would make the writing and reading of narratives relevant, interesting, and purposeful. For many students, the events of summer vacation are unreportable when compared to other events in their lives. And even when a vacation has been memorable, the details may be growing dim in September. In desperation, some children resort to *inventing* details. When completing the "summer vacation" assignment (and many other narrative writing assignments as well), students:

- rarely study models

- rarely purposefully connect narrative reading and writing to other genres

- rarely conduct inquiries to uncover the details of past experiences (by consulting newspapers or archives, talking with family members, or making phone calls to relevant experts, for example)

In contrast, Carmela's project and other genre-with-purpose narrative projects are a process of inquiry. When writing narratives students must do more than simply close their eyes and remember the past: They need to conduct research, for example by reading books (including other narratives), talking with family members (and often listening to their stories), viewing archival materials (including photographs), phoning experts to get a term or description right for a story, and so on (Hillocks 1996). When students engage in inquiry as part of narrative writing, they are following the practices of expert narrative writers (Lamott 1994).

The Purposes of Narrative Texts

Students in Carmela's classroom developed general academic skills; they conducted research; planned, designed, revised, published, and presented their work; and read and interpreted a range of texts and accompanying images. They also developed their knowledge of and ability to read, write, speak, and listen to many kinds of fictional and nonfiction narratives. When teachers take a genre-with-purpose approach, students become immersed in, and in some cases explicitly learn about, purposes for and communicative possibilities of narrative forms that have been:

- designed to share and interpret a wide range of experiences (personal, family, communal, historical, and fictitious) with readers

- composed by someone who either lived through, conducted research about, or has deep vicarious knowledge about the experience being shared

- interpreted by someone who is interested in learning about others' past and present experiences (either real or imagined)

Typical uses of narrative reading and writing in classrooms tend to foreground retelling personal experiences, writing personal narratives, and/or reading fiction. By contrast, genre-with-purpose projects take advantage of the full range of social and historical actions and interactions that narratives can accomplish in classrooms, schools, and communities (Daiute 2004, 2010; Juzwik 2009; Kamberelis 1999). Rather than using narrative exclusively to dig into students' personal pasts, these projects employ narratives for all sorts of other real-world purposes, like sharing and comparing family cultural experiences and exploring the significance of events and places in the community.

Truth-Telling and Narrative Texts

From a genre perspective, both fictional and nonfiction narratives share the same purposes, a point made clear in the Common Core State Standards Initiative (CCSI 2010a) on narrative writing. Because we don't see the fiction versus nonfiction distinction as central to narrative, we refer to a range of fictional and nonfiction narrative texts throughout this chapter. The chief difference between a nonfiction narrative and a fictional narrative is the truth claim made for the narrative.

When narratives are presented as fiction, veracity does not matter. However, when narrative texts are presented as real-life events, truth telling and sometimes even evidence of veracity (e.g., artifacts from or photos of the event) are expected. We worry when we hear teachers encouraging students to embellish their personal stories so that they are more entertaining or, depressingly, more likely to receive a high score on a high-stakes test. Some literacy researchers suggest that how much students and families value "telling the truth" on the one hand and "telling a good story" on the other can vary according to class, culture, and religious faith (e.g., Heath 1983). Truth telling should be explicitly addressed when teaching narrative writings, for not all students share the same notions of narrative truth and falsity.

Although writing embellished or entirely imagined stories is worthwhile even at the early elementary level, children can also produce nonfiction ("true") stories and identify them as such. It is especially important to emphasize to upper-elementary and middle school students the need for truth and accuracy in historical projects. For example, the students working on Barney Brawer's Evacuation Day project (described later) initially drafted this lead for their narrative: "Can you imagine that there was a battle with no blood—just victory for the Americans?" But then they ran into a truth-telling problem: They discovered historical evidence that several people had, in fact, died. Blood had been shed. To remain true to what really happened, they changed their lead to "Can you imagine that there was a battle with almost [emphasis added] no blood—just victory for the Americans?"

Now that you've seen one of our favorite narrative projects, compared that to an example of how narrative texts are commonly taught, and considered a definition of narrative genres according to their purpose, let's look at another great project and use it as a model for how to teach narrative reading and writing.

GENRE PROJECT

What Genre with Purpose Looks Like:
The Evacuation Day Project, Grades 4 and 5

Barney Brawer, principal of the Michael J. Perkins Elementary School in South Boston, is constantly coming up with new ways to make United States history meaningful for elementary students.

Evacuation Day is celebrated in the Boston area on March 17 (the same day as St. Patrick's Day). The holiday honors the British army's departure from Boston in March 1776, the colonists' first victory after the bloody but inconclusive Battle of Bunker Hill. Although the Perkins students and their parents were well aware of the annual Saint Patrick's Day parade (South Boston is heavily Irish American), they knew little about the history of Evacuation Day, often dismissed as "just an excuse to get the day off on St.

Patrick's Day." Mr. Brawer decided to help his students and the school community explore the events that took place in their neighborhood while the country was being formed. So, with the help of parents, teachers, and community members, a group of fourth and fifth graders in the school collaboratively wrote and illustrated the children's book Why Do We Celebrate Evacuation Day?

Why Do We Celebrate Evacuation Day? is available for purchase at amazon.com, or directly from Michael J. Perkins School (in which case the school makes more money for their scholarship fund), for $14.99. To order one or more copies, write, call, or email the Michael J. Perkins School:

Michael J. Perkins School
50 Burke Street
South Boston, MA 02127
(617) 905-3156
perkins@boston.k12.ma.us

How to Teach Narrative with Purpose: Five Principles for Instruction

We turn now to discussing how our five principles can be enacted in projects involving narrative texts. In Appendices A and B of this book, you'll find planning sheets to help you teach genre with purpose. These planning sheets offer resources for each genre. We encourage you to use them as you develop your own projects using the principles in this book.

PRINCIPLE ① Design compelling, communicatively meaningful environments.

Involve students in something bigger than themselves.

The kindergartners through eighth graders in Carmela's room and the fourth and fifth graders in Barney's school were all participating in collective enterprises bigger than themselves: They contributed quilts and narrative texts as artifacts to a museum and collectively authored a narrative about a little-known historical event. They did far more than write personal narratives about what they did on their summer vacation; they became deeply engaged in product-driven, collaborative activities (Heath 1998). Such activities are a critical first step in creating communicative environments that motivate children and adolescents *to use narrative texts to learn* and *to learn about the uses of narrative texts.*

Design opportunities for collaboration among students and with adults.

Genre-with-purpose projects demand intensive collaboration among students and between students and adults other than teachers. For example, Carmela's students used family members' oral histories as the basis for their quilts and family stories. In the Evacuation Day book project, "helpful grownups" (28) worked side by side with the students to research the central events of Evacuation Day, which were available only in texts written for grownups, such as *1776* (McCullough 2006). The adults learned alongside the students, which made the project an exciting process of inquiry for *all*. As the adults related information from the source material (the fact that one cannon fell through the ice of the Hudson River, for example), the students wrote their version of the narrative in their own words:

> When they had to take the cannons across the Hudson River, they were worried the ice was not strong enough to hold them up. Henry Knox did something smart. He had the soldiers cut holes in the ice. Then water would rise up and freeze and the ice would get thicker and thicker, so the cannons will not fall. But one fell. They still didn't give up. They pulled the cannon up and cleaned it, then kept on moving.

The children asked wonderful questions ("Why didn't the British know the cannons were coming?") that led to other questions ("How did *anyone* in Revolutionary times know *anything* they hadn't personally observed?"). This led the team of children and adults to visualize how people communicated across distances (or didn't) in a no-telephones, no-TV, no-radios, no-Internet era!

The adults and children together compiled all the separate episodes. They created a big list on chart paper, numbered the episodes in sequence, and identified which parts of the story needed to be fleshed out more fully. For example, the students realized they had written too much about all the snow on the journey and about sneaking the cannons up the hill but needed a description of what happened *after* the cannons were installed on the hill. Groups of adults and children were commissioned to go back to the history books to find details that would fill in missing parts of the story (how long it took for the British to leave, for example). The children also made illustrations to accompany each of the episodes to be included in the book.

Provide many tools and materials.

Populating the classroom with rich and varied tools and materials is also critical for studying and designing narrative texts (pages 34–35 discuss using model and sample texts). Certainly Carmela's classroom was filled with written narratives (not uncommon in K–8 classrooms), but it is equally important to include a range of narrative tools and resources beyond printed texts. Carmela's classroom included story quilts, a sewing machine, and a computer on which students called up and reviewed their family oral narratives. An important resource for Barney's project was the Evacuation Day memorial on the hill behind the school: The book project began when the whole student body and faculty hiked up the hill to visit it and became curious about the event it memorialized. (A communicatively meaningful environment can expand beyond school walls!) Other tools that can contribute to communicatively meaningful environments include photos and paintings; videos and video games; cameras and video cameras; computers, e-books, or other digital devices; scanners; and artistic supplies for generating, illustrating, or enacting stories in various media (paint, pencils, pens, clay, colorful paper, leaves, fabric, costumes, and so on). Materials like these help students realize that written narrative texts intertwine creatively with other media and modes of communication.

≡ *More Project Ideas for Teaching Narrative with Purpose*

1. *Have adolescents write and illustrate modern-day fairy tales, personal narratives, or other children's stories to share with younger children—one classroom donated their books to a pediatrician's office (e.g., Stone 2005).*

2. *Have children read and write fictitious and autobiographical narratives centering on social conflicts as part of a broader project about violence prevention (Daiute 2004).*

3. *Have children write their own stories about the joys and hardships of learning to read and write, compile them with similar stories by others, and share them with students in other classrooms (Mitchell 1995).*

4. *Have adolescents use video cameras and other inquiry tools to create stories that critically question and reframe a specific urban area; neighborhood gentrification in Harlem, for example (Kinloch 2009).*

5. *Have students create comic strips on www.MakeBeliefsComix.com and enter them in the site's Facebook wall competition. The strips can also be posted on students' own Facebook walls.*

≡ *Try These Digital Resources!*

Digitally mediated environments are excellent resources for narrative genre projects in the twenty-first century, with burgeoning interest in digital storytelling and digital archiving of life stories:

- *The StoryCorps project (http://storycorps.org/) is an oral history resource for K–8 teachers. The project has collected and archived over 30,000 oral histories that are freely available and searchable by theme.*

- *The Center for Digital Storytelling (www.storycenter.org/index1.html) is a collection of resources related to digital storytelling. (For a blog post about uses of digital storytelling in education, see http://jorivas.wordpress.com/2010/03/16/digital-storytelling/.)*

- *Digital Storyteller (www.digitalstoryteller.org/aboutus.htm) is a resource provided for teachers and students by the Curry School of Education at the University of Virginia.*

- *The Digital Clubhouse Network (www.digiclub.org/mission/index.html) helps people use digital resources, including digitally mediated narratives, to improve their communities.*

- *Born in Slavery: Slave Narratives from the Federal Writers' Project, 1936–1938 (http://memory.loc.gov/ammem/snhtml/) is an online collection of more than 2,300 first-person accounts of slavery and 500 black-and-white photographs of former slaves.*

PRINCIPLE ② Provide exposure and experience.

You may feel you'll have an easier time designing purposeful exposure to and experience with narrative texts than some of the other genres, because many students have been saturated with oral and written narrative texts from a very young age. Yet literacy research since the 1980s suggests that children's exposure and experience with written narrative texts varies enormously by social class and culture (e.g., Heath 1982). So don't assume students read or listen to stories with their families every night; create many opportunities for your students to listen to stories, handle and interact with narrative texts, read narrative texts aloud (if children are able to read), retell stories they hear and read, and produce stories of their own.

Many K–8 classroom libraries are well stocked with fictional narratives, and this is important. But it's also important to share a wide variety of narrative text types *beyond* fictional narratives: personal narratives and autobiographies (see text box on pages 40–41 for further discussion), family narratives, community narratives, and historical narratives. Sometimes the genre distinctions blur, as in the texts listed in the box on page 34. Studying these "hybrid" texts can show young readers and writers how authors creatively manipulate genres for their own communicative purposes.

Recommended Model and Mentor Narrative Texts for K–8 Classrooms

Many of these books can be used across the K–8 span and even the chapter books, like Seedfolks, may be read aloud to younger children.

Ten for Primary Grade Readers

1. A Chair for My Mother *by V. B. Williams. Mulberry, 1982. (fiction)*
2. Little Panda: The World Welcomes Hua Mei at the San Diego Zoo *by J. Ryder. Simon and Schuster, 2001. (nonfiction)*
3. One Smile *by C. McKinley, Illumination Arts, 2002. (fiction)*
4. On My Way to Buy Eggs *by C. Chen. Scholastic, 2001. (fiction)*
5. Owen & Mzee: The True Story of a Remarkable Friendship *by I. Hatkoff, C. Hatkoff, & P. Kahumbu. Scholastic, 2006. (nonfiction)*
6. Swimming with Dolphins *by L. Davis. Blue Sky Press, 2004. (fiction)*

7. The Man Who Walked Between the Towers *by M. Gerstein. Square Fish, 2003. (nonfiction)*

8. Tell Me a Mitzi *by L. Segal. Scholastic, 1970. (fiction)*

9. Wangari's Trees of Peace: A True Story from Africa *by J. Winter. Harcourt, 2008. (nonfiction)*

10. Zoo *by A. Browne. Sunburst, 1992. (fiction)*

Ten for Upper-Elementary and Middle School Students

1. Children of the Dust Bowl: The True Story of the School at Weedpatch Camp, *by J. Stanley. Crown Books for Children, 1993. (nonfiction)*

2. Crow Boy *by T. Yashima, Scholastic, 1965. (fiction)*

3. Exploring the Titanic *by R. D. Ballard. Scholastic/Madison Press, 1988. (nonfiction)*

4. Holes, *by L. Sachar. Bloombury, 1998. (fiction)*

5. Mama Went to Jail for the Vote *by K. Kerr. Hyperion, 2005 (historical fiction)*

6. Martin Luther King, Jr. and the March on Washington *by F. Ruffin. Scholastic, 2001. (nonfiction)*

7. Seedfolks *by P. Fleischman. HarperTrophy, 2004. (fiction)*

8. Spies of the Mississippi: The True Story of the Spy Network That Tried to Destroy the Civil Rights Movement *by R. Bowers. National Geographic, 2010. (nonfiction)*

9. They Called Themselves the K.K.K.: The Birth of an American Terrorist Group *by S. C. Bartoletti. Houghton Mifflin, 2010. (nonfiction; because of disturbing content, probably best reserved for middle schoolers)*

10. The View from Saturday *by E. L. Konigsburg. Atheneum, 1998. (fiction)*

Ten Genre-Blurring Narratives

1. Bad Kitty vs. Uncle Murray, *by N. Bruel. Square Fish, 2011.*

2. The Complete MAUS: A Survivor's Tale *by A. Spiegelman. Pantheon, 1994. (because of disturbing content, probably best reserved for middle schoolers)*

3. Crossing Borders: Stories of Immigrants *by T. Lang. Celebration Press, 2005.*

4. Dawn Land, *by J. Bruchac & W. Davis. First Second, 2010.*

5. The Kids' Invention Book *by A. Erlbach. Scholastic, 1997.*

6. Knucklehead: Tall Tales and Almost True Stories of Growing Up Scieszka *by J. Scieszka. Viking, 2008.*

7. Paddle-to-the-Sea *by H. C. Hollings. Sandpiper, 1980.*

8. Persepolis *by M. Satrapi. Pantheon, 2004.*

9. The Secrets of Vesuvius *by S. C. Bisel. Scholastic, 1990.*

10. The Trapp Family Book *by H. Wilhelm. Heinemann, 1983.*

Use model or mentor texts.

Carmela's and Barney's projects used model narratives in different ways, but in both projects students examined models to inspire writing and to develop reading and listening skills. Carmela's students studied the published narratives, *The Keeping Quilt* (Polacco 1988) and *The Whispering Cloth* (Shea 1996), to see how family stories could be organized around a meaningful object. The books included many of the features of narrative genres outlined above. But sometimes, as in an ambitious project like the *Why Do We Celebrate Evacuation Day?* book, there are no model texts for children to examine. This is good in that it motivates the project, but it means you need to search for model texts about related historical topics. Because there were no children's books about Evacuation Day, Barney and his students looked at books about Bunker Hill Day. They made the fascinating discovery that there is more to celebrate about Evacuation Day than there is about Bunker Hill Day, because the Battle of Bunker Hill included many deaths and was not a turning point in the Revolutionary War. The discovery led students to come face to face with the power of storytelling: Which stories are told, and how they are told, can influence our understanding of the past and sometimes the present. Barney's students had the power to change perception by telling a neglected but important story in local and national history.

Filling a classroom with model texts can be time-consuming and expensive. Teachers have long consulted with school, public, and university librarians. In addition, local, national, and international digital teacher networks, such as the National Writing Project (www.nwp.org/) or the Bread Loaf Teacher Network (www.middlebury.edu/blse/bltn/), can be extremely helpful in identifying and sometimes even locating model narrative texts for a new project, as are the digital repositories listed on pages 32–33.

Grant writing is also an important professional skill for you to develop in an effort to create a "slush fund" (in addition to your own pocket) for purchasing model narratives and other materials and resources. And receiving a grant may have the added benefit of connecting you with other teachers working on similar projects. Mary's Stories in the Land grant from the Orion Society supported her work on the Boulder book project (described later in this chapter and in the Coda) and connected her with eight teachers from around the country who received a grant for the same period of time. Literacy researcher Judith Langer (2001) lists participation in multiple professional networks as a key characteristic of teachers who "beat the odds" to cultivate student growth and achievement in schools where student success is not predicted by socioeconomics and other demographics.

PRINCIPLE ③ Explicitly teach genre features.

By explicitly teaching narrative genre features and designing opportunities for students to learn about them, you can orchestrate increasingly sophisticated encounters with narrative genres. To decide which features to teach explicitly (a critical step), you first need to understand the characteristics of narrative texts.

What do I need to know about narrative text characteristics?

You'll benefit greatly from an understanding of narrative genres (oral as well as written) that goes well beyond the genre features you teach your students. You needn't (and *shouldn't*) teach your students all the terms on page 36, but just being aware of them will allow you to introduce your narrative writers to ever-more sophisticated moves and to provide ongoing coaching and feedback with confidence.

Common Characteristics of Narrative Texts*

Elements

- *Abstracts* encapsulate the gist of the story at the beginning of the text (Labov 1972; e.g., "You'll never believe what Janie did yesterday! What shocking behavior!").

- *Setting: When and where does the story take place?* Setting, as well as characters, are introduced in sections called *orientations*, usually at or near the beginning of the narrative (Labov 1972).

- *Characterization: Who does the action involve?* Characterization refers to how characters are described and developed and how they interact with other characters.

- *Plot: What happens?* Plot describes the general sequence of events that happen in a story.

  - *Problem situation or conflict: What is the problem or conflict in the story?*

  - *Rising action: How does the plot develop?*

  - *Resolution: How is the story problem or situation resolved?*

- *Theme: What is the point of the story?* Theme describes why the action matters to the narrator or to others. Authors and speakers communicate themes through *evaluations*, or strategies that help readers and listeners interpret story events (Juzwik 2009; Polanyi 1985).

Language Characteristics

- *Detailed descriptions* are created using adjectives, vivid verbs, metaphors, and any number of other techniques to evoke images for readers and listeners.

- *Temporal and causal transitions* show relationships between and among sentences and sections of a narrative. Narratives rely on temporal transitions (e.g., *very soon* and *suddenly*) to manage the passage of time and on causal transitions (e.g., *because*) to specify logical links.

- *Special language devices* typical of narrative include beginning a story with the time-honored fairy- or folktale cue *once upon a time*, using rhyming words, constructing dialogue, and posing rhetorical questions.

- *Play with language for the sake of language.* Narrative is a great vehicle for studying expressive stylistic choices at the sentence level (e.g., "Not by the hair on my *chinny chin chin!*").

- *Verb structures* in narratives tend to be simple past or present tense verbs rather than more complex verbal phrases, especially when narrators are moving the plot forward (e.g., "The next day, the wolf *came* again").

- *Clauses and sentence structures* in oral narratives and stories written for children also tend to be simple rather than complex (e.g., "And [the wolf] gobbled up the little pig").

---

* *Any given narrative text is unlikely to, and needn't, have all of these characteristics.*

Narratives in *The Three Little Pigs* and *Why Do We Celebrate Evacuation Day?*

- *Characterization: Who does the action involve?*

The characterization component of narrative texts encompasses how characters are described and developed and how they interact with other characters. Fictional and nonfiction stories alike are populated with protagonists (main characters), minor characters, and antagonists (villains). In *The Three Little Pigs* (Marshall 1989), the third little pig is the protagonist and "hero" of the story: Early on, we see that he is sensible because in contrast to his happy-go-lucky and casually dressed brothers, he wears a dapper suit and carries a handsome bag to sally forth into the world. The antagonist is, of course, a "lean and hungry wolf."

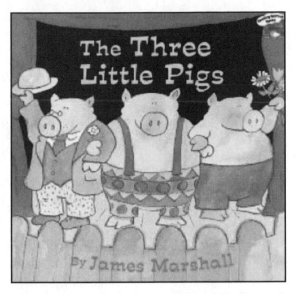

Figure 2.10 Cover of James Marshall's *The Three Little Pigs*

Notably, nonfiction narratives also have protagonists. For example, the protagonists of *Why Do We Celebrate Evacuation Day?* (Michael J. Perkins School 2007) are Henry Knox and General George Washington. Some object to calling the persons in nonfiction narratives (especially personal narratives) *characters*; however, labeling nonfiction protagonists, antagonists, and villains *characters* helps students realize that even in narrative writing, real people (including narrators) become characters and that writers have choices about how they portray these characters. Students in difficult circumstances can even be empowered by invitations to imagine their life, family, and national stories in new ways (Daiute 2010).

- *Setting: When and where does the story take place?*

The setting of *The Three Little Pigs* is folktale land rather than a specific time and place. The long-ago time is cued with, "Once upon a time."

- *Plot: What happens?*

The plot of the story is the general sequence of events that take place. Plot includes the commonly taught story elements of problem or conflict; rising action; and resolution or ending. Keep in mind that the "beginning, middle, end" structure is not the only option for structuring plot. Sometimes narrators choose to start a story "in medias res"—in the middle of the action.

- *Problem situation or conflict: What is the problem or conflict in the story?*
  In stories, the plot is often realized in three distinct and identifiable sections: an instigating problem, rising action (or exposition), and resolution. Problem situations put the plot into motion. In *The Three Little Pigs*, the problem—a *conflict* between each pig and the wolf—is established when the "mean old wolf" blows the first pig's home in and gobbles him up.

- *Rising action: How does the plot develop?* More complex narratives tend to develop through connected episodes. In *The Three Little Pigs*, three major episodes—one featuring each of the three pigs—begin "The first little pig," "The second little pig," and "Now the third little pig."

- *Resolution: How is the story problem or situation resolved?* Story plot is usually resolved as characters respond to those conflicts: The third little pig outwits the wolf three times and ultimately gobbles *him* up!

■ *Theme: What is the point of the story?*

Themes are the broad point or points a story addresses—the "so what?" This *meaning-making* dimension separates narrative from similar genres, such as *recounts*. Some "my summer vacation" narratives become lists of vacation events (with the structure "and then . . . and then . . . and then . . .") that simply *recount* past events, rather than stories showing why the events matter to the narrator or to others. Theme is constructed through a wide range of textual resources, often described as "voice." Through voice, authors show their stance on story events. Marshall uses dialogue as a key means to convey his stance on events in *The Three Little Pigs*. For example, on the penultimate page of the story, the wolf announces, "Here I come! Dinnertime" next to an illustration of the sensible third pig putting a boiling pot into the fireplace, the book *How to Cook a Wolf* lying nearby. The pig's rejoinder ("You can say that again!") at the top of the final page projects Marshall's signature comically ironic authorial voice extolling the virtues of planning, cleverness, persistence, and skill exemplified by the third pig—the themes of the story.

Narrative Evaluation in the Evacuation Day Project

As noted on page 36, evaluation facilitates narrative meaning-making. When Barney's Evacuation Day project was nearing completion, the group realized they hadn't yet answered the "so what?" posed in their book title. Why *do* we celebrate Evacuation Day? Why does this story matter? Why should people today care about these long-ago events? This became a "juicy" (Barney's word) exploration about the past in relation to narrative and led to a text box at the end of the book that reads:

Why do we celebrate Evacuation Day?

We celebrate Evacuation Day because it was a victory with almost no blood!

We celebrate Evacuation Day because the British soldiers had taken over Boston. When they left, the Americans could be in charge of our own city. Now people could make their own laws and stand for their own rights!

We celebrate Evacuation Day because one clever idea—and a lot of hard work—can change history!

Note that this evaluation occurs in a nonfiction narrative. As already discussed, fictional and nonfiction narrative texts share the same characteristics. The distinction between *fictional* and *nonfiction* narratives has no bearing on text characteristics; rather, the distinction hinges on whether a narrative is *real* or *imagined*.

Narrative Text Characteristics and Development

Not all narrative texts include all the narrative elements and structural features discussed in this section; texts written by young children rarely do. Often young

Figure 2.11–2.12 Narrative features of two pages of *Why Do We Celebrate Evacuation Day?*

The abstract: short encapsulation of the gist of the whole story

Orientation: provides scene-setting detail for the story to come

Rising Action: A problem is introduced.

Can you imagine that there was a battle with almost no blood – just victory for the Americans?

This amazing victory happened in 1776 right behind our school, in the neighborhood that is now called South Boston. In 1776, our school was not built yet, and back then South Boston was called Dorchester Heights.

It all started in 1768 when the British soldiers came to Boston. That was their first mistake.

Orientation: Uses special devices, such as a rhetorical question addressed directly to you, the reader.

Evaluation of the events of the story from a particular point of view. This point of view does not just represent the personal, school, or community perspective; it also reflects a widely accepted national theme or "moral stance": the American colonists and Revolutionaries were good and the British soldiers and loyalists were bad.

Temporal transition words, such as "then," are typical in narrative texts.

Characterization is developed through brief description.

Plot is developed through past tense verbs and fairly simple sentence constructions. The event in this sentence (and all the events on this page) are part of the *rising action* in this story.

Then Henry Knox had a brilliant idea. Henry Knox was a young man who was a soldier with the colonists. He used to own a bookstore in Boston, and he read many books about guns, battles, and wars. He knew there were lots of cannons at Fort Ticonderoga in New York State.

The Americans had just taken Fort Ticonderoga away from the British.

Henry Knox asked General George Washington if he could go to Fort Ticonderoga to get the cannons and bring them to Boston to fight the British. The cannons were more than 300 miles away, and they were very heavy.

General Washington said, "Yes. Do it."

Henry Knox

Evaluation of the events of the story from a particular point of view. This is an example of "embedded" evaluation, given within the frame and plot line of the story events.

Detailed pictures of important characters contribute to character development.

Constructed dialogue is another special language device used in narrative texts. Sometimes "constructed dialogues" are invented to represent real speech events, even when the characters didn't say those exact words, in an attempt to personalize these events.

The juxtaposition of images and text in the layout supports the storyline. The choice to convey Knox's "brilliant idea" as a text box coming out of Knox's head invokes comic strips and visual novels, where a text box (or bubble) is used to represent what a character is saying or thinking.

children's earliest efforts at writing narratives—and sometimes their later efforts—produce *recounts* rather than stories. Other times, as in Ravneet's "My Family Story" (Figure 2.6), attempted narratives are arranged as purely descriptive pieces rather than temporally sequenced and causally linked narratives. The text elements and structural features outlined on pages 37–38 are simply characteristics that frequently typify "fully formed" narrative genres.

Narratives are written and spoken toward the broad social purposes of sharing and making meaning of experience with others, and the features of narrative texts are driven by these purposes. Students who are taught genre with purpose begin to realize that narrative texts make a point (or several points) about the teller or the world through temporally ordered events, told from one or more points of view. Although students can rarely explicitly label the structural elements of their own narrative texts, many do *enact* several structural narrative genre features in their writing. Furthermore, once children have learned some of the key genre features, they are more likely to enjoy story parodies, such as Wiesner's version of *The Three Little Pigs* (2001), which purposefully violate the typical narrative genre features to delightful effect.

Biography and Autobiography: Narrative or Informational Genre?

Many teachers wonder how to categorize biographical texts. It's easy to see why. Biography and autobiography share some features of both narrative *and* informational *texts: They serve the purposes of communicating a perspective on a person's life and conveying information.*

Biography has been defined as an "account of a person's life written by another person" (National Assessment Governing Board 2008, 59). Biographies and autobiographies can retell a person's life from birth onward, focus on particular episodes, or arrange facts to support a specific interpretation of that life. Biographies are usually written in the third person and feature well-developed main "characters." Autobiographies, on the other hand, are typically written in the first person. The author is the protagonist. Both biography and autobiography include details about the protagonist and his or her social context. Both typically rely on research. Many biographies and autobiographies also include graphics, artifacts, dialogue, descriptive headings, themes or messages, and/or elements such as genealogy charts or footnotes.

Although K–8 students often write personal narratives focused on a discrete series of life events, writing compelling autobiographies about "a life" is rare at this age. Having students read and write biography with purpose, however, can be a highly effective teaching strategy. Possible projects include:

- *a class-authored biography to inform the rest of the students and faculty about the person for whom the school is named*

- *group-created biographies of community members whose lives exemplify an important character trait, to be used to teach students in younger grades about character development*

- *individual biographies that document the lives of students' favorite family members that they can copy and give to their relatives*

- *group-created biographies of people students know who have made a difference in the lives of others, to be posted on a website that tries to convince other children to become advocates for their community*

Here are a few favorite biographies for sharing with students (and some of the "genre-blurring" narratives also have biographical or autobiographical components—see page 34):

Abe Lincoln: The Boy Who Loves Books *by K. Winters & N. Carpenter. Aladdin, 2003.*

Cesar Chavez: The Farm Workers' Best Friend *by S. B. Collard. Benchmark Books, 2009.*

Frida Kahlo *by M. Venezia. Children's Press, 1999.*

Leonardo Da Vinci *by D. Stanley. Morrow Junior Books, 1996.*

Odd Boy Out: Young Albert Einstein *by D. Brown. Houghton Mifflin, 2004.*

A Weed Is a Flower: The Life of George Washington Carver *by Aliki. Aladdin, 1988.*

Wilma Unlimited: How Wilma Rudolph Became the World's Fastest Woman *by K. Krull. Sandpiper, 2000.*

How do I teach narrative text characteristics?

Use models and ineffective texts

To teach *detailed description*, Carmela first played the telephone game with her students to illustrate why detailed description is important in narrative texts and how changing details can alter the meaning of a story. She also shared written narratives that contained little or no detail. As she read these "nonmodels" aloud, she thought aloud about how hard it was for her to envision the story because it had so little detail. She had her students examine detail in *The Keeping Quilt* (Polacco 1988), a text that also modeled an immigration story similar to the one she was inviting students to write.

Call attention to text characteristics in the models

Carmela read the passage about Anna going to school in a new country (a passage with which many of her English language learners could relate): "When Anna went to school, English sounded to her like pebbles dropping into shallow water. *Shhhhhh . . . Shhhhh . . . Shhhhhh*" (3). Carmela pointed out how author Patricia Polacco uses a *special language device*, onomatopoeia. She showed them how, rather than writing, "When Anna went to school, she had a difficult time understanding English," Polacco shows the reader just *how* Anna experienced English as difficult. She also pointed out how the details of the illustration (Anna is in color, and the other children at school are in black and white) enhances the narrative experience for the reader: One interpretation is that not understanding the language around you can make you feel that the world is "in black and white" rather than "in color." She pointed out that detailed description can be used to develop characters (like Anna), make the plot entertaining (not boring), and communicate a point of view and the meaning of events (the text characteristic *evaluation*, although Carmela did not introduce this term). In small groups, students then explored detailed description in other trade books.

Design engaging activities

The meaning of narrative events can be ambiguous; readers interpret them based on the details and other textual and visual cues provided by rich description. Explicitly teaching detailed description can be approached in different ways. Educator and writing researcher George Hillocks (2006) uses seashells: He brings in many kinds of conch shells and has middle school students write descriptions of them. Students start with basic descriptions that apply to all the shells. After discussing these "nonmodels" and being shown how generic they are, the students write highly detailed descriptions; then they read them aloud while their classmates try to identify which shell is being described. Although Hillocks uses this activity in a personal narrative unit, it can be used to teach other types of narrative as well.

Plan for teaching text characteristics

Prepare to teach text characteristics explicitly by:

- reading widely in the genre

- writing texts of the sort you will ask your students to create (Hillocks 1996)

- *analyzing* the texts you have read and written and identifying their characteristics; then asking, "What do students need to *do* in order to learn what they need to know to write such a text effectively?" (Hillocks 1996).

- anticipating potential problems, misunderstandings, or confusions students may develop

- collecting and generating materials to share with students

- designing experiences, including many opportunities for collaboration, that will:

  - teach and review the text characteristics of the genre

  - prompt the inquiry necessary to design and create meaningful texts (for narrative texts, this could include gathering historical artifacts, talking with family members, and telephoning relevant experts)

Invite students to articulate metatextual knowledge

Students need opportunities to articulate their metatextual knowledge about narrative genre features throughout and at the end of a project, both in informal conversations and in formal assessments. Middle school students invited to articulate the genre-specific features of their narrative reading and writing (and their purposes), whether in whole-class discussions, one-on-one conferences, cover letters or writer's memos, or other written or spoken reflections, often surprise us with their metatextual knowledge. But even when they cannot articulate explicit genre features, they may still enact those genre features brilliantly in their writing. Producing and interpreting texts that include appropriate genre features is far more important than being able to provide metatextual labels for these features. Many of us spend far too much time asking students to learn the names and definitions of narrative tools and not enough time having them use those tools.

Use the story-mapping strategy

One way to teach some of the elements of narrative is through story mapping, an approach that helps young readers improve their recall and comprehension of narrative texts. Jim Baumann and Bette Bergeron (1993) focused on five elements and accompanying questions (415):

Story Element	Key Question(s)
Characters	Who?
Setting	Where? When?
Problem	What's the problem?
Major Events	What happened?
Ending	What's the solution?

They organize the instruction in four steps:

1. Describe, define, and give an example of the story-mapping process.

2. Explain the importance of the process.

3. Teach students how to map stories: Explain, model, and collaborate.

4. Explain when story mapping should be used.

Teach this cycle in several lessons, gradually spending less time on the first steps and more time on the last steps—always helping your students become independent story mappers. Don't neglect students' reading responses; give them opportunities to discuss the author's craft and their connections to the story.

PRINCIPLE ④ Explicitly teach genre-specific or genre-sensitive strategies.

Research shows that strong readers and writers use a range of strategies for making sense of, composing, and revising narrative texts (e.g., Graham & Perin 2007; Pressley & Afflerbach 1995; Roberts & Wibbens 2010; Wolf 2004). Research also shows that teaching many of these strategies, even to young children, helps improve their reading comprehension (Shanahan et al. 2010).

Teach reading and listening strategies.

Reading strategies include:

- *Previewing the narrative and activating background knowledge.* For example, strong readers examine the front and back cover and make connections to previous books or previous experiences ("What do we know about quilts?" for example). They note whether they've read other books by the author.

- *Visualizing the setting, characters, and events in the narrative.* Teaching students to visualize characters and settings can be effective even in the primary grades. This strategy is especially effective when used in connection with nonprint genres such as drawing or dancing.

- *Building "envisionments" during reading.* Strong readers speculate why characters do certain things; connect characters' actions to real-world actions and experiences they have had; pose questions, including questions to themselves; predict what will happen next; and infer motives and actions (Langer 1995). Carmela frequently asked her students while reading, "What do you think will happen next?"

- *Monitoring, clarifying, fixing.* Strong readers pay attention to whether the narrative is making sense. When it doesn't, they use strategies to help, such as stopping to picture what is happening. Strong readers also realize that some narrative texts intentionally confuse or surprise readers, forcing them to readjust their developing understanding.

- *Reviewing the story after reading.* Strong readers ask, *what happened?* They retell or summarize the events of the story aloud (see the box on page 45 for a fuller explication of this strategy), in writing, or mentally. Asking "Who can recap what happened in the book?" activates this strategy.

- *Evaluating the significance of reading.* Strong readers interpret and analyze. They usually determine the theme or "moral" of the story (or when the text is richly ambiguous, a number of thematic possibilities). Strategies include analyzing the actions and motivations of characters ("So what does this quilt mean to the family in the book?" for example), comparing the narrative with other works, noting and interpreting formal dimensions of the text, to name just some (Langer 1995). The box on pages 45–46 features one specific strategy, theme scheme, found to be effective.

Teach these strategies using the gradual release of responsibility model, in which ownership or application of a strategy gradually transfers from teacher to student over time (Pearson & Gallagher 1983; see also Duke, Pearson, Strachan & Billman 2011):

1. *Explicitly describe* the strategy and when and how it should be used.

2. *Model* the strategy in action (show students how to use the strategy by thinking aloud as you read).

3. *Use the strategy collaboratively* in action (apply the strategy together with your students).

4. *Guide students as they practice* the strategy (let students take increasing responsibility for applying the strategy; coach as needed).

5. *Let students use the strategy independently* (bookmarks or similar devices can be used as reminders).

You'll cycle through these stages many times as the complexity of the text increases.

☰ *How Do I Help My Young Students Retell a Story?*

In the mid-1980s, Lesley Morrow (1985) taught kindergartners to retell stories and found that they significantly improved their comprehension, story structure knowledge, and oral language skills. She used the following prompts to guide their retellings (659–60):

- *"A little while ago I read the story [name the story]. Would you retell the story as if you were telling it to a friend who has never heard it before?" (Even better, provide an audience that really hasn't heard the story before.)*
- *"What comes next?" or "Then what happened?"*
- *"Who was the story about?"*
- *"When did the story happen?"*
- *"Where did the story happen?"*
- *"What was [name the main character]'s problem in the story?"*
- *"How did [she/he] try to solve [her/his] problem? What did [she/he] do first? next?"*
- *"How was the problem solved?"*
- *"How did the story end?"*

Because narrative texts have a wide range of purposes (personal, family, community, biographical, historical), narrative reading and writing strategies also vary with the specific text being read.

☰ *The Theme Scheme*

Strong readers usually infer the theme or "moral" of the story (whether fiction or nonfiction), even when it is not explicitly given (as it is in Aesop's fables, for example). Joanna Williams and her colleagues (1994, 2001) have developed a teaching approach to help students identify the theme of a narrative. Although the approach focuses on fiction, it can also be used with nonfiction. The approach has been shown to be effective with at-risk second graders as well as fifth through eighth graders with and without disabilities (e.g., Williams, Brown, Silverstein & deCani 1994). Called the theme scheme, the approach involves careful scaffolding and uses the same four-part framework for each lesson:

1. **Introduce the theme and text.** *Focus on students' background knowledge, and provide less support over time. For example, in the initial lessons introduce the idea of theme, justify its importance, and describe the text's theme; later, help students identify the theme themselves through collaborative discussions.*

2. **Read the narrative.** *Read the narrative aloud, stopping frequently to ask questions, elicit student predictions and event summaries, and discuss the text.*

3. **Lead a postreading discussion.** *Focus on the plot and theme by asking questions such as:*

   "Who is the main character?"

   "What is the main character's problem?"

   "What did the main character do about the problem?"

   "And then what happened?"

   "Was what happened good or bad?"

   "Why was it good or bad?"

   "What did the main character learn?"

   "Is this something everyone should do?" (Williams, Hall, Lauer & Lord 2001, 76–77)

4. **Provide a three-part conclusion:** *(1) Help students transfer what they are learning by asking them to find the theme in another short text, (2) review the organizing questions and extend the discussion by generating examples of the theme in their own life experiences, and (3) include a wrap-up enrichment activity—such as writing, drawing, or role-playing—to stimulate further reflection on the theme.*

Teach writing and speaking strategies.

Writing strategies used by expert narrative writers include planning, drafting, revising, and editing. Although not a great deal of narrative-specific research on writing strategy instruction has been undertaken, several genre-specific approaches are promising.

Steven Graham, Karen Harris, and their colleagues have developed a program called *self-regulated strategy instruction* (Graham, Harris & Mason 2005; Harris, Graham & Mason 2006; Sawyer, Graham & Harris 1992). This approach targets students' planning and drafting skills and has been tested with various elementary and middle school grades (e.g., second grade in Harris et al. 2006) and student populations (e.g., students with autism spectrum disorders in Asaro-Saddler & Saddler 2010). You begin by introducing two important strategies: POW and WWW, What = 2, How = 2. In POW students "*P*ick my ideas (i.e., decide what to write about), *O*rganize my notes (i.e., organize possible writing ideas into a writing plan), and *W*rite and say more (i.e., modify and upgrade the plan while writing)" (Graham et al. 2005, 217). In WWW, What = 2, How = 2, students ask themselves, "*W*ho are the main characters? When does the story take place? Where does the story take place? *What* do the main characters want to do? *What* happens when the main characters try to do it? *How* does the story end? *How* do the main characters feel?"—some of the same questions used in story mapping—and record their responses to these questions (Graham et al. 2005, 217). During this phase, you also discuss the elements of high-quality narratives. Next, you and your students practice identifying story elements, setting goals, and monitoring drafting activities. You then model POW and WWW, What = 2, How = 2, and students, working together, use the strategies to plan and draft their own narratives. Finally, students craft narratives independently.

Researchers also identify the importance of *criteria-based narrative revision* strategies and explicit instruction about revision (Fitzgerald & Markham 1987; Hillocks 2006). Hillocks, for example, finds that teaching middle school students to use detailed rubrics with narrative text characteristics helps them give one another substantive feedback in peer review sessions and monitor their own revision process. The overall quality of narrative writing improves.

Other genre-specific instructional strategies, such as discussing high-quality literature, may also increase elementary students' ability to write narrative texts (Corden 2007; Dressel 1990).

☰ *Gathering Writing Ideas by Reading Model Texts*

Help your students explore high-quality literature by:

- *reading a mentor text aloud, leading discussions about the author's use of literary devices, and using these literary devices during shared writing*

- *asking small groups of students to examine the author's craft in more detail*

- *having the small groups share their findings with the whole class*

- *asking all students to record their insights in their author's notebook (Corden 2007)*

PRINCIPLE ⑤ Offer ongoing coaching and feedback.

Divide the process into steps with appropriate check-ins.

Intensive coaching and feedback is a critical aspect of a genre-with-purpose approach, because it allows you to tailor your instruction to your students' individual processes and needs. Mary structured numerous opportunities for ongoing coaching and feedback in a project in which her students researched and wrote a tour guide about Boulder (each student wrote about one place in the community). Because the project was so big, she broke it down into parts—requiring students to turn in lists of five sources and their two-column research notes, for example (see Juzwik 1999 for more detail). If students only used Internet sources (they were required to use at least three non-Internet sources) or if they had only very dated sources, Mary pushed these students to consult more varied or more recent resources. She also responded to students' drafts both in writing and in short conferences, pushing them to polish the pieces for book publication.

Respond individually.

Students will encounter particular challenges in writing and revising their texts. In Mary's Boulder Book Project, for example, Julia produced a draft that was heavy on telling and listing but light on narrative action and description (see Figure 2.13). Mary's feedback included two key points:

- The piece needs to be further developed as a narrative. Here are some questions to help you: What is the story and history of the mall? Can you provide more descriptive details about its history, especially the expansions? Why should readers care about the mall?

- Develop your own voice as a credible narrator of the story of the mall.

Figure 2.13 A draft of Julia's narrative

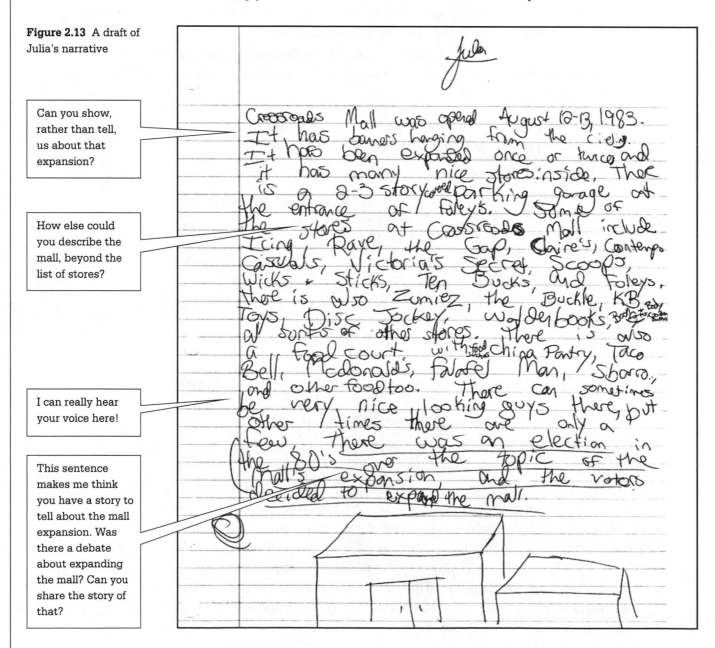

Can you show, rather than tell, us about that expansion?

How else could you describe the mall, beyond the list of stores?

I can really hear your voice here!

This sentence makes me think you have a story to tell about the mall expansion. Was there a debate about expanding the mall? Can you share the story of that?

Our Beloved Mall

by Julia

Crossroads Mall is the only indoor shopping mall in Boulder. It is called "Crossroads" because it is located at the intersection of the Boulder Bypass and State Highway 7.

It was constructed by W.R. Grimshaw Company in 1961. The mall officially opened on March 14, 1963. When Crossroads opened, it had 394,000 square feet, which is still a part of the mall, and can be found south of JCPenney. Between 1981 and 1983, Macerich/BURA added on Foley's (which used to be May D&F) and two levels of stores. Then, along came Mervyn's a mere three years later. And only four years after that, in 1990, the mall grew again, this time expanding Foley's and adding a parking garage.

After all this expansion, the mall is currently 860,000 square feet. This year, in 1998, more development is being planned, and the mall is going to be "made over" and get a fresh new face!

Now that you know the basic history of our beloved mall, let's talk about its contents. When

This is a main mall entrance with the Crossroads logo displayed proudly on the blue banner.

...roads Mall's finest stores.

In Julia's final version (see Figure 2.14), the story is a recognizable narrative text and the voice is quite strong, particularly the tongue-in-cheek humor: "Ah, the mall. A landmark that will forever stand in the hearts and wallets of Boulder County citizens." By using terms like *landmark* and *citizens*, Julia evokes the ceremonial tone (characteristic of what rhetoricians call *epideictic* genres) assumed by public officials at ribbon-cutting ceremonies.

Give genuine, real-world feedback.

One of the beauties of establishing a compelling communicative purpose for narrative writing is that students become more open to ongoing coaching and feedback. Motivated to "get it right" as they imagine the impression they will make on a broader real-world audience, they are eager for feedback that will help make their writing the best it can be. In Mary's project, the goal of book publication created this motivation. Mary assumed the real-world role of editor. She was

Figure 2.14a
Final text of Julia's contribution to *The Boulder Book*, "Our Beloved Mall"

This is Andrew, one of the many fine mall employees.

I interviewed random shoppers in the mall bout their favorite stores, a store most frequently mentioned was Rave. Other favorites: The Gap, The Buckle, Scoops, and the food court. Some of the best stores in this mall (or at least in my opinion) are: Rave, Contempo Casuals, The Gap, Claire's, The Limited, Scoops, The Buckle, Bath and Body Works, Victoria's Secret, Garden Botanika, and, of course, the food court.

Yes, our mall is something to be proud of. It has given a retreat from the outside world into a place where shopping and fun abound. It is the key to unlock the

④⑦

One of the many fine dumpsters of the Crossroads Mall.

world of fashion. (Whatever kind of fashion it may be.)

Ah, the mall. A landmark that will forever stand in the hearts and wallets of Boulder County citizens. It is known as a place to hang out, meet new people, greet old friends, relax, have fun, and most importantly, shop. There are cash machines in the mall for your convenience. One is right outside Disc Jockey, and the others, well, I'm not sure. You'll have to find out for yourself.

If you are in Boulder, you must see the mall. It is a priority! It is just one of the many great things Boulder has to offer. Let's all salute the mall!

④⑧

Figure 2.14b

Final text of Julia's contribution to *The Boulder Book,* "Our Beloved Mall"

direct and explicit and honestly enthusiastic. She focused on improvements over accomplishments. Because of the purposeful context for writing, students welcomed the feedback.

Narrative Text: The Power of Sharing and Making Meaning with Others

Teaching narrative genres with purpose can, to quote James Moffett (1987), expand students' "universe of discourse." Barney's project took on a publishing life of its own. After the first black-and-white, photocopied edition of the book (completed in 2007) was distributed, the group revised it in subsequent years to include more illustrations (in color) and glossy paper. They also obtained an ISBN number with its own bar code. The third edition of the book is currently sold at the school, in local bookstores, and at amazon.com, where it has received a four-star review that concludes with a point we endorse: "The story is fascinating and the illustrations are delightful. We need more kids writing history books."

Moreover, approaching genre with purpose can connect meaningfully with students' own life goals and trajectories. The archival inquiry Julia did at the Carnegie Library in Boulder, Colorado, for the Boulder Book Project became an enduring interest. When this book went to press, she was a graduate student at the University of Iowa, conducting archival research and writing a thesis on how Iowa public libraries changed the way they developed their collections and sponsored patriotic activities when the United States entered the First World War.

3

Learning How and Teaching Others: Procedural Genres

GENRE PROJECT

What Genre with Purpose Looks Like: Earth Day How-to Books, Grade 1

First graders gape at the marquee over the entrance to Horrocks, a local farm market, which proclaims "Delta Center Authors' Books Sold Here." They walk into the store and very soon a voice on the PA system announces, "We have real writers in the building! Stop by the front of the store now if you would like an autographed copy of Saving the Earth One Piece of Trash at a Time." Their teacher, Katie Davis, doesn't recall any moment in the year in which children showed as much pride in their work as they did that day.

Designing a compelling, communicatively meaningful environment During an Earth Day read-aloud about garbage, Katie Davis' first graders expressed disgust about all the waste being generated. "Too much garbage!" was their reply when Katie asked them to identify the problem. Their solution: "Recycling!" The students bemoaned that there was no recycling program at their school. Katie mentioned that she had been talking to some friends who wished they had a book about how to recycle or reuse some of the things in their house. Katie asked, "Do you think you could write a book about that?" The students responded with an enthusiastic yes.

Katie began her project by establishing a reason for students to write procedural text that went well beyond simply learning how to do so. Her students would teach others how to recycle or reuse some of the things in their home. This would, in turn, reduce garbage—the students' goal. Katie also identified an audience for students' writing that went well beyond the classroom—at first her friends but later broadened to include the customers at Horrocks—and a way to earn money to help fund a recycling program at the school.

Providing exposure and experience Katie began reading students simple published procedural or how-to texts about making things, such as Fleming's *Make a Paper Hat* (2000) and Clyne and Griffiths' *Let's Make Music* (2005). As she read, Katie pointed out important strategies for this kind of reading (e.g., "It helps to look ahead to see what the finished product will look like") and key characteristics of this kind of text (e.g., "There is usually a section at the beginning that tells what we need, or the *materials*, to do the procedure"). She set aside these and other procedural texts in a bin in the classroom library so students could refer to them as models.

Katie also gave students time to think of ways to reuse items that would otherwise be thrown away. They had studied reducing, reusing, and recycling garbage during their science lessons, and this helped them identify especially good candidates for reuse (e.g., paper, cardboard, plastic). Once each pair of first graders had settled on the trash item they would reuse, Katie had them make a list of the materials they thought they would need and then sent an email to teachers, parents, and others asking for donations of the items needed.

Explicitly teaching genre features and genre-sensitive strategies Katie knew that authors need to know how to do something well before they can write a text teaching others how to do it, so she wanted to give students the opportunity to make the item (a key strategy for writing and revising procedural text is repeatedly carrying out the procedure oneself). Katie asked students to write down steps and details as they worked and use these notes to draft their texts. Katie coached them as needed.

Another key strategy is peer feedback. Katie arranged for the much-admired fourth graders in the classroom of her mentor teacher, Kathleen Jayaraman, to try out her students' procedures and provide feedback on the

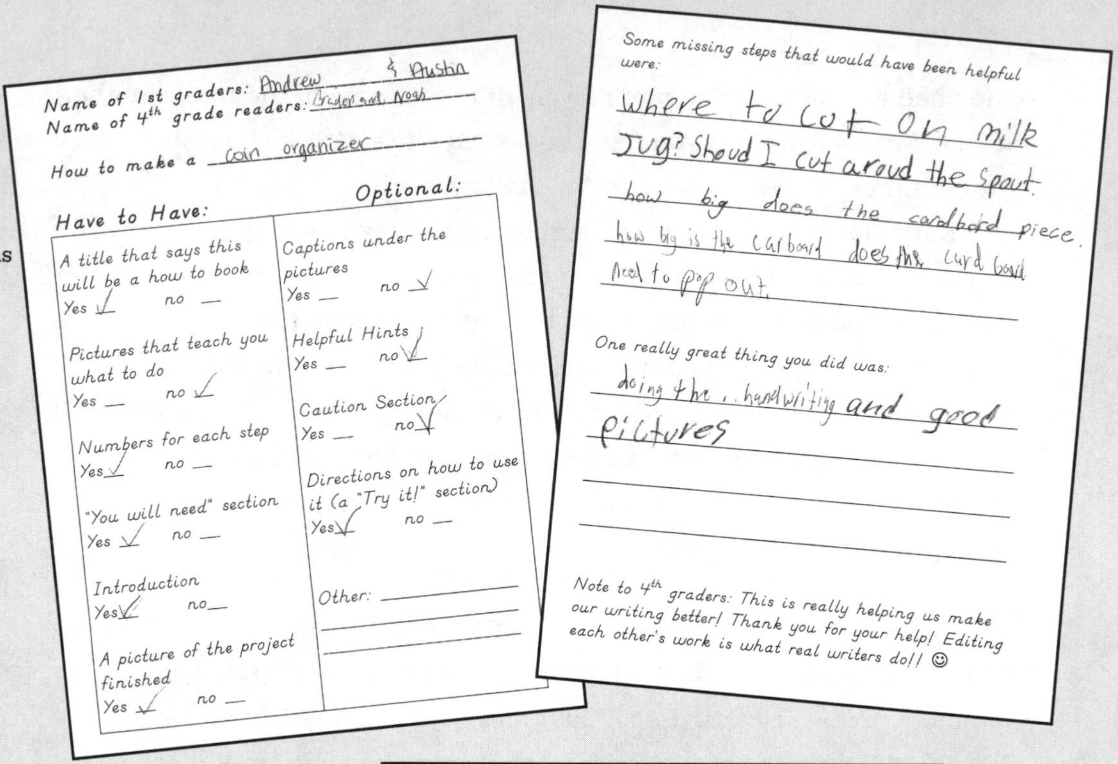

Figure 3.1 Feedback sheet for the fourth graders to complete as they read and carried out first graders' procedures

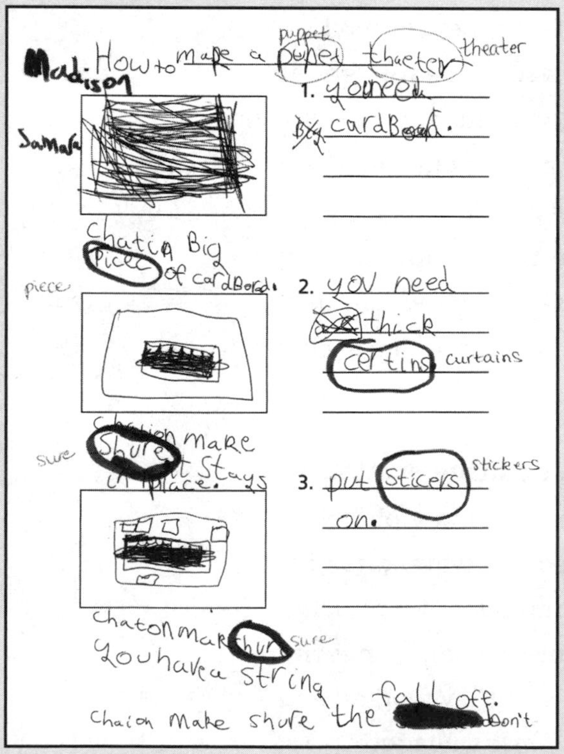

Name of 1st graders: Andrew   & Austin
Name of 4th grade readers: Brandon and Noah

How to make a _Coin organizer_

Have to Have: Optional:

A title that says this   Captions under the
will be a how to book   pictures
Yes ✓   no ___   Yes ___   no ✓

Pictures that teach you   Helpful Hints
what to do   Yes ___   no ✓
Yes ___   no ✓
                                Caution Section
Numbers for each step   Yes ___   no ✓
Yes ✓   no ___
                                Directions on how to use
"You will need" section   it (a "Try it!" section)
Yes ✓   no ___   Yes ✓   no ___

Introduction
Yes ✓   no ___   Other: _____

A picture of the project
finished
Yes ✓   no ___

Some missing steps that would have been helpful were:

where to cut on milk jug? Shoud I cut aroud the spout.
how big does the cardbord piece.
how big is the carbord does the curdbord
Need to pop out.

One really great thing you did was:

doing the handwriting and good pictures

Note to 4th graders: This is really helping us make our writing better! Thank you for your help! Editing each other's work is what real writers do!! ☺

Figure 3.2 Excerpt of a draft of *How to Make a Puppet Theater*

Madison
Samara
How to make a puppet theater

1. you need cardBord.

Chatin Big Piece of cardBord.
piece

2. you need thick certins curtains
sure

Chation make sure it stays in place.

3. put Sticers stickers on.

chaton make sure
Youhavea string
Chaion Make shure the ___ don't fall off.

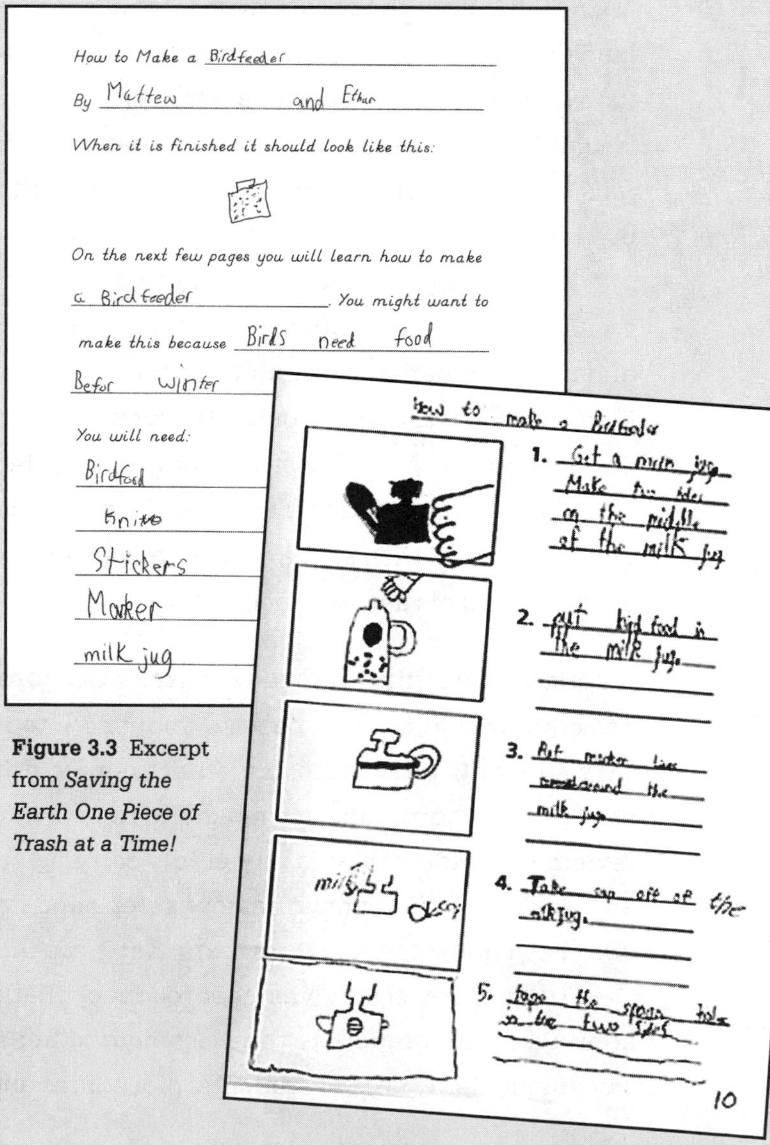

How to Make a Birdfeeder

By Mattew   and Ethan

When it is finished it should look like this:

On the next few pages you will learn how to make
a Birdfeeder . You might want to
make this because Birds need food
Befor winter

You will need:
Birdfood
Knive
Stickers
Marker
milk jug

Figure 3.3 Excerpt from *Saving the Earth One Piece of Trash at a Time!*

how to make a Birdfeeder

1. Get a milk jug Make an slit on the middle of the milk jug

2. put bird food in the milk jug.

3. Put marker line around the milk jug

4. Take cap off of the milk jug

5. tape the spout into two sides

10

form in Figure 3.1. She also asked the first graders to read over their own writing with a critical eye, for example by circling five words on their drafts they thought might be misspelled (Figure 3.2). Knowing that their book would be reproduced and sold in a real store, for real money, students worked diligently on their final drafts, scrutinizing both their illustrations and their writing.

Katie also developed students' knowledge of text features by using models from published books to help them create a cover page, table of contents, introduction, and index for their book. Spiral-bound copies were produced at a local copy shop (see Figure 3.3 for an excerpt), and Katie brought the copies to Horrocks. Sales of the book at the market came to $44. Students presented the check to the principal in a school assembly, and the principal promised the funds would be used to start a recycling program at the school in the fall.

Rethinking Popular Procedural Text Assignments: Beyond Making Peanut Butter and Jelly Sandwiches

A popular way to introduce procedural writing—a technique Nell used herself—is to have students write down how to make a peanut butter and jelly sandwich, then choose one student's version and follow it exactly, trying to get peanut butter on the knife without first opening the jar, spreading jelly on your arm because the instructions don't specify bread, and so on. Although this is amusing, the activity is problematic from a genre-with-purpose perspective. You already know how to make a peanut butter and jelly sandwich, so you don't need the students' instructions. And even if you didn't, the students are right there; they could demonstrate the procedure in person. Also, recipes often, and appropriately, assume some knowledge on the part of the reader; something like opening the jar first is understood.

The Purpose of Procedural Texts

Like all genres, procedural texts are the products of specific rhetorical situations (Miller 1984). In this case, they exist because people need to learn how to do things they don't yet know how to do. When the people teaching and learning are together physically, these texts may be oral. Written procedural texts allow people who are separated in time or space to teach and learn how to do something.

Katie Davis had her students read and write procedural text for the same reasons people read and/or write procedural texts outside school:

- to learn how to do something you want or need to know how to do

- to teach others how to do something (make a particular food or get to a particular place, for example)

Procedural texts are written by someone who knows how to do the procedure to be read by someone who does not (Duke et al. 2006/2007). Effective procedural reading and writing instruction reflects these real-world characteristics.

Now that you've seen one of our favorite procedural projects, compared that to an example of how procedural texts are commonly taught, and considered a definition of procedural texts according to their purpose, let's look at another great project and use it as a model for how to teach procedural reading and writing.

GENRE PROJECT

What Procedural Texts with Purpose Looks Like: Organizing Your Desk, Grade 5

Four fifth graders stand before a class of younger students eager to hear what the "big kids" have to say (see Figure 3.4). The fifth graders are giving a presentation on how to clean and organize your desk— and keep it that way. The second graders are mesmerized by these much-admired senior students of the school and can't wait to get their hands on the booklet the fifth graders made for them (see the example in Figure 3.5). The second graders' teacher thanks the fifth graders for their help.

Figure 3.4 Students present about organizing desks.

Designing a compelling, communicatively meaningful environment: Sometimes, you don't have to look far. Fifth-grade teacher Sheila Bell at Delta Center Elementary had some students who had difficulty keeping their belongings organized, and with the organizational demands of middle school looming, she was concerned. She didn't have to look far to identify a compelling context for students to write procedural text!

Sheila first had the students, with her help, create a rubric and use it to rate, clean, and organize their desks. Then she told them that other teachers in the school were complaining that their students had messy desks as well and asked whether they were interested in helping these teachers address the problem. Sheila's students designed a program in

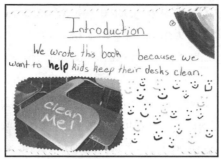

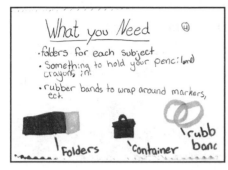

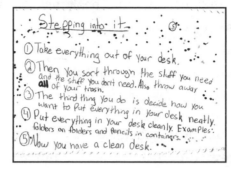

Figure 3.5 Kylie, Savanna, and Nicole's book about keeping their desks organized

which student teams would go to second- and third-grade classrooms, make presentations about organizing desks and keeping them organized, and leave behind a written how-to text on the topic for reference.

Providing exposure and experience: Study text characteristics with a focus on how they help or hinder a reader. Sheila engaged students in studying as many how-to books and manuals as they could find, making notes on their features, purpose, and usefulness to the reader (see Figure 3.6). Then the students determined which features best served their audience.

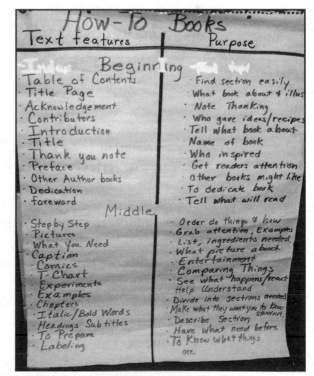

Figure 3.6 A chart paper generated as students studied features of how-to text

Explicitly teaching genre features and genre-sensitive strategies, without discouraging innovation. Sheila made sure not to treat the genre features students had identified as a rigid formula that could not be modified or expanded. Instead, she encouraged students to be innovative about how to help their audience. One book included a list of dos and don'ts related to keeping your desk clean, a feature not often seen in procedural texts but one that worked very well for this purpose and audience. Another book included results of a class survey about desk organization and a "germ fact" about the cleanliness of school desktops. Sheila encouraged her students to avoid dull, formulaic texts and use their textual knowledge to make their voices heard in interesting ways.

Offering ongoing coaching and feedback: Use the audience to inspire revision. Teams used the rubric they'd developed and their experiences organizing their own desks to inform their writing. Sheila circulated, coaching and providing particular feedback with regard to their audience: "Will this be clear to second or third graders?" "How can you grab the attention of second and third graders?" "What else will second or third graders need to know?" Sheila also coached students on presenting procedural text orally, emphasizing audience first and foremost.

How to Teach Procedural Text with Purpose: Five Principles for Instruction

We now discuss how our five principles apply to projects involving procedural text.

PRINCIPLE ① Design compelling, communicatively meaningful environments.

To teach students to read and write procedural text with purpose, you need to create situations in which someone wants or needs to know how to do something that your students know (or can learn) how to do. In Sheila Bell's and Katie Davis' classrooms, reading and writing procedural text did not arise solely from students' desire to learn "school stuff," earn a good grade, and/or please the teacher. Although these factors probably contributed, each project was carefully crafted to provide opportunities for other motivations. Although providing the opportunity does not mean students will accept it, students who repeatedly experience achievement tied to nonschool motives are likely to begin to adopt these motives (Guthrie, Wigfield & Perencevich 2004b).

A Three-Step Process for Designing Communicatively Meaningful Contexts for Reading or Writing Procedural Text		
Three-Step Process	**As Evidenced in Katie Davis' Earth Day Project**	**As Evidenced in Sheila Bell's Organizing Desks Project**
1. Identify a need or problem within or outside the school community.	Humans produce too much waste (later, there's no recycling program at the school).	Students have messy desks.
2. Identify a solution that involves teaching others how or learning how.	Teach people how to reuse some household waste to make different, useful items (later, raise money for a recycling program at the school).	Teach students how to organize their desks and keep them organized.
3. Use procedural text to help achieve the solution.	Write procedural texts about how to reuse household trash and sell them to members of the community.	Student teams give a presentation and provide a written procedural text on how to organize desks and keep them organized.

Five Surefire Ways to Get Students Reading Procedural Text with Purpose

1. *Offer students the opportunity to read how-to texts or watch how-to videos (on sites such as www.activitytv.com or www.ehow.com) to learn how to do something they'd like to do.*

2. *Invite students to write you a note about something they'd like to, but don't know how to do. Recommend (or ask the media specialist or a volunteer to recommend) related texts they can read independently at home or at school.*

3. *Engage students in reading procedural texts you have posted for classroom routines (how to operate the equipment in the listening center or how to do a particular activity in the math center, for example). These can be published texts or texts you or students have written (pictures only for emergent readers).*

4. *Provide manuals for students that you have developed on how to do each classroom job, so they're well prepared when it's their turn to do that job.*

5. *Offer texts on how to play particular games or do particular exercises or stretches in P.E., how to do particular art projects or use particular media in art, how to play particular instruments in music, and so on.*

Students have to be (or be able to become) experts in what they're writing procedures for.

Part of creating a communicatively appropriate context is ensuring that students are knowledgeable in the procedure they're writing about. Katie Davis had her students make their new product from reusable materials before writing a procedural text on how to do so. Sheila Bell had her students evaluate and organize their own desk before they wrote a text showing others how to do so. (In contrast, we have seen elementary school children write procedural texts on how to drive a car! They can't be experts on that without violating the law!)

Ten Compelling, Communicatively Meaningful Procedural Text Writing Projects

1. Students design a series of science investigations and write texts about how to do the investigations for another class or the following year's class.

2. Students write reader-friendly technical manuals about how to use particular pieces of technology (a partnership with a senior citizen home, a local business, or community group would create an audience).

3. Students write procedural texts for a school event (the annual carnival or ice cream social, for example).

4. Students collect and publish procedural texts on things their families know how to do—hobbies, cultural traditions, vocational or technical skills, and so on. For example, students might collect family recipes related to their cultural traditions and publish them in a cookbook.

5. Students research and write a collection of seasonally themed craft projects that buddies in another class can take home and do with their families.

6. Students publish a manual for new immigrants, and those interacting with new immigrants, about the school and/or school customs.

7. Students publish a manual for native-born students on how to interact productively and sensitively with immigrants.

8. Students create, collect, and publish texts that teach classmates a favorite hobby (e.g., making friendship bracelets, hairstyling, pitching a baseball).

9. Students provide clear, concise directions for how to play the available games on community game night (community game night, not family game night, so students whose families don't attend won't feel out of place).

10. Students write a manual of classroom or school procedures to give new students (this could include lunchtime procedures, the words to a school pledge, a map of the school, school rules, and so on).

PRINCIPLE ② Provide exposure and experience.

Procedural texts are common outside school: manuals for operating TVs and DVD/VHS players; recipes; directions for various crafts projects and games; instructions for organizational tools like label makers; step-by-step illustrations for exercises such as do-it-yourself yoga therapy. To develop students' ability to read and write procedural text, you need to surround them with procedural texts:

Classroom libraries: Procedural texts in the classroom library will feed students' growing interest in learning how to do things from text and provide models for their own procedural writing. But—unless they are currently being referenced for elements of genre or authors' craft—group them by area. Students are unlikely to think "I want to read a how-to text today," but may think "I feel like reading about art today" and come across a book about how to carry out various arts and crafts projects, or, "I feel like reading a sports book" and come across a book about how to draw sports figures or improve a particular game. Sources for procedural texts for the classroom library are highlighted in the box on page 63.

Classroom walls and other surfaces: Because how-to texts tend to be short, they are easier to post on classroom walls and other surfaces than many other text types. Idea 3 in the box on page 59 provides one reason to have procedural texts on classroom walls. Idea 10 in the box on page 60 provides how-to texts that would make sense clipped to the wall or placed on tables or other surfaces in the classroom.

Classroom activities: Whenever you tell students how to do something, you are using procedural text, so students in your classroom have lots of experience listening to it. Give students opportunities to deliver procedural text orally by having them teach other interested students how to do something they're especially good at (e.g., using a particular computer program, playing a particular recess game). Or, at the beginning of the week, teach table or center captains how to do the weekly assignments and have the captains teach the rest of their group (rotate the captain role). For other classroom activities involving writing or reading procedural text, see the boxes on pages 59 and 60.

Home reading programs: No matter how little a family reads, there are probably procedural texts in the home that can become a bridge between home and school literacies (Duke & Purcell-Gates 2003). As a lead-up to the organizing desks project, Sheila Bell had her students complete a survey about the reading done by their family members over the weekend, either filling out the survey themselves (Figure 3.7) or having family members fill it out (Figure 3.8). Many examples of procedural text surfaced, among many other types of reading. Students became remarkably metatextual as they and Sheila compiled the broad range of texts and purposes for reading in their homes (Figure 3.9). This exercise also validates students whose families perhaps don't read novels or more "academic" texts but do read in some form. For more about drawing on home literacy practices, see Purcell-Gates, 2011.

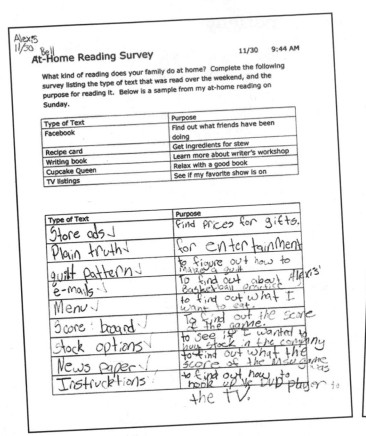

Figure 3.7 At-Home Reading Survey developed by Sheila Bell and completed by Alexis

Figure 3.8 At-Home Reading Survey developed by Sheila Bell and completed by Kristin and members of her family

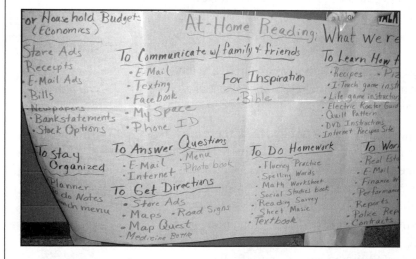

Figure 3.9 Students compile the results of the At-Home Reading Survey, identifying purposes and texts for reading.

Megan Menzynski, a third-, fourth-, and fifth-grade Title One teacher at Cashton Elementary School, takes advantage of her students' families' familiarity with procedural texts by inviting each family to write down how to do something other families might want to know how to do. These texts are compiled in a book and shared with the larger school community. Every family has a hobby, cultural tradition, vocational skill, or technical skill that is part of their "funds of knowledge"—"the historically accumulated and culturally developed bodies of knowledge and skills essential for household or individual functioning and well-being" (Moll, Amanti, Neff & Gonzalez 2001, 133). For example, a family member may know how to do a particular kind of weaving or be a master electrician or know how to can fruits and vegetables. Procedural writing offers one means of enabling families to share this know-how with others.

Recommended Model and Mentor Procedural Texts

High-quality procedural texts aimed at adults are everywhere: cookbooks, driving directions, self-help books, first-aid instructions, home and auto repair manuals, gardening books, fitness manuals, training manuals, appliance operating manuals, instructions for dealing with emergencies. Ones intended for children and adolescents are more difficult to find but still readily accessible. Here are some suggestions (roughly in order of difficulty):

Ten for Primary-Grade Readers

1. Dig In *by T. B. Morton. Pearson Education, 2005.*
2. Do the Loops Trick *by S. Fleming. Cambridge University Press, 2000.*
3. Hairy Harry *by B. Perez. National Geographic Society, 2001.*
4. Let's Make Music *by M. Clyne & R. Griffiths. Pearson Education, 2005.*
5. Let's Play: Games Around the World *by T. B. Morton. Pearson Education, 2005.*
6. Make a Paper Hat *by S. Fleming. Cambridge University Press, 2000.*
7. Pretend Soup and Other Real Recipes: A Cookbook for Preschoolers and Up *by M. Katzen & A. L. Henderson. Tricycle Press, 2004.*
8. Thumbprint Critters *by S. Tatler, illustrated by Bob Barner. Scott Foresman, 1993. (Please note: This one doesn't have a materials section; you can have an interesting discussion about whether or not it needs one.)*
9. What Is It? *by L. Kimmelman. Pearson Education, 2005.*
10. You Can Make a Pom-Pom *by M. Buckley. National Geographic Society, 2001.*

Ten for Upper-Elementary and Middle School Readers

1. Fabulous Hair: Find Your Best Look! *by M. Neuman. DK Publishing, 2006.*
2. Fairytale Things to Make and Do *by L. Pratt. Usborne, 2006.*
3. Here's How, *edited by Jennifer Hirsch. Pleasant Company Publications, 1996.*
4. How to Be a Spy in 7 Days or Less *by J. Smith. Kingfisher, 2007.*
5. Janice VanCleave's 200 Gooey, Slippery, Slimy, Weird and Fun Experiments *by J. P. VanCleave. Wiley, John & Sons, 1992.*
6. Make Gifts! *by K. Solga. McGraw-Hill Ryerson, 1991.*
7. Nature for Fun Projects *by S. Hewitt. Copper Beech Books, 2000.*
8. Rainy Day Activity Book *by A. Pinnington. Priddybooks, 2004.*
9. A Smart Girl's Guide to Friendship Troubles *by P. K. Criswell. American Girl Publishers, 2003.*
10. Travel Smart *by L. Buller. Pearson Education, 2005.*

Use problematic as well as model or mentor texts.

High-quality examples of the genre students are learning to read and write are important, but *poor-quality* examples are also valuable (e.g., texts that are ineffective at teaching someone how to do something because individual steps are unclear or not detailed enough). Students can learn a great deal about effective procedural writing by studying ineffective examples. Also, critiquing published texts reinforces the notion that not everything published can be trusted.

Fortunately (or unfortunately, depending on how you look at it), ineffective procedural texts abound. It's difficult to get permission from publishers or companies to use their work as an example of ineffective procedural text (!), but it's not hard to find these texts. Dollar stores are one good place to look (at their games, toys, crafts, kitchen materials). Low-cost crafts, toys, and games from overseas sold in bulk from catalogs and online (sources your school might use for ice-cream social prizes, incentives for reading programs, or the like) are another good place to find not fully effective procedural texts. Although they've improved in recent years, manuals that go with some electronic devices are also a good source. Common characteristics of ineffective procedural texts are:

- no materials list when one is needed

- incomplete materials list

- individual steps unclear

- steps missing altogether

- hard-to-read or altogether-absent graphics

≡ *How to Catch an Elephant*

Amy Schwartz has written a parody of procedural text called How to Catch an Elephant *(1999). If students are aware of the function and characteristics of procedural texts, it's fun to read this book with them. Materials needed include "3 cakes and 2 raisins"; the first two steps are "First, pack up your equipment. / Then ask your Uncle Jack to bring you to the place where elephants go."*

≡ *Informational and Procedural Genres: A Match Made in Monopoly*

Informational and procedural texts are often found together. For example, many information books also contain one or more procedural texts related to the topic being discussed, as in the brief Try It Out *boxes in the* It's Science! *series from Children's Press or the more traditional procedural discussions in* How People Learned to Fly *(Hodgkins 2007). The immediate purpose of these procedural features is to teach readers how to perform an investigation, but the results of the investigation provide further information on the topic being addressed. Students themselves may include procedural texts within the information books they write (as Kathleen Jayaraman's students did; see the discussion in Chapter 4). A genre-of-the-month approach precludes working with both informational and procedural text at the same time, but in a genre-with-purpose approach, both genres may be invoked whenever the project calls for it.*

As an alternative to the problematic fifty-states report, third-grade teacher Jill Hoort of Greenwood Elementary capitalized on her students' strong interest in board and video games. She asked whether they wanted to develop games featuring the Northeast United States, the region they were studying, and got their immediate buy-in. They were especially excited about the proposed audience for these games—parents who would be attending their authors' celebration. Students loved the idea of stumping parents with challenging questions about the Northeast.

Jill first had students bring in board games from home (she brought in some of hers as well). Students, working in groups, completed a "game study" in which they identified the object of the game, the materials, and so on. Jill asked them to pay close attention to the directions, emphasizing that clear directions are important if people are to be able to play a game successfully. Students noticed that many game directions were less than ideal in any number of ways. These ineffective texts helped them see what not to do in their own directions. Effective game directions provided models for what to do.

Jill also provided a board game rubric (see Figure 3.10) that students used to guide them in their work. They drafted, revised, and rewrote their game directions a number of times. Jill coached and gave feedback, and a "test group" of students in another third-grade classroom tried the games and completed a feedback sheet, answering such questions as "Were the directions written in a way that made sense and was easy to follow?" and "Did you clearly understand the object of the game?" and providing specific examples. The students' finished game directions conformed to conventions and were generally clear (see Figure 3.11).

Much of this project also focused on reading and writing informational text about the region. Students read about the Northeast to discover facts and information they could use to develop their game. They then wrote game questions based on this knowledge and understanding (comparable to the information they would have included in a "report"): "What is an important resource of the Northeast region?" (answer "the Atlantic Ocean"); "What is a coast?" (answer: "where land is next to the ocean").

Board Games

Group member's name: _____

Assignment

You are a board game manufacturer and you have been assigned the task of creating a board game that will help students review everything they read in _____ in a fun and interesting way.

Requirements

_____ Using a file folder, colored paper, colored pencils, and markers, create a game board. Put the name of your game on the tab of the folder and decorate the inside so that it is a game board. Make it neat, colorful, interesting, and creative.

10 Points	8 Points	6 Points	4 Points	2 Points
Everything is neatly created and directions were followed completely.	Game board is excellent, but some parts are a little sloppy.	Game board is complete, but 1 or 2 elements are missing and it could be neater.	Most of the directions were ignored and the board is sloppy.	There is a game board, but it is not colored and no extra efforts were made at creativity.

_____ Create 25 questions and answers for your game that relate to the Northeast region. These questions must be somehow incorporated into playing the game.

10 Points	8 Points	6 Points	4 Points	2 Points
There are 25 questions and answers and they are well incorporated into the game.	A couple of questions or answers are missing or incorrect.	Some questions are missing OR one could play the game without answering most questions.	Half of the questions are missing OR questions are hardly used in the game.	Many questions are incorrect or missing and very few are required to play the game.

_____ The format and purpose of your game must relate in some way to the region. Example: Game board is in the shape of the Northeast region OR the purpose is to sail a ship through the region.

10 Points	8 Points	6 Points	4 Points	2 Points
The purpose of the game relates directly to the region and the game board represents the theme.	The purpose closely relates to the region and the game board somewhat represents the theme.	The purpose partially relates to the region and the game board doesn't clearly represent a theme.	The purpose slightly relates to the region but does not represent a theme.	It is unclear what the purpose and theme of the game are from the appearance.

continues

Figure 3.10 The rubric Jill Hoort and her students used to evaluate the Northeast region games. It is a slightly modified version of a rubric provided by Erin Crisp of New Palestine, Indiana on ReadWriteThink.org, a joint project of the International Reading Association and National Council of Teachers of English.

_____ Write directions for your game that would make it perfectly clear how to play the game. Type the directions and glue them to the back cover of the file folder.

10 Points	8 Points	6 Points	4 Points	2 Points
Directions make it perfectly clear how to play the game. They are neatly typed with minimal grammatical errors.	Directions are typed, but have 2–3 grammatical errors. They are somewhat unclear or 1 step is missing.	There are more than 3 errors. Directions are unclear and 2–3 steps could be added to clarify.	Errors in grammar interfere with understanding of the directions. Much revision is needed.	Complete revision needed. Many steps are missing or incomplete and it is very difficult to understand how to play the game.

Content and difficulty

10 Points	8 Points	6 Points	4 Points	2 Points
Questions and rules of play are of an appropriate level—not too difficult and not too easy.	Rules of play are age appropriate, but some questions are too easy or too difficult.	Game is a bit too simple for the grade level and some questions are too easy.	Game is very simple and most questions are too easily answered.	Game is not appropriate for the grade level and questions are too easy or too difficult.

Total: _____ / 50 points

TURN IN THIS RUBRIC WITH YOUR GAME.

Figure 3.10 *(cont.)*

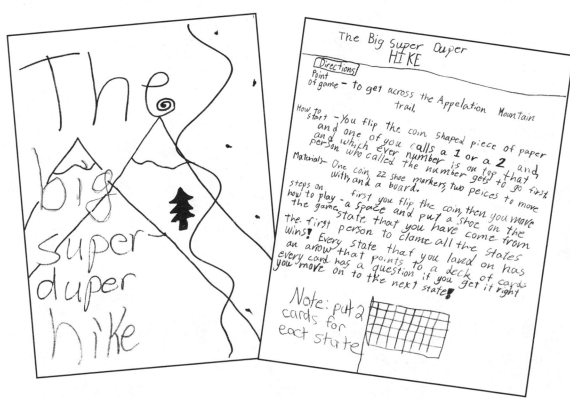

Figure 3.11 A board game about the Northeast region: the Big Super Duper Hike. The images shown are the front and back of a file folder. The inside of the folder consists of a map of the Northeast region.

Common Characteristics of Procedural Texts*

(Taken from Purcell-Gates, Duke & Martineau 2007)

Content Characteristics

- provides information about how to do something
- can occur in any number of domains, from cooking to crafts to science to sociology and so on

Structural Characteristics

- has a statement of goal (sometimes in the title; e.g., *How to Grow a Plant*) and/or inquiry question
- has a materials section
- includes methods/procedures/steps
- uses letters or numbers to indicate the order of the steps (less often, may use temporal terms such as *first, then, next, before, after*)
- has an evaluation of the outcome (e.g., *Now look at your two plants. Which one grew better?*)
- indicates the expected results and/or provides a scientific explanation for the results (a characteristic specific to procedural texts in science)

Language Characteristics

- has an explicit, clear description of materials
- has explicit information about procedures (how, when, etc.; e.g., *In two weeks, look at your plant* versus *Look at your plant later*)
- uses the *you* personal pronoun (or none at all)
- employs imperative verbs (e.g., *put, make*)
- uses units of measure (e.g., centimeters, inches)

Graphical Characteristics

- has graphics, and the graphics are almost always demonstrative
- has a graphic of the end product (e.g., a grown plant)

Navigational Features

- has headings/subcategories
- lists materials in order of use

* *Any given procedural text is unlikely to, and needn't, have all of these characteristics.*

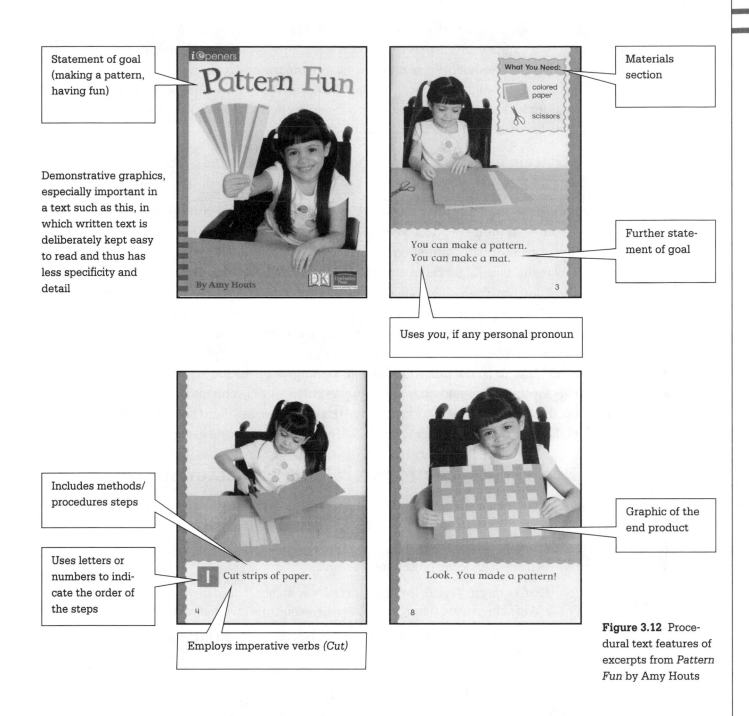

Statement of goal (making a pattern, having fun)

Demonstrative graphics, especially important in a text such as this, in which written text is deliberately kept easy to read and thus has less specificity and detail

Pattern Fun

By Amy Houts

Materials section

What You Need:
colored paper
scissors

You can make a pattern.
You can make a mat.

Further statement of goal

3

Uses *you*, if any personal pronoun

Includes methods/procedures steps

Uses letters or numbers to indicate the order of the steps

Cut strips of paper.

4

Employs imperative verbs *(Cut)*

Look. You made a pattern!

8

Graphic of the end product

Figure 3.12 Procedural text features of excerpts from *Pattern Fun* by Amy Houts

PRINCIPLE ③ Explicitly teach genre features.

Procedural texts have specific features different from those found in other types of text. A study of second and third graders reading and writing procedural texts in science (Purcell-Gates et al. 2007) found that explicit instruction in characteristic features improved students' writing (but not reading) of procedural texts—but *only* in classrooms in which reading and writing activities more often had a clear purpose beyond learning to read and write and texts were similar to texts found in the world outside school (those you might find in a bookstore or library).

We strongly advise that you explicitly teach procedural text features only as needed. Some students pick up some features on their own but need instruction in others. Some students recognize features easily; others need ongoing support. In order to respond to each text and each reading and writing situation, you need to be knowledgeable about procedural text features.

What do I need to know about procedural text characteristics?

Purcell-Gates and colleagues (2007) analyzed procedural texts appropriate for second and third graders in science (mainly procedures for conducting science investigations). The features on page 68 commonly appeared in these texts. Figure 3.12 is a published procedural text annotated to point out these characteristics.

Hart-Davidson (2009) divides characteristics of procedural text (he uses the term "writing to guide action") into three major categories: (1) staging, which includes setting the goal of the text/procedure and helping readers prepare for the procedure; (2) coaching, which includes using words and/or pictures to show the reader how to do the procedure; and (3) alerting, which includes providing warnings for the reader and noting how to prevent or solve problems that may come up. If you like, you might try to place the text characteristics listed here, or the parts of the texts shown in Figures 3.3 and 3.5 into these three broad categories.

How do I teach procedural text characteristics?

We suggest four components to teaching text characteristics explicitly (Purcell-Gates et al. 2007), as illustrated in the following about the materials section characteristic:

Name it: "This is the materials section. It tells the materials, or things, that are needed to do the procedure."

Model using it: "I want to make sure I have everything I need to make [whatever]. I'm going to read through the materials section to see a list of what I need."

Describe it: "The materials section often lists the materials in the order you will use them." (This is an important point; some young children list the materials in the order of interest—clay, even if not needed until late in the procedure, is likely to get first billing!)

Explain its function: "Readers need to know what they need to do the procedure. If readers don't know what they need, they might get to a step and find they can't do it because they don't have what they need. If they can't get what they need quickly, they may not be able to finish the procedure at all. Once I was making bread. . . ."

> There's no point in having features for features' sake; features should be included for your readers' sake.

We can't stress enough the importance of the final component. Always emphasize what the feature does for the reader—there's no point in having features for features' sake; features should be included for your readers' sake. Just as we don't want students who can recite phonics rules but aren't able to apply them, we don't want students who can rattle off features but can't use them, can't see their value or utility.

You might think of teaching genre features as falling under the larger umbrella of teaching author's craft. Don't lose sight of the other aspects. For example, in a project described earlier in this chapter (pages 56–58), some students wanted to reach out to readers in their opening. Their final draft began:

> Are you sick of your desk being messy? Are you getting frustrated because of your desk? If so, listen very closely to us. We're going to guide you through a step-by-step instruction to clean your desk.

From a characteristics perspective, this is "statement of goal," but it is more than that—it is an opening designed to grab readers' attention and act, essentially, as an advertisement for the pamphlet. Encourage students to include these kinds of thoughtful innovations rather than simply check off genre features they've "covered" in their text.

PRINCIPLE ④ Explicitly teach genre-specific or genre-sensitive strategies.

Procedural texts have a unique purpose and unique features, and there are strategies uniquely appropriate for reading and writing them.

Teach reading strategies.

We know of no published research on strategies good readers use when they read procedural texts, but observation tells us the following are effective practices:

Preview the text. Look ahead to see what materials, time, and expertise are needed and to see what the finished product looks like.

Gather or ensure that you have the materials or ingredients needed. Although this isn't always necessary, it is usually a good idea.

Read steps in order from beginning to end. Unlike informational texts (described in Chapter 4), it is usually necessary to read procedural texts linearly. If it is a compilation of a number of procedural texts, readers may read selectively and nonlinearly (selecting only particular procedures, and perhaps reading those in a different order). But within a given procedure, assuming they are reading English, readers need to begin at the first word and read from left to right and top to bottom until they reach the end of that section.

Pause frequently. It is generally best for readers to read a chunk of text (e.g., a step), pause to follow that instruction, and then read the next chunk. As they do this, they will use the order markers (such as 1, 2, 3 or a, b, c) when these appear to guide their movement from step to step.

Use the illustrations. In many procedural texts, the photographs, diagrams, and illustrations contain important information, and readers usually look at the graphic accompanying each step (if applicable). After each step it is a good idea to compare what you have done with what is shown in the illustration.

Reread. It is often helpful to reread a step or part of a step several times before attempting to implement it.

Take notes. When the procedural text is more a self-help guide (providing advice about how to deal with bullies, for example), it can be useful to take notes on key points.

Use other strategies. Many other reading strategies that apply to a variety of texts, such as strategies for decoding or ascertaining the meaning of unfamiliar words, can also be applied in reading procedural text.

Students may implement some or many of these strategies without instruction; you should talk with and observe students to decide which ones you need to teach, preferably using the gradual release of responsibility approach (Pearson & Gallagher 1983) described in Chapter 2. In the following section, we focus on one phase of the approach—modeling or thinking aloud.

Think aloud to model reading procedural text.

Making the strategy or process transparent to students through modeling is a crucial part of teaching. With procedural text, it may be tempting to read each step to students and then do that step. But you should also think aloud as you read and perform the steps, voicing what you are thinking. Students get to see an expert reader's otherwise invisible thought processes in action as you pay attention to certain things, voice specific kinds of questions or comments, and selectively employ strategies. A procedural text think-aloud might begin:

> Okay, I'm going to start by looking through the text. I need a sense of what I'm going to need for this, how long this is going to take, and what this is going to look like when I'm done. Oh, I see I'm going to need dried beans. I'm not even sure I have those. I'm going to check my supply closet before we go any further. . . .

Effective think-alouds can be difficult to enact. They often need to be planned and rehearsed. As you page through the text, think about the strategy (or set of strategies) you want to target and identify places where this strategy would "naturally" be employed. Sticky notes with "reminder" phrases are a useful tool for marking places to stop and think aloud.

Think-alouds are not limited to specific grade levels. They are appropriate at every grade level, but their subjects, complexity, and vocabulary will change as students' comprehension, world knowledge, and interests change. And think-alouds are more than demonstrations. For a think-aloud to be effective, you have to reveal your underlying thought processes. Often, novices report their conclusions (e.g., "That character is from Japan") without explaining how and why they arrived at the conclusion (e.g., "He is wearing a kimono and looks similar to many people from Japan"). Omitting the intervening process prevents students from seeing how expert readers combine background knowledge, local text knowledge, and picture clues to arrive at a reasonable interpretation. Taking the time before the lesson to think through (and verbalize) the step-by-step application of the targeted strategy and its outcome can yield high dividends.

☰ *Using a Think-Aloud to Demonstrate Mistaken Thinking*

Some teachers like to do silly or uninformed think-alouds from time to time, thinking aloud the wrong things to do and waiting for students to correct them. For example:

Ms. Smith: *Okay, I'm going to start reading right here at step 3 because three is my favorite number.*

Students: *No! No! No!*

Ms. Smith: *What? What's wrong?*

Student 1: *You can't start at step 3.*

Student 2: *You have to start at step 1.*

Student 3: *You have to do the steps in order!*

Obviously, this works best after you have done some regular explicit teaching and modeling so that students have begun to learn how to read the text effectively (and thus can correct you). This approach can be engaging and help students really own effective reading strategies for that genre. You might wear a funny hat or have some other signal to indicate you are going to play the role of the uninformed reader.

Teach writing strategies.

Five strategies we believe are useful to teach students to use when writing procedural text are:

1. *Conduct the procedure, taking notes or writing in the process.* A writer is more likely to think of everything a reader needs to know to conduct a procedure by doing the procedure him- or herself.

2. *Use a template or outline.* Younger or struggling writers may benefit from using a template with a space for the title, the materials, steps, graphics for each step, and a graphic of the final product (see Figure 3.3). Older students may simply need an outline or other reminder to organize their draft into materials and ordered steps.

3. *Write from a rubric or list of characteristics of effective procedural text.* A rubric (e.g., Figure 3.10) or a list of characteristics of effective procedural writing (e.g., clear and explicit steps) can help focus writing and revision. Ideally, students should help create this as you examine published procedural texts together.

4. *Revise in rounds.* Writers should engage in several read-throughs of their text, each focusing on different aspects that may need to be revised or edited. This is often more effective than read-throughs that focus on everything at once. This is especially true of procedural text, in which

there are so many different things to read for—clarity and specificity of course, but also the accuracy of the materials section and procedures, the effectiveness of the graphics, the accessibility of the layout, the mechanics, and so on.

5. *Have someone else try to do the procedure based on your text.* Those who write and publish cookbooks, for example, often have test cooks carry out the procedures to see whether they are written correctly and thoroughly. Testers should note when they have difficulty and/or send you notes or complete a feedback sheet (e.g., Figure 3.1).

PRINCIPLE ⑤ Offer ongoing coaching and feedback.

Nell often says she'd stack a great teacher up against an assessment any day of the week. That is, no assessment can tell us as much as a knowledgeable teacher who carefully observes her students. Because there are so few assessments for procedural reading or writing, you need to especially rely on your observations. The following project shows how two second-grade teachers used observations of students' procedural reading and writing to guide their teaching.

GENRE PROJECT

What Genre with Purpose Looks Like:
The Weather Tools Project, Grade 2

Students are excited about a new batch of letters from their pen-pal classroom (a second-grade classroom in another district school). The letters thank students for the great weather tools books they sent (Figure 3.13) and share plans to make the tools to report on weather at their school. At an end-of-year picnic at which students get to meet their pen pals, the weather tool books come up again, as students report to one another which tools they made and how it went. Not the usual picnic conversation!

Figure 3.13
Excerpts from Meaghan, Avery, Alex, and Melanie's text on how to make an anemometer (a type of weather tool)

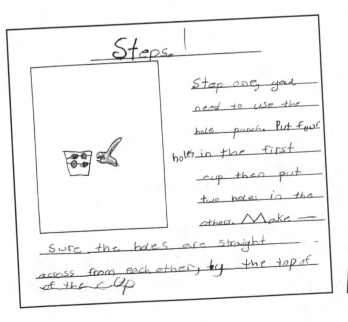

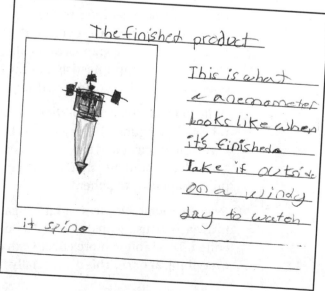

Designing a compelling, communicatively meaningful context: One text inspires another. As part of a unit on weather, Denise Dufort and Jamie Slear's students at Greenwood Elementary gave a weather report each day over the school's PA system. Students used weather tools to gather information about the weather right outside their school building. One of their challenges was to construct their own wind vanes, using the National Geographic Science procedural text *How to Make a Wind Vane* (see Figure 3.14). Of course, meteorologists measure much more than just wind direction, a point made at the end of the book (see Figure 3.15). Denise

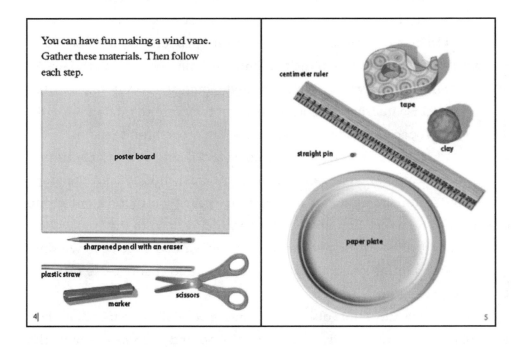

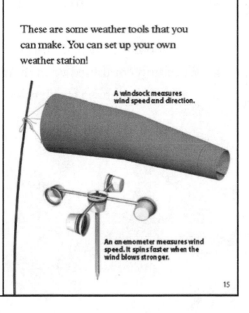

Figures 3.14 and 3.15
How to Make a Wind Vane: A Procedural Text. Copyright © 2010 by The Hampton-Brown Company, LLC, a wholly owned subsidiary of the National Geographic Society. Used by permission of the publisher. All rights reserved.

and Jamie lamented that they didn't have instructions for how to make any other weather tools. Students quickly volunteered to figure out how to make other weather tools based on the pictures in the book and then write detailed directions for doing so that their classmates, as well as their second-grade pen pals in another school, also studying weather, could use.

Explicitly teaching genre features and genre-sensitive strategies: Let observation guide what you teach and to whom.
Based on their observations of students' work with instructions for other classroom assignments, as well as their approach to informational text, Denise and Jamie realized that most or all students would need to be explicitly taught certain strategies for reading procedural text, such as previewing the text and gathering needed materials. As students began writing their own text, some strategies also merited whole-class instruction, such as using a template to guide their writing and specific headings to structure the procedural text.

There were also strategies Denise and Jamie taught only to subsets of students. For example, although most groups read the steps in order from beginning to end without explicit instruction, one group needed help resisting the temptation to skip ahead to the "fun" steps. Similarly, although some students were clear and specific in wording the steps, others needed lots of coaching and feedback to be sufficiently clear and detailed.

Denise and Jamie observed students carefully and modified their instruction accordingly. When they observed students taping the arrow head and end to the straw horizontally, though it needed to be vertical, they reminded students to compare the graphic after each step with what they had done in each step. Denise and Jamie's careful kidwatching combined with their knowledge of genre-specific strategies allowed them to teach the right strategy at the right time.

Procedural Text: The Power of Teaching a Genre Everyone Reads

One of the most widely read genres is procedural texts, which, in and of itself, is an argument for teaching them. Although quantity and quality of books vary in students' home environments, you will find that every student's home contains at least one procedural text. The ubiquitous nature of these texts reflects their foundational role in our lives. We teach and learn how to do things. In order to be successful citizens of the world, students must be able both to acquire new skills from others and to pass along their new skills to others.

Developing and Communicating Expertise:
Informational Genres

What Genre with Purpose Looks Like: The Zoo-Animal Guidebook Project, Grades K–2, Lansing School District

On a bright summer day dozens of K–2 students, all boys, stream into the city zoo. With them are their summer school teachers, as well as the high school students who are the boys' mentors (Figure 4.1). Field trips to zoos are commonplace, but this is no ordinary field trip and no ordinary day. The K–2 students are there to deliver "animal guides" they developed for the zoo. Exhibits throughout the park will now include guides providing additional information about the animal(s) on display (Figure 4.2).

Former kindergarten teacher (now assistant professor) Kate Roberts led this special summer school experience for a group of at-risk boys in Lansing, Michigan. In twenty half-day sessions over five weeks,

Figure 4.1 *(left)* Children and their mentors at the zoo, ready to carry out their research!

Figure 4.2 *(right)* A first grader and his mentor show off their completed guide to animals living on the Coral Reef.

teachers in six classrooms taught students to design and create their own zoo-animal guidebooks—a compelling, communicatively meaningful purpose for researching and writing informational text.

Providing exposure and experience Students worked with informational text in a variety of ways and formats.

- They read letters from the head veterinarian at the zoo and sent her letters in return.

- They emailed questions to zoo personnel and interviewed them in person.

- They listened to presentations by zoo personnel.

- They listened to factual books that were read aloud to them.

- They observed animals and took notes or drew pictures of what they saw.

- With help from their mentors (three to five in each classroom) and their teacher, they gathered information from books and websites about animals.

Explicitly teaching genre features and genre-sensitive strategies
As students read and wrote informational text, their teachers presented daily lessons on informational text features (e.g., index, table of contents, captions, diagrams), comprehension, research strategies, and writers' craft, as well as phonological awareness, sound–letter relationships, and sight word vocabulary. All lessons, worksheets, textbooks, or other materials were related to preparing students to do research, communicate with experts, or create the zoo-animal guides in an enjoyable way.

Getting Results

On average, students in this demographic group lose ground academically over the summer (Cooper, Nye, Charlton, Lindsay & Greathouse 1996). But students in this program made significant gains in comprehension, letter–word identification, word attack, and attitude toward writing. Just as important, students connected with and contributed to their community in a way few children in the United States have the opportunity to do.

Rethinking Popular Informational Text Assignments: Beyond "Reports"

Now that you've seen what an informational text project can look like, let's consider more typical informational text assignments. Writing informational text in school often falls under the banner of "reports" (as in "a report about cheetahs"). Report used in this way is a school-bound term. People don't say they are going to the bookstore or a library to look for a "report" on pandas. Better to use terms found in the real world (*field guide, atlas, encyclopedia, pamphlet, information book/booklet, informational website*) and reserve "report" for how it's used outside the classroom (for example, if you and your students collaboratively write and submit a grant proposal that is indeed funded, the class might need to write a report to the funding agency on how the grant money was used).

In addition, informational writing in schools too often lacks a compelling audience or format. Animal and other reports (the "fifty-states reports" in Chapter 1, for example) usually have no audience beyond teacher, classmates, and family. Worse, they are usually created in a format one rarely finds outside school (e.g., the five-paragraph essay) or that all too closely imitates, if not copies from, the sources students used for their writing in the first place!

The writing in Kate's summer school program was different. The pieces were called *animal guides*. Many different kinds of texts informed the writing—factual books about animals, yes, but also interviews, letters, emails, and other sources. The children had a compelling context for their writing (zoo exhibits featuring a particular animal or habitat) and a compelling audience—visitors to the zoo.

The Purpose of Informational Texts

The summer school project involved students in developing expertise and sharing that expertise with others. It engaged students in reading and writing what we call informational genres, and doing so for the same reasons people read and/or write informational texts outside of a schooling context. Outside of schools:

- Informational texts are written for the primary purpose of conveying information about the natural or social world to a person or people who want or need to know that information.

- Informational texts are read for the primary purpose of obtaining information one wants or needs to know.

- Informational texts are written by someone who knows the information to be read by someone who does not (Duke et al. 2006/2007).

- In the summer school project, students read to gather information on the animals about which they were going to write their guides. They wrote guides that would teach visitors to the zoo about the animals they saw there. They developed expertise and conveyed it to an audience who did not possess that expertise. Many teachers create opportunities like this for informational writing. We can get beyond reports.

Understanding the Term Informational Text

Some people use the term informational text *to mean* nonfiction—*any text that is true or purports to be true. A menu is nonfiction if the restaurant really serves those dishes, an account someone writes about what happened to her over the weekend is nonfiction, and so on. Yet these texts do not share the same purpose or features. They are different in important ways, and we shouldn't use the same term for all of them. It is better to talk about different types of nonfiction: informational text, biography and autobiography, memoir, and so on.*

Other authorities—including the National Assessment of Educational Progress (NAEP) Framework (National Assessment Governing Board 2008) and the Common Core State Standards (2010a)—use informational text, *only slightly less broadly, to refer to texts that convey information about the natural and social world and texts that teach others how to do something* (procedural or how-to texts) and *texts meant to persuade (such as editorials). (The NAEP Framework's other big category is* literary text, *which includes fiction, literary nonfiction—such as essays, speeches, and autobiographies or biographies—and poetry.)*

We use the term informational text *more narrowly, because we believe there are important reasons to distinguish* procedural, persuasive, *and* informational texts; *two of them are that they have different purposes and different characteristics (see the discussions of procedural text in Chapter 3 and persuasive text in Chapter 6). Although we sometimes use the term* expository text, *we prefer* informational text *because it gets right at its purpose—to inform. In* What Genre with Purpose Looks Like *on pages 82–83, we describe another project in which students are engaged in writing to inform.*

What Genre with Purpose Looks Like:
The Books of Hope Project, Grades 2 and 4

A group of students in Michigan are looking, entranced, at a collection of photos. In the photos, students in Uganda are holding books the Michigan students wrote. These Michigan students have made a difference half a world away.

This our city. It is called Lansing.

Lansing is the capital of our state.

Figure 4.3 A page from the class-written book *Delta Center on the Map*

Designing a communicatively meaningful environment: Invite rather than assume participation. Fourth-grade teacher Kathleen Jayaraman and second-grade teacher LeAnn Thelen offered their students the option of working with Books of Hope (www.booksofhope.org), a service-learning program in which students in U.S. schools create books for students in foreign schools that provide English-language instruction. Once Kathleen's and LeAnn's students learned that children "just like them" had so few books, they were eager to help—and to learn what life is like for children in another part of the world. LeAnn and the second graders created a sample book (Figure 4.3). After the book was reviewed and accepted by the Books of Hope staff, the Michigan students were matched with a sister school in Uganda. Kathleen and her fourth graders then took the lead in writing a series of books about light and sound, topics relevant to the students in both schools.

Providing exposure and experience: Texts and content. To write about a topic you often have to know a lot about it. Kathleen filled her classroom with excellent informational texts on light and sound. She also designed related hands-on experiences based on state science standards (investigations with flashlights and mirrors, for example).

Providing explicit teaching of genre features and genre-sensitive strategies: Use peer feedback to improve writing. Kathleen emphasized that one important strategy in writing is to obtain feedback from others and to revise, as appropriate, based on that feedback. LeAnn's second graders were ideal reviewers for evaluating the clarity of the fourth graders' explanations and graphics, and both groups of students learned that feedback from their peers helps make their writing more effective. There were also several adult reviewers.

In all, students revised their books six, eight, even ten times! Looking at the photos of students in Uganda holding their books, students felt it was well worth it. (Figure 4.4 shows students hard at work; Figure 4.5 contains excerpts of the final products.)

Figure 4.4 Students hard at work

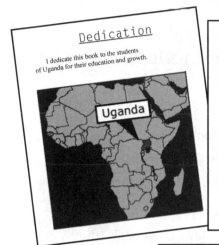

Dedication

I dedicate this book to the students of Uganda for their education and growth.

Uganda

Inside of your Ear

You hear many different sounds every day. You hear people talking, you hear music, and sounds of cars. You have learned that sound is made by vibrations. Vibrations send sound waves through the air. But how do your ears turn these sound waves into the sounds we hear? Your ear has three main parts, the outer ear, the middle ear, and the inner ear. The sound waves start out as a vibration then they travel as a sound wave, they go into your ear and hit what is called your eardrum. Then you can hear the sound.

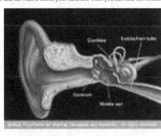

Figure 4.5 Excerpts from students' books written for children in Uganda. Notice the attention to audience evidenced in the excerpts.

BOOK SUMMARY:

Learn all about sound in this **amazing** book. Also look at some COOL pictures. Learn about VIBRATIONS, TROUGHS, RAREFRACTIONS, CRESTS, and MORE. How do we hear? The answer is **in this book.** Do you like COOL FACTS ? This book   has cool facts too. OPEN THIS BOOK to LEARN ALL ABOUT SOUND.

Dedication

I dedicate this book to the kids in Uganda because they give me the strength to make this book great.

LIGHT

On earth our light comes from the sun. The light travels to the earth in a straight line.

The color of the light is white. The white light is really made from six different colors. The colors are red, orange, yellow, green, blue, and violet.

Ro G. Biv

Red | Orange | | Green | Blue | Indigo | Violet

To remember the order of the colors in a rainbow, we use the term Roy G. Biv

Narrative-Informational Text

Some books appear to have two purposes—to convey a fictional experience and to convey information. We call these narrative-informational texts. They are also called dual-purpose texts (Donovan & Smolkin 2001), pseudonarrative texts (Jetton 1994), and hybrid books (Pappas 2006). Classic examples are the Magic School Bus series, by Joanna Cole, and the Magic Tree House series, by Mary Pope Osborne. It's certainly all right to include these kinds of books in the classroom, but make sure there are also plenty of purely informational texts and purely narrative texts as well. And remember that some young children will have difficulty distinguishing the nonfiction information from the fictional elements. Also, a recent study of third and fourth graders found that students answered more comprehension questions correctly and recalled more key concepts when scientific information was presented as informational text than when it was presented in a fictional narrative (Cervetti, Bravo, Hiebert, Pearson & Jaynes 2009).

How to Teach Informational Text with Purpose: Five Principles for Instruction

We turn now to discussing how our five principles apply to projects involving informational text.

PRINCIPLE ① Design compelling, communicatively meaningful environments.

Informational texts are written by and for people who want or need to know information. In a classroom where reading and writing informational texts is compelling and communicatively meaningful, students want or need to know information.

Introduce interesting topics.

Introducing an interesting topic is a straightforward way to create the desire for information. Informational texts on sports, the human body, and animals (think sharks, snakes, bunnies, horses) are good bets. But interest is also an individual matter. Taking an interest inventory early in the year can help you connect texts with students' interests. Maybe one student loves books about art and architecture, another is interested in books about skateboarding, and still another is fascinated by the history of hip hop. Keene (2008) identifies becoming passionately interested in reading about specific topics as a key dimension of comprehension.

But what about the student who seems to have no interest in reading informational text of any kind? These students are probably relatively uncommon (as Mohr 2006 suggests), but when you do encounter them, try to find books related to stories they like. For example, if the student loves fantasy, give him *Unicorns* (Clarke 2006) or *Dragons* (Tatchell 2005). Or if the student is crazy for Angelina Ballerina books (written by Katherine Holabird and illustrated by Helen Craig), she might eagerly open *My First Ballet Book* (Castle 2006).

Introduce interesting graphics.

You can also create the desire to know with interesting graphics. For example, *Let's Find Out About Ice Cream* (Reid 1996) has photographs from the Ben and Jerry's ice-cream factory. Once students see a few of these photographs, their interest in reading the book or having it read to them is palpable.

Design projects around pressing issues.

Pressing issues in children's and adolescent's lives are also compelling reasons for reading and writing informational texts. When working with a class of second graders on a project about microscopic animals (lice, fleas, dust mites—maybe gross to you, but a huge hit with second graders!), Nell met a boy completely absorbed by reading about and making a poster featuring dust mites. He'd been told for years that he was allergic to dust mites but had no idea what they were!

Reading specialist Ann Castle of Greenwood Elementary used current events to get her students to want information. The community, faced with major financial problems, was going to have to close a number of schools, and students were understandably worried that theirs might be one of them. Ann incorporated their concern into her teaching. Students read an article from the local newspaper about new district boundaries. They read several informational pieces about the history of Michigan schools, including the ones in their area. Children were surprised to learn that their school was formerly the site of a one-room schoolhouse and that there were over fifty one-room schoolhouses in their area at one time! These "struggling" readers became resident experts on a topic of wide interest to the entire school community.

Reading Level and Interesting Text

When you go out of your way to provide students with texts of high interest to them, students are likely to be able to read at a higher level than you would otherwise expect. Laura Jiménez (Jiménez & Duke 2011) found that fourth graders reading texts they found very interesting used many more comprehension processes, a greater range of comprehension processes, and had better recall (scores nearly doubled!). Already knowing quite a bit about a topic also seems to support reading comprehension (Hollingsworth & Reutzel 1990; Pritchard 1990). Among other things, this suggests we shouldn't stick rigidly to students' "reading level," as that level may depend to some degree on their interests, background knowledge, even how much sleep they got the night before!

When the texts students want to read are too difficult, you can use a variety of instructional moves to make them more accessible. For example, Ann used the following strategies:

Rereading: *Rereading increases fluency and comprehension. Once Ann's students had reread a text to the point they were able to do so fluently, she had them read it to someone else interested in the looming school closings (which included everyone in the school!).*

Rewriting: *Ann wrote her own, easier-to-read versions of some of the texts. This doesn't take as long as you might think and greatly increases the range of accessible information.*

Coaching and scaffolding: *Ann cued students to chunk a word into parts or reminded them to use a helpful comprehension strategy.*

Writing in response to reading: *Comprehension and learning can be supported by writing (see Collins, Lee, Fox & Madigan 2011, for example). Ann followed up the students' research by helping them create a digital text about the school then and now; they gathered photos from the past, took photos of the school now, and compared the two.*

Create need-to-know situations.

Kate and the team of Kathleen and LeAnn created situations in which students needed to know information in order to write their zoo-animal guides or books for their peers in Uganda. But there are less elaborate ways to create need-to-know situations. During flu season, *Germs Make Me Sick!* (Berger 1995) is compelling reading. An upcoming field trip can trigger a need to know. An infestation of a particular bug in the classroom may prompt students to consult a field guide on insects. Wanting to know whether they'll be able to conduct tomorrow's outdoor science investigation might lead students to read an online weather report. Do these examples sound familiar? They should. Many of the reasons you need to consult informational text in your daily life are also reasons to consult informational text in the classroom.

Provide a real audience.

Audience is central to compelling, communicatively meaningful writing of any kind, certainly informational texts. Periodically, you can be that compelling audience—for example, you might bring in your childhood rock collection (or re-create it) and ask students to research and write a guide to the rocks in it, so you can display the guide along with the collection. But typically you alone—or even the class—is not a sufficiently compelling audience.

Here are ten potential audiences for students' informational writing:

1. students in another classroom studying the same or a related topic

2. students in younger grades who are interested in the topic

3. new teachers who will be teaching a unit on the topic

4. the larger school community (Lynn Bigelman, Principal of Jayno Adams Elementary School, a Michigan and National Blue Ribbon School and recipient of the International Reading Association Exemplary Reading Award for the state of Michigan, hosts "living museum" nights in which students give workshops and presentations on topics on which they've become experts.)

5. local businesses relevant to the topic (restaurants for texts about foods, banks for texts about money, pet stores for texts about animals)

6. local nonprofits relevant to the topic (visitor centers for texts about the region, state, city, town, or tourist attractions; community gardens for texts about plants)

7. electronic or paper pen pals (a group of students wrote books about Michigan for students in a school in China; the Chinese students sent books about their province in return)

8. readers of websites

9. book authors, publishing companies, entertainers, website authors—anyone who has made an informational error students recognize and want to correct or who would for any other reason be interested in the topic on which students are writing

10. your family and/or friends (for example, a teacher asked her students to write a pamphlet about how to move heavy objects for her father, who was about to move to a new home)

Follow through.

Whoever the audience, you need to follow through. If you say you're going to send students' letters to the Chinese government, it's important you do so. If you say your son's preschool teacher is going to show her charges the video your students made, arrange for that. It only takes one or two failures to follow through to ruin it for students and teachers later on. Students lose trust and, along with it, buy-in.

If possible, students should receive tangible proof of follow-through. A favorite example comes from classroom teacher and reading specialist Christina Trotochaud of Holbrook Elementary. Second graders in Chrissy's school wrote books about Michigan for a hotel in Michigan's Mackinaw City, which attracts many out-of-state tourists. Chrissy made sure the books were available to guests in the hotel lobby. One guest wrote the students, telling them how much she enjoyed the books and sharing facts about her own state. Students were thrilled, and the experience likely helped develop their belief that they can touch the world through writing.

PRINCIPLE ② Provide exposure and experience.

A number of studies suggest that elementary-age students get relatively little exposure to and experience with informational text (e.g., Jeong, Gaffney & Choi 2010), on average only 3.6 minutes per day in first grade according to one study (Duke 2000), even less in classrooms in economically deprived areas. It's critical to include informational books:

> *In classroom libraries.* Informational texts on interesting topics should be available in the classroom. We recommend that at least a third of the classroom library be informational text. Libraries, secondhand book sales, Web texts (onscreen or printed), magazine subscriptions, and free informational brochures provided by organizations are among the low-cost ways to increase the volume of informational text in your classrooms. If you can't yet achieve the 1:3 ratio, at least increase the number of informational texts you display; students gravitate toward texts that are more visible.

> *On classroom walls and other surfaces.* Informational posters, informational magazine articles, informational "wall books" (a book is taken apart and taped along the wall where students can read it as they wait in line, move to a different room or activity, and so on), students' own informational writing—all these and more can and should grace classroom walls and other surfaces.

> *In classroom activities.* Every recurring activity that involves extended text (three or more related sentences) should feature informational text—at least one-third of the time, we suggest. For example, if you read aloud every day, some of the texts should be informational. If students write every day, some days they should be writing informational text. Informational text should

also be spread throughout the day, rather than concentrated only in English language arts or only in science (in the former, content may get less attention; in the latter, text-as-text may get less attention).

In home reading programs. Some parents prefer reading informational text with their children (e.g., Caswell & Duke 1998; Xu 1999), and parents seem to attend more to vocabulary and concepts when reading informational text (Pellegrini, Perlmutter, Galda & Brody 1990). Yet too often teachers give students only narratives or basic descriptive texts ("I like apples. I like bananas. . . .") to read at home. Make a point to include information books, magazines, printed excerpts from websites, downloadable books, and similar texts.

Use model or mentor texts.

A myth even adults buy into is that writing informational text is cut-and-dried—"Just the facts, ma'am." However, there is a great deal of art to conveying information engagingly and effectively. We have all read informational texts that are real snoozers, as well as ones we couldn't put down—check out Nicola Davies' *What's Eating You? Parasites—The Inside Story* (2009). We've all read informational texts that have left us scratching our heads and others that were so clearly written we finally understood a concept that had long eluded us. It is not just the content but the writing and presentation that make the difference.

There are whole books about how to use model or mentor texts when teaching students to write informational text. Here are just three strategies:

1. ***Make model texts readily available.*** You might designate a special area for model texts or obtain several copies of a key mentor text so each student or group can have one. Some teachers send potential model texts home and have students ask parents, siblings, or other family members what they think of them.

2. ***Get metatextual.*** Although informational text should be read primarily for information, you should also evaluate the text as text. LeAnn has students finish these stems:

   • One thing I noticed about this book that made it easy to understand was. . . .

   • One thing that would make this book easier to understand is. . . .

   Fifth-grade teacher Niki McGuire asks:

   • What do you like about the way this book presents the information?

   • Is there anything you think would make the book better?

   Questions about the author's intent, which have been shown (in McKeown, Beck & Blake 2009, for example) to improve reading comprehension in upper-elementary students (their effect on writing ability has not been examined), include:

   • What is the author trying to say?

   • What is the author's message?

   • What is the author talking about?

- Does that make sense?

- Is that said in a clear way?

- Did the author explain that clearly? Why or why not?

- What's missing? What do we need to figure out or find out?

(Beck, McKeown, Sandora, Kucan & Worthy 1996; see also Beck & McKeown 2006)

3. ***Study the author.*** Examining several works by an author for common elements as well as variations in how he or she conveys information is a powerful way to help students understand the role of craft and voice. Authors whose work is well worth studying include Steve Jenkins, Seymour Simon, and Aliki, to name just a few. A great resource for informational text author study is www.inkthinktank.com. Students can learn about the work of award-winning nonfiction authors and you can even arrange live videoconferencing and webinars with authors.

Excellent Informational Texts for Young Children

A trip to any library or bookstore will yield plenty of informational text for intermediate and middle school students, but informational text for primary-grade students is a bit harder to come by. Here are some favorite informational texts for reading aloud to K–2 students (titles are available individually or as the Buzz About IT collection/libraries through Scholastic).

Kindergarten

All Kinds of Books, *Berger*

Big & Little, *Jenkins*

From Seed to Plant, *Gibbons*

Hello! Good-bye!, *Aliki*

Insects and Crawly Creatures, *Royston*

Let's Find Out About Ice Cream, *Reid*

The Busy Body Book, *Rockwell*

Two Eyes, a Nose, and a Mouth, *Intrater*

What Do You Do with a Tail Like This?, *Page*

Wonderful Worms, *Glaser*

First Grade

Babies: All You Need to Know, *Heiligman*

Chameleons Are Cool, *Jenkins*

Earthworms, *Llewellyn*

Germs Make Me Sick, *Berger*

Good Enough to Eat: A Kid's Guide to Food and Nutrition, *Rockwell*

Night-time Animals, *Royston*

Surprising Sharks, *Davies*

Throw Your Tooth on the Roof, *Beeler*

United States of America: State-by-State Guide, *Nelson*

What Do Authors Do?, *Christelow*

Second Grade

Ah, Music!, *Aliki*

Animals Nobody Loves, *Simon*

A Cache of Jewels and Other Collective Nouns, *Heller*

A Drop of Water: A Book of Science and Wonder, *Wick*

Everyday Mysteries, *Wexler*

Ice Cream Including Great Moments in Ice Cream History, *Older*

The Life and Times of the Peanut, *Micucci*

Machines We Use, *Hewitt*

Oh Baby! Amazing Baby Animals, *Hirschmann*

You're Tall in the Morning but Shorter at Night and Other Amazing Facts About the Human Body, *Berger*

Excellent Informational Texts for Older Students

We couldn't resist sharing some favorite information books for grades 3 to 8 . . .

The Brain: Our Nervous System *by S. Simon. Morrow Junior Books, 1997.*

Celebrations! *by B. & A. Kindersley. DK Publishing, 1997.*

Deep Sea Creatures, *by P. Batson & B. Batson. Tangerine Press, 2008.*

Extreme Dinosaurs *by R. Mash. Atheneum, 2007.*

Immigrant Kids *by R. Freedman. Scholastic, 1980.*

National Parks *by S. Fear. Celebration Press, 2005.*

A Street Through Time: A 12,000 Year Walk Through History *by A. Millard, illustrated by S. Noon. DK Children, 1998.*

Rocks and Minerals *by R. F. Symes and the staff of the National History Museum. DK Children, 2004.*

Talking Walls *by M. B. Knight, illustrated by A. S. O'Brien. Tilbury House Publishers, 1992.*

Women and Girls in the Middle Ages *by K. Eastwood. Crabtree Publishing Company, 2004.*

PRINCIPLE **3** **Explicitly teach genre features.**

Informational texts have specific characteristics that accomplish their purpose of conveying information about the natural or social world.

What do I need to know about informational text characteristics?

Understanding the characteristics of the texts you expect your students to learn to read and write helps you more easily recognize why students may be struggling and decide how to guide them more effectively. If you are reading this book with a friend or study group (or even by yourself), you may want to have some information books from your classroom at hand to look at as you study the list of characteristics broken out on pages 93–94. (Figure 4.6 contains excerpts from an information book with key features annotated.)

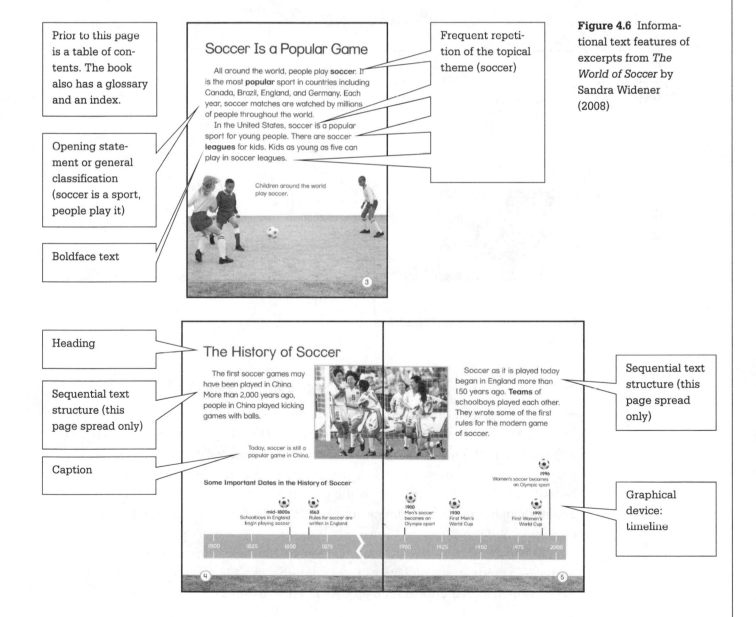

Figure 4.6 Informational text features of excerpts from *The World of Soccer* by Sandra Widener (2008)

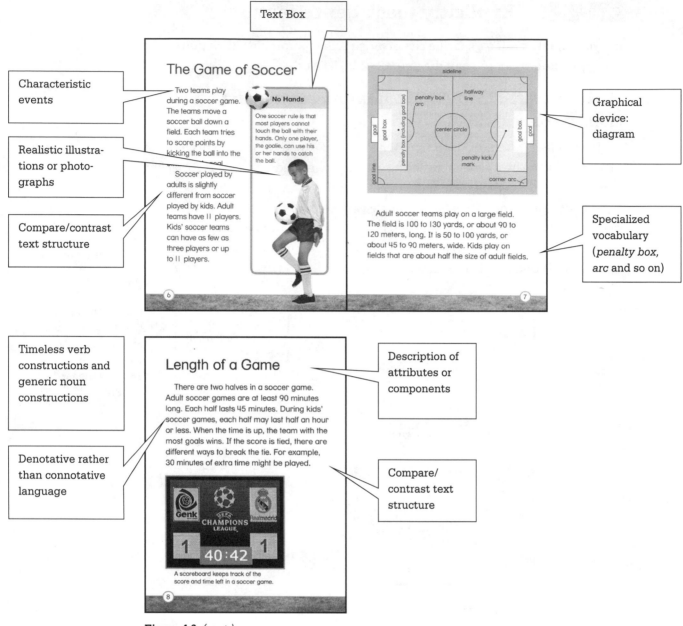

Figure 4.6 *(cont.)*

How do I teach informational text characteristics?

A favorite phrase of ours is *children aren't born knowing*: Children aren't born knowing that "(tie-RAN-oh-SORE-us)" is telling you how to pronounce the word it follows, that "a gorilla has" means that *all gorillas have,* or that the bars on a graph represent relative amounts. These are all things that children and adolescents have to learn. Some learn these things without anyone ever saying anything about them, but many children need to be told explicitly about these and other conventions of text.

Driven by this thinking, some years ago Nell and Vicki Purcell-Gates designed a study in which classes were randomly assigned to receive, or not, instruction in informational (and procedural) text features during science class

Common Characteristics of Informational Texts*

(Taken from Purcell-Gates, Duke & Martineau 2007 unless otherwise noted)

Content Characteristics

- information about the natural or social world
- information that is true or purports to be true

Navigational Features

- table of contents
- headings and subheadings
- numbered pages
- index

Structural Characteristics

- opening statement or general classification (e.g., "Dragonflies are a type of insect.")
- description of attributes or components of the subject (e.g., "Dragonflies have six legs and two pairs of wings.")
- characteristic events (e.g., "Dragonflies eat flies and other small insects.")
- compare/contrast structures and classifications either within a sentence (e.g., "Dragonflies are a type of insect") or from sentence to sentence (e.g., "Some dragonflies live in forests near streams. Some dragonflies live in fields near marshes. Some dragonflies live in deserts near pools.")
- other text structures such as enumerative (lists), sequential, problem–solution, and cause–effect (Duke & Kays 1998; Meyer & Rice 1984)
- final summary (Pappas 2006) and general statement or closing (e.g., "There is so much to learn about this amazing insect!")

Less Common Structural Characteristics

- prelude (a short narrative or comment designed to capture readers' attention and draw them into the text, such as an anecdote about a sneeze at the outset of a book about germs; Pappas 2006)
- afterword (additional information about the topic in a section at the end of the text; Pappas 2006)
- addendum (e.g., excerpts of the journal of a beekeeper in an information book about beekeeping; Pappas 2006)
- short historical accounts (e.g., explanation of the origin of a term; Pappas 2006)

* *Any given informational text is unlikely to, and needn't, have all of these characteristics.*

Language Characteristics

- frequent repetition of the topic of the text (e.g., if the text is about dragonflies, the word *dragonflies* is used repeatedly; Duke & Kays 1998)

- generic noun constructions and timeless verb constructions (e.g., "Dragonflies lay eggs," rather than "Daisy Dragonfly laid her eggs")

- denotative rather than connotative language (e.g., "Most dragonflies are between one and four inches long," rather than "Dragonflies are small creatures")

- specialized or technical vocabulary (e.g., *thorax, wingspan, larva*); key terms may be repeated more often, and the text may provide more clues to word meaning such as explanations (e.g., "omnivores, or animals that eat both plants and other animals") and graphics (e.g., a diagram with the thorax labeled)

- definitions in running text and/or glossary (e.g., "Herbivores are animals that only eat plants")

Graphical Features

- realistic illustrations or photographs

- labels and/or captions

- boldfaced and italicized vocabulary

- graphical devices such as the following:

  - Timelines (graphical devices that identify specific historical events or epochs within a period of time, arranged in chronological order)

  - Surface diagrams (illustrations or photographs of the surface of an animate or inanimate object or scene in which specific, individual parts are labeled)

  - Cross-section diagrams (illustrations or photographs that include normally unseen interior portions of an animate or inanimate object or scene in which specific, individual parts are labeled)

  - Flowcharts (graphical devices that depict the stages of a process in a chronologically ordered set of illustrations or photographs, typically connected by lines or arrows)

  - Tables (graphical devices containing columns and rows, whether labeled or unlabeled)

  - Insets (smaller pictures within or near larger pictures)

(descriptions of graphical devices from Roberts, Norman, Morsink, Duke, Martin, and Knight 2011) from the beginning of second grade to the end of third grade (Purcell-Gates et al. 2007). Students in classes assigned to the explicit teaching group showed no greater growth in informational text comprehension and writing ability over the two years. This is only one study, and there are many possible explanations other than that explicitly teaching genre features doesn't work: Maybe there wasn't enough explicit instruction (the science periods were forty-five minutes twice a week, and text features were dealt with during only a small portion of that time), or maybe the explicit instruction wasn't presented the way it should have been. Nevertheless, it is a cautionary tale. A long string of minilessons on informational text characteristics is probably not the way to go. Rather, let the following factors influence your decision about what to teach:

The students' own writing. If many students are struggling to organize their writing, then explicitly teaching text structure may make sense. If students want to show something close-up, that might be the time to teach insets.

The needs of the audience. When students are writing a book that the audience is supposed to use for reference, teach students (and only those students) who don't already know how to create an index how to do so.

State or national standards. Many states require students to have specific knowledge and skills related to informational text features. These standards too can guide your instruction—not to "cover" each expectation, but to monitor whether individual students are meeting them and adjust your instruction accordingly.

See box below for a great technique for teaching text characteristics.

Technique for Deepening Knowledge of Text Features: Improve-a-Text (Instead of Conventions Notebooks)

Some teachers ask their students to keep "conventions" notebooks in which they name and describe particular text features and collect examples. Often this approach separates the features too much from their context and the purposes they serve. Rather than writing content-less informational text about these conventions, students might better write content-based informational texts that use these conventions.

Students can also deepen their knowledge of text features and the purposes they serve through a technique called "improve-a-text." Whenever an informational text lacks a feature that would convey the information more effectively or engagingly, students, using sticky notes or sticky tape, improve the text themselves. For example, if a text fails to define an important term or lacks helpful navigational or organizational headings, the students provide the definition or the headings on the spot. An added benefit is that this approach encourages students to read published text with a critical eye.

PRINCIPLE ④ Explicitly teach genre-specific or genre-sensitive strategies.

As we've explained, strategies need to be taught in the context of the specific genre in which we want students to apply them. It doesn't work to teach comprehension strategies only with narrative text, for example, and expect students to transfer them automatically to informational reading or vice-versa. Then, too, some strategies apply to some genres and not others (for example, skimming is an important strategy in informational reading but generally not appropriate when reading a story or a novel).

Teach strategies for reading and listening.

The following comprehension strategies should be taught in connection with informational text (though not necessarily all in the same year):

- previewing
- skimming and scanning
- searching
- monitoring, clarifying, fixing up
- activating background knowledge
- predicting (what the author will tell you next, not what will happen next)
- visualizing
- visually representing (e.g., using graphic organizers, drawing, role-playing)
- inferring
- questioning
- summarizing (as you read and at the conclusion of reading)

In teaching any of these strategies, follow the gradual release of responsibility model discussed in Chapter 2.

Is it better to teach comprehension strategies one at a time, spending a long time on each, or in groups or clusters, teaching them individually only very briefly and immediately expecting students to apply several strategies more or less at once? The only study we're aware of that directly addresses this question does so in connection with second-grade science (Reutzel, Smith & Fawson 2005). The researchers found there was no clear advantage either way with regard to most strategies; the few instances in which an advantage was discernible, it was in favor of multiple-strategy instruction.

There are a number of effective approaches to multiple-comprehension-strategy instruction for informational text (see Gajria, Jitendra, Sood & Sacks 2007 and Martin & Duke 2011 for reviews). The box on pages 97–98 highlights an approach for social studies; the box on pages 98–99 highlights one for science.

A Technique for Improving Comprehension of Social Studies Texts: Collaborative Strategic Reading

Collaborative Strategic Reading (CSR) was developed by Janette Klingner, Sharon Vaughn, and Jeanne Schumm (1998), and enjoys considerable research support (e.g., Klingner, Vaughn, Arguelles, Hughes & Leftwich 2004; Klingner, Vaughn, Dimino, Schumm & Bryant 2001; Klingner, et al. 1998). The strategies used in CSR were deliberately chosen for informational texts.

Students are taught to use four comprehension strategies simultaneously (some of which entail more than one procedure):

Strategy	Strategy Description	Key Questions to Ask Yourself*
Preview	Think about what you already know about a topic and predict what the text might teach you.	"What do I think I will find out about the topic when I read the passage?" "What do I already know about the topic?"
Click (things are making sense) and *clunk* (they're not)	Identify sections you found challenging to read and select fix-up strategies to solve words or improve your understanding.	"Were there any parts that were hard to understand (clunks)?" "How can I fix the clunks?"
Get the gist	Identify important people, events, and concepts.	What is the most important *who* or *what?*" "What is the most important idea about the *who* or *what?*"
Wrap-up	Brainstorm questions that highlight important ideas and reflect on what you have learned from the text.	"What questions would show I understand the most important information?" "What did I learn?"

* Content is drawn from Klingner et al. (1988), and the questions in the third column are taken directly from Klingner et al. (1998, 19–20).

Here's how it works. First explain and model the strategies for the whole class. Then give students, still as a class, opportunities to practice applying these strategies before reading (previewing), while reading (click and clunk, get the gist), and after reading (wrap-up). Next, have groups of students take turns using the strategies (with your support) in front of the rest of the class. Afterward, ask students, in small groups, to apply the strategies while reading informational text about social studies. During these sessions, students take on roles (in rotation), such as group leader and clunk expert (student who helps when other students run into a clunk). You circulate, scaffolding students' thinking and learning as needed.

Technique for Improving Comprehension of Scientific Texts: Concept-Oriented Reading Instruction

Teaching and learning content is the purpose of informational genres. Concept-Oriented Reading Instruction (CORI) has proven highly effective at raising reading comprehension as well as improving motivation and science knowledge (e.g., Guthrie, Anderson, Alao & Rinehart 1999; Guthrie, Meter, Hancock, Solomon, Anderson & McCann 1998; and Guthrie, Wigfield & VonSecker 2000; see Guthrie, McRae & Klauda 2007 for a review), even as compared to good strategy instruction in the context of English Language Arts.

CORI focuses on five comprehension strategies particularly appropriate for science-related informational text (Guthrie, Wigfield & Perencevich 2004a, 14–15):

1. **Activating background knowledge:** *Thinking about previous experiences and knowledge relevant to the text, using its features as a guide*

2. **Questioning:** *Generating questions related to the text's content that take its structure into account*

3. **Searching for information:** *Setting goals to find information, using the text's features to achieve the goals and integrating information with other texts and your knowledge of the world*

4. **Summarizing:** *Using the text's structure and linguistic cues to retell main ideas and identify supporting evidence*

5. **Organizing graphically:** *Identifying and creating visual depictions, such as concept maps and diagrams, that mirror the text's structures*

These strategies are taught within six-week integrated reading/science units that focus on a conceptual theme. Students progress through four phases (Guthrie et al. 2004a, 7–8):

- observe and personalize *(weeks 1 and 2)*

- search and retrieve *(week 3)*

- comprehend and integrate *(weeks 4 and 5)*

- communicate to others *(week 6)*

During these phases, students participate in hands-on science activities and do a great deal of guided and independent reading. Together they research their own questions, collect and analyze data, and teach others (e.g., classmates who focused on a different topic within the theme) what they have learned.

For example, in one unit, students think about how their previous and current science experiences connect with stories about birds (week 1), generate questions about how birds survive on land (week 2), identify information in texts that might answer their questions (week 3), record and organize what they have found in the texts (weeks 4 and 5), and create written syntheses of what they have learned, such as concept maps and posters (week 6). Throughout, students make choices about their learning, have opportunities to learn about something that interests them specifically, read interesting informational texts, and collaborate with their peers.

For more information about the CORI approach, including videos of CORI in action and instructions about how to arrange for professional development in the CORI approach, see www.cori.umd.edu.

Introduce strategies for writing and speaking.

Writers and speakers use many strategies while composing informational text. Three areas are especially important: researching, planning, and revising.

Researching

Almost always, authors of informational text need to do research. For students, some of this research may occur as a matter of course during hands-on investigations, artifact exploration, and interviews.

The "octopus" approach. When students are gathering information for their writing, they should, as a general rule, gather different kinds of information from different kinds of sources. Informational author Stephen R. Swinburne, as quoted in Robb (2004), explains:

> I have what I call an "octopus" or "multi-armed" approach to research. I get in lots of field time [for observing]. I read books and magazines. I check references in the library. I surf the Internet. I telephone experts and scientists. I interview people. I rely on all these sources to give me a foundation of fact on my subject. (82)

The recursive nature of the research process. There may be a phase when writers are "wandering around"—they don't yet know enough about the topic to be aware of what they already know and what they want or need to know. So they move on to planning—figuring out what specifically they want to say and roughly how they want to say it, thus determining what they already know and what they still need to know. This plan guides their further research, although what they learn often further informs the plan. The process of writing informational text, and most texts, is recursive. There isn't a rigid steplike progression; rather, the author revisits steps as she or he spirals toward the final text.

Using trustworthy information. A significant challenge in the research process is getting students to draw on trustworthy sources. Middle and high school students tend to trust anything that has been published (see Henry 2007; Wallace, Kupperman, Krajcik & Soloway 2000). This problem is even more acute in the age of the Internet, in which anyone can publish anything. There are many professional resources that can help you teach students at different ages to be critical consumers of information on the Internet, including professional books (e.g., Eagleton & Dobler 2007), articles (e.g., Coiro 2003) and websites (e.g., www.shsu.edu/~lis_mah/documents/TCEA/hoaxtable.html, which lists "hoax" websites; use it to illustrate that students can't trust everything they find on the Web). In the WWWDOT (*W*ho wrote this?; *W*hy did they write it?; *W*hen was it written?; *O*rganization of site; *T*o-do list for the future) approach (Zhang & Duke 2011) students answer a series of questions (see Figure 4.7) about a website to decide whether or not to use it as a source of information. Fourth- and fifth-grade classes randomly assigned to learn the WWWDOT approach in just four thirty-minute sessions (two to learn the six elements, two to practice applying the framework and debate the relative trustworthiness of different websites) became much more aware than a control group of the need to evaluate information on the Internet for credibility and were much better able to evaluate the trustworthiness of websites in numerous areas. For a more detailed explanation of the approach, see Zhang and Duke (in press).

Transforming information. A perennial problem in informational writing is plagiarism (or at least too-heavy borrowing from other sources). The "octopus" approach to research is one way to prevent this: Having many and varied sources encourages synthesis and reframing. Another important strategy for reducing plagiarism is to have students transform the information in some way. They might enter it onto a map or web (see below) and write from that. They might use text-based sources to make a video, or massage a videotaped interview into a written text. They might use texts written for fourth graders as sources for texts for second graders. Having a compelling, communicatively meaningful context for writing also makes a big difference; students are more likely to tailor the information to their specific purpose and audience. In planning a project, teachers need to ask: Is there already a text students could use to meet the want or need? If so, plagiarism is more likely; if not, it is less so.

Name ______________________ Date ____________

URL ______________________

WWWDOT: A Tool for Supporting Critical Reading of Internet Sites

Who wrote this (and what credentials do they have)?

____

____

____

____

____

Why did they write it?

____

____

____

____

____

When was it written and updated?

____

____

____

____

____

Figure 4.7 WWWDOT worksheet for evaluating the trustworthiness of websites

Does this help meet my needs (and how)?

_____

_____

_____

_____

Organization of site (you can write and/or draw).

_____

_____

_____

_____

_____

_____

_____

To do list for the future.

_____

_____

_____

_____

_____

_____

Figure 4.7 *(Cont.)*

Planning

Planning is critical to guiding (and being guided by) research and also to composing. Two preliminary questions essential to planning are (Englert, Raphael & Anderson 1992):

- Who am I writing for?
- Why am I writing?

In a genre-with-purpose approach, your students should be able to answer these questions easily and compellingly.

The most traditional form of planning after answering these questions is the outline. An outline works for some students and texts, but other approaches are more spatial and more flexible. One approach supported by research (e.g., Sturm & Rankin-Erickson 2002) is mapping. A planning map (see Figure 4.8) typically has the central topic of the planned text in a circle in the center, with spokes and circles coming out for different categories of information or subtopics within the central topic. Those circles may in turn have their own spokes and circles, or they may have adjacent lines on which to write key points or information to include. As described by Graham and Harris (2005, 128–29), mapping has six steps:

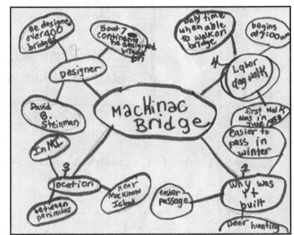

Figure 4.8 Example of a map for planning writing

1. *Brainstorming* what you already know about the topic.

2. *Organizing* what you know onto a map.

3. *Gathering additional information* to correct and fill in the map as needed.

4. *Numbering information* on the map in the order it will be presented.

5. *Adding to or revising your map* as you write (e.g., if, in writing, you realize that an important piece of information for readers' understanding is missing).

6. *Reviewing your map* to be sure you included everything you intended to (using check marks, a highlighter, or the like).

For more about planning strategies, please see pages 104–106.

For more about planning strategies, please see pages 104–106.

GENRE PROJECT

What Genre with Purpose Looks Like:
Human Body System Texts, Grade 5

Fifth-grader Josh walks into class eager to share a story. He is on a baseball team made up of students from a number of schools in the district. A teammate has found out that Josh is from Greenwood School and in fifth grade. The teammate says, "Hey, that's where our human body books are from! They're gross, especially the digestive section with all the nasty pictures of the esophagus!" To Josh, and many students in this class, this is highly funny and high praise.

Designing a communicatively meaningful environment: Looking just down the road for a compelling audience. Niki McGuire, a fifth-grade teacher, received an email from another fifth-grade teacher seeking advice on planning a unit on human body systems, a new districtwide fifth-grade unit. When Niki read this email to her students, they responded, "We have to help!" In the middle of their own unit on human body systems and aware that there weren't books that addressed precisely and only the district-required topics, the students immediately understood the need and had clear ideas of what to do to help.

Explicitly teaching genre-sensitive strategies: Planning especially suited to informational writing. Niki emphasized teaching students to plan their writing. She had students examine a collection of information books she had gathered on body systems using "informational book walk" questions she developed (see Figure 4.9). Students looked closely at the books' characteristics and noted what they liked and didn't like. Using their book walk sheets, a mentor text they selected—*You're Tall in the Morning but Shorter at Night and Other Amazing Facts About the Human Body* (Berger & Berger 2004)—and the district guidelines (include the respiratory system, don't include the reproductive system, etc.), they came up with the preplanning sheet in Figure 4.10. Because the students would be using websites as sources of information, Niki also taught lessons about identifying trustworthy websites, citing digital sources, and other concepts her careful observations told her needed specific attention.

Because graphics and navigational features are such important characteristics of informational texts (most are not exclusively linear), Niki taught an additional phase of planning—text layout—in which students decided where graphics, headings, and text blocks would be positioned on a page (see Figure 4.11). A book-length layout would

---

Names:

Body Systems Informational Book Walk

How is this book organized?

How does the author use headings? [You could select any number of features to ask about here.]

What does the author include in each body system section?

What different kinds of pictures/illustrations/photographs does the author use?

What do you like about the way this book presents the information?

Is there anything you think would make the book better?

Figure 4.9 Informational book walk questions from Niki McGuire. Students used this to gather ideas and approaches for their own books.

also show where the table of contents, index, glossary, references, addendum, and so on (as applicable) might be placed. As this was a class book (students worked on the project in groups of four, each group writing about one body system and providing feedback on the others), groups showed their layout to the class (and to Niki) for feedback. Students used their planned text layout to help them draw information from their science folders (e.g., notes from their hands-on investigations), from books, and from websites (which Niki taught them to evaluate critically). In total, drafting from the layouts (a two-page spread is shown in Figure 4.11) took six days, forty-five minutes to an hour each day. Final product excerpts are shown in Figure 4.12.

Preplanning Sheet   Name _____

The information that will be provided in the _____ text will be:

nervous system	excretory system
digestive system	respiratory system
muscular system	cardiovascular system
skeletal system	systems working together
Table of contents	glossary and index

Under each section the following information will be provided:

- The main function of each system
- The main organs involved in each section
- How the main organs work together to make the system successful

To make each section more interesting the following will also be included:

- Pictures
- Diagrams
- Explanation of the system in fifth graders' terms
- Facts interesting to fifth graders
- Keeping yourself healthy tibdit
- Heading to keep the reader informed and our writing focused
- Vocabulary boldfaced to stand out
- Quick Quiz

My group's section is _____.

The types of pictures I want to include will be about:

The types of facts I want to include will be about:

I would explain the main function of the system to be . . .

I think the main organs of this system are:	This is how the main organs work together:

Figure 4.10
Preplanning sheet for sections of the body systems book

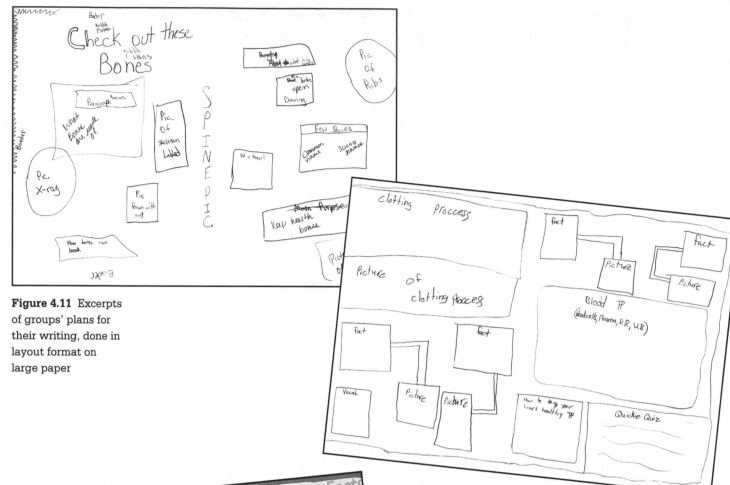

Figure 4.11 Excerpts of groups' plans for their writing, done in layout format on large paper

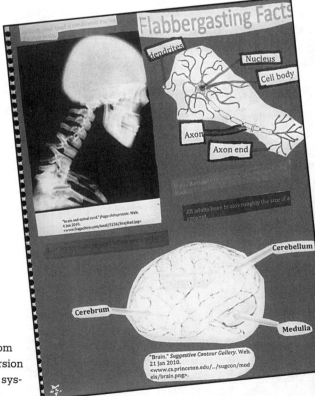

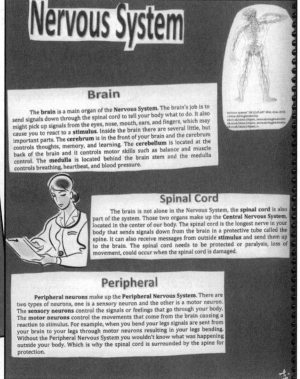

Figure 4.12 Excerpts from the final version of the body systems book

> ### ☰ *Niki Reflects*
>
> *Niki is the first to say that this project was challenging; there were some missteps (taking students to the computer lab before they had done sufficient planning, for example) and sometimes it was hard to see the light at the end of the tunnel. But the project was gratifying. "I didn't have to pull teeth. They were excited to work on it every day." Niki encourages teachers to just try one project like this and see the impact it has.*

Revising

The key to revision is focus. As Donald Murray explains, "Trying to read for content, form, and language simultaneously causes the writer to do an unnecessary amount of scurrying back and forth. There is an enormous waste of motion and a great deal of doing over" (quoted in Robb 2004, 255). If this is true for expert adult writers, it most certainly is true for K–8 students, whose automaticity with and ability to think about many aspects of writing simultaneously are still in early stages. You need to guide their focus as they revise—have them read through several times, each time concentrating on a different aspect.

A genre-with-purpose perspective also means tailoring revisions to the text's genre and the specific purpose and audience it is to serve. For example, when revising a comic, a big concern is how funny it is; when revising a recipe, the concern is how clear and accurate it is. When revising information books for second graders, a key concern is whether the information is understandable to second graders; revising information books to be read by adults, the concern is whether the material is sophisticated enough for that audience.

Particularly for younger students, it's helpful to organize revision guides by "reads"—what to focus on in read 1, read 2, read 3, and so on (but students should be able to alter the order as appropriate). Focus elements are often presented as questions:

- Does the text grab the reader's attention?

- Does the text alert the reader to the topic?

- Does the text help the reader find the information she/he wants or needs to know?

- Does the text (sentence by sentence or paragraph by paragraph) present the information clearly?

- Does each graphic help the reader learn and understand? Are there additional graphics that would be helpful?

- Does the text, page by page, keep the reader's attention on the information?

- Do mechanical issues (sentence by sentence or in the text as a whole or both) get in the way of focusing on the information?

Depending on the students, you may need to create subquestions or make the questions more specific (e.g., Does the text have a table of contents to help the reader find the information she or he wants or needs to know?). Whatever the format, the questions should be phrased in terms of *the reader's experience*. Checklists of features with no indication of the purpose or function they serve divert attention from the compelling, communicative context you've worked so hard to create.

PRINCIPLE ⑤ Offer ongoing coaching and feedback.

There is certainly a place for whole-class instruction in your pedagogy. But instruction, coaching, and feedback that occur one-on-one and in small groups should be at the heart of your teaching, as it was for the teachers who designed and presented the projects in this chapter. As Professor Emerita Lilian Katz says, "When a teacher tries to teach something to the entire class at the same time, chances are one-third of the kids already know it, one-third will get it, and the remaining third won't. So two-thirds of the children are wasting their time."

For one thing, there is wide variation in knowledge and skill in any classroom. Our assessments of primary-grade students' informational comprehension (available free to download at http://msularc.educ.msu.edu/what-we-do/projects/mai-coca/ and http://msularc.educ.msu.edu/what-we-do/projects/isca/), as well as our research on visual literacy development, clearly show how differently students perform. It makes little sense to teach the table of contents to students who can already use and produce one effectively *or* to students who are still unsure what informational text is even for. Providing coaching and feedback to students one-on-one and with small groups of students grouped based on their specific needs (Taberski 2000) allows you to differentiate instruction for these different levels of knowledge.

Another reason to differentiate instruction, coaching, and feedback is that students appear to struggle with informational reading and writing for different reasons (e.g., Riddle Buly & Valencia 2002). Some may have limited understanding of informational text characteristics and how to use them. Others may have this knowledge but don't apply it to informational reading and writing. Others may struggle primarily because they lack the background knowledge or vocabulary the text assumes. Still others may struggle because they find informational text dull and unappealing.

Some teachers create a chart with the knowledge and strategies they want students to learn as column headings and students' names as row headings. Then, using a code, they indicate which knowledge and strategies each student has demonstrated. Based on these and other observations, they form temporary groups and establish instructional focuses. Other teachers have a more informal system, making anecdotal observations in notebooks or on sticky notes. The key is to maximize your instructional time with each student by tailoring your teaching to each student's strengths and needs.

Why You Need to Add Informational Projects with Purpose to Your Curriculum *Now*

Informational reading and writing are a major focus of the Common Core State Standards, NAEP, and any number of other standards documents and assessments. Informational reading and writing are keys to success in content-area classrooms, our working lives, and citizenship. Most important, some students (many or all students in the classrooms we have profiled here) enjoy reading and writing informational text. We can't afford to neglect informational reading and writing, and we can't afford to teach informational reading and writing with anything other than purpose.

5

Exploring Meaning Through Performance:
Dramatic Genres

What Genre with Purpose Looks Like: Putting on a Play, Grade 4

Blue sheets of paper, sprinkled with fluffy white clouds, form a backdrop. Chairs indicate a waiting room above the clouds. Dawn Kennaugh's students at Holbrook Elementary fidget in the hallway outside the gym, dressed in summer shorts or kingly robes, checking their props: a pair of glasses, a beach ball, an umbrella. After numerous run-throughs, painting backdrops on poster paper in art class, and developing introductions for each play (another genre!), these actors are ready for their debut. Parents are seated in chairs along the sides of the school gym, and classes of first through fifth graders sit on the floor. After Maddy presents her introduction, the actors, finally able to be their characters for an audience, begin the first scene and reveal the inspired bits of comic business they have honed over weeks of work. While half the class performs Seasonal . . . Whether, *the other half provides technical support. The actors in the first play provide support for* Punctuation Proclamation. *Each play is performed twice, so that all classes in the school can see one*

Figure 5.1 *(top)* June, May, and April react to Father Time's roar in rehearsal.

Figure 5.1 The tutor looks worried as the king dictates the proclamation that abolishes punctuation.

play. Despite the gym's poor acoustics, students' enthusiastic perform-ances and their physical comedy carry the day, and students finally get that sweet reward: applause.

—–·—–·—–·—–·—–·—–·—–·—–·—–·—–·—–·—–·—–

Because one of her goals in fourth-grade English language arts was to improve her students' fluency, Dawn Kennaugh had long made a version of readers theater available to her students. It was a popular option for pair work. Hoping to magnify the effects on reading and fluency by putting on a show outside her classroom, Dawn asked her students if they wanted to try it. They enthusiastically signed on.

After discovering a source of royalty-free plays, searchable by grade level and topic (*Plays* magazine, www.playsmagazine.com), Dawn began the challenging task of choosing the right one, with a role for each of her twenty-two students. Confident that she knew her students and their tastes, Dawn chose two short comedies (a choice her fourth graders heartily approved): *Seasonal . . . Whether*, by Frank V. Priore (ten characters), and *Punctuation Proclamation*, by Claire Boiko (twelve characters). Everyone had an onstage role in one comedy and an offstage role in the other. While Dawn worked on choosing the plays and finalizing the calendar, Samantha held a couple of short workshops. Students played rehearsal games that introduced them to ways of focusing on a scene, responding to their acting partners, and combining speech and movement.

Explicitly teaching genre features Students' prior experience with readers theater prepared them for the genre conventions of the play script: Speakers are identified at the beginning of each line; stage directions are in italics and not read aloud. Later in the process, they examined the genre of the theater program using models from other school and community groups, and wrote brief synopses, cast and crew lists, and acknowledgments of help received.

Explicitly teaching genre-specific strategies Using copies of two short readers theater scripts that featured stock characters and a minor conflict, students practiced reading lines before and after working on some basic character analysis, asking themselves: "What does this character want? What does the character do to get what he or she wants? What does he or she want the other person to do?" Identifying motivation and a central action gives the actor a focus and a goal found in the script, one with playable consequences.

The class did the same sort of work with pencil and paper and copies of their plays. Reading the plays aloud with the class, Samantha and Dawn paused often to model the sort of questions actors and directors ask: "What is the opening conflict, and how can you tell? Who is friendly with whom? Why? When is the conflict settled?" The students were eager to dig into this analysis: They had not considered before that actors had textual work to do to get ready for their roles.

Offering ongoing coaching and feedback The students moved smoothly through the rehearsal process. They quickly placed the set pieces and blocked the characters' movement. To help students think creatively about staging, Samantha brought in some more rehearsal exercises from Viola Spolin's books (see text box on page 134). Up to the final week, students were making improvements during rehearsals, coming up with new ideas; in the theater, interpretation is an ongoing process. As they became more confident in their roles, they were able to focus more on articulation, projection, and sharing the scene.

Rethinking Popular Drama Assignments: Beyond the Class Reading

It's common to teach plays as though they were just oddly formatted short stories in the grade-level anthology. Plays have characters, plots, and themes, like short stories or novels, and the textbook includes comprehension and thinking questions after each act, like it does for short stories. Teachers often assign roles each day, have students read their parts aloud with no preparation, and then answer questions in journals or on worksheets. But a play is not a stand-alone text: It is more like an architect's blueprint, needing to be fleshed out in the course of its intended use. This can cause problems for the inexperienced play reader.

A short story or a novel offers signposts. The setting is introduced and described, and the author keeps us informed about how the character moves within and uses the setting. Characters are described physically at the beginning, and we are reminded at intervals what they are doing, how they move, how they feel, what they are thinking, and how they speak. Speech is presented in numerous ways, depending on the character's state of mind and feeling: *said, shouted, whined, squeaked, roared, cried, whispered, murmured* (with any number of modifying adverbs). A play offers a fraction of that information: dialogue, plus a few clues in the form of stage directions. The rest is inferred from the dialogue. Given the interpretive leaps required by dramatic texts, reading and writing them effectively demands instruction and practice.

When dramatic texts are taught with their authentic purposes in mind, students have the opportunity to practice the sorts of critical reading and inference actors and directors undertake—to integrate reading, writing, speaking, and listening in a coherent and meaningful way.

Purposes of Dramatic Genres

Dramatic genres involving a performer and an audience—such as drama, the recitation of epic poetry, and oral storytelling—predate written language by thousands of years. Epic poems, such as the Iliad or Beowulf, originated as oral texts passed on from generation to generation. They relied on rhythm and memorable images to help the performer and the audience remember long, complex tales of myth and history. The earliest plays we know, from ancient Greece, were both religious observances and reasons for the community to gather: Everybody came.

Plays are still an opportunity for people to gather and interact as a community, both onstage (performing a play is the ultimate collaborative act) and as part of an audience. In these days of sitting in front of a screen, enacting plays and viewing live people performing can be an electrifying experience.

Drama is like narrative in that most dramas tell a story. However, the experience of watching characters live through the conflicts and interactions in a play is not the same as reading about those characters. We are watching someone move through space and time, and we can identify in a special way. Identification with character is even more intense for an actor, who has to consider the character's past in light of present circumstances and imagine how this person would respond at every moment of the action.

Drama provides opportunities to integrate reading, writing, speaking, and listening. Speaking and listening are rarely assessed using standardized instruments (at least outside the speech pathologist's office). Teaching dramatic genres with purpose helps restore the spoken word to the curriculum. Students are introduced to the skills learned from reading aloud and rehearsing readings. Discussing the text's meaning and interacting while working together to prepare a performance provide many opportunities for using oral language.

Meeting Standards Through Teaching Drama

The Common Core State Standards (CCSS) (2010a) refer to drama forty-three times and also emphasize reading abilities that drama supports. In grades 3–12 students are expected to know how the craft and structure of dramatic texts differ from the craft and structure of other narrative texts and poetry. Reading: Literature, Standard 10, Range, Quality, Complexity explicitly states that all reading standards are to be applied to "stories, drama, and poetry." In grades K–5, students are to be familiar with "staged dialogue and brief familiar scenes"; in grades 6–12, with "one-act and multi-act plays, both written and on film." The focus on film is further developed in Reading: Literature, Standards 6.7 and 7.7, which expect students to compare and contrast reading a play or story with watching a film version, and in Standard 8.7, which expects them to "analyze the extent to which a filmed or live production of a story or drama stays faithful to or departs from the text or script, evaluating the choices made by the director or actors."

Drama can also help your students meet the reading standards in other ways. The foundational skills of reading, grades 1–5, highlight fluency (e.g., read grade-level prose and poetry orally with accuracy, appropriate rate, and expression), as well as the ability to "read grade-level text with purpose and understanding."

At all grade levels after grade 4, developing skill in making inferences is a high priority (Reading: Literature, Standard 4.1, "Refer to details and examples in a text when explaining what the text says explicitly and when drawing inferences from the text," as well as Standards 5.1, 6.1, and 7.1). Dramatic play scripts, which are open to interpretation on a number of levels, are ideal vehicles for building inferential skills. Students are also expected to build more sophisticated understanding of how plot, character, and setting interact over time. When preparing a script for performance, actors and directors analyze how character goals motivate action, how characters interact, how plot and setting provide obstacles to character goals, and how characters overcome obstacles.

Finally, the narrative writing standards for grades 3 and higher are also well served by drama. For example, in grade 4, students are expected to "orient the reader by establishing a situation and introducing a narrator and/or characters; organize an event sequence that unfolds naturally" and "use dialogue and description to develop experiences and events or show the responses of characters to situations." The middle school playwrights (see the vignette below) are learning how to meet these standards, and the experience of performing their plays for one another provides a real-life assessment of how well they are doing so.

What Genre with Purpose Looks Like:
Writing One-Act Plays, Grade 7

It is the day when the Humbugs will be revealed. Seventh graders have written a one-act play with at least two scenes (and one scene change) that includes a character known as "The Humbug" (a device that ties these scenes together in much the same way that recurring characters or situations do in comedy sketch shows on TV). What the Humbug is and what it might do is left to each group of three or four writers to determine. The Humbug wears a mask made from a paper bag—an excuse to use glitter, paint, glue, and pipe cleaners. When performance day arrives, all questions are answered about each group's Humbug and his or her adventures: Will the Humbug be rejected by the popular Pink and Purple bugs? Will the Humbug be Santa Claus? A bank robber? These details, tightly guarded secrets during the rehearsal process, are now revealed to an eager audience of their fellow playwrights, so far the only audience for these masterworks. However, the teachers leading this effort are aware of how opening drama to a wider audience ups the ante and prompts more intense engagement, so who knows where the Humbugs might travel in future?

—————————————————————

Judy Jackson, Jill Mitchell, and Cheryl Sunday, a team of teachers designing curriculum for their seventh-grade writing workshop at Flushing Middle School, together oversee a project in which students write and perform their own one-act plays for one another. There are few rules: Include the Humbug, and everyone in the group must have at least one part to play.

Providing exposure and experience: Reading and performing lead to writing. The project begins with reading, rehearsing, and performing short, humorous plays found on the Internet and discussing the similarities and differences between plays and other kinds of reading the students have done. Students identify genre features (dialogue, stage directions, props), learn the specialized vocabulary of scenes and acts, and look at how plot structure (exposition, turning point, and climax) work in short plays and in television shows. They cast and perform a stage version of *The Christmas Carol*. After this immersion in the genre, they are ready to write and perform their own one-act plays.

Explicitly teaching genre-specific strategies: Providing scaffolding. Each group of students begins by creating a storyboard on a piece of twelve-by-eighteen-inch paper—images of each stage in the action linked by sticky-note transitions and comments. They then write their first drafts on templates with spaces for character names, dialogue, and stage directions (piles of these photocopied forms are readily available).

Offering ongoing coaching and feedback: Coaching writing and performing. Revision is a major part of the process. After a couple of read-throughs (just like real playwrights!), groups begin rehearsing to see how the dialogue works, play with stage movement and stage directions, and rewrite as needed. The three teachers move from group to group, helping when groups get stuck, handing over tissue boxes and other supplies to use as props, and coaching students in narrowing or elaborating the plot, as needed.

How to Teach Dramatic Text with Purpose: Five Principles for Instruction

We turn now to discussing how our five principles apply to projects involving dramatic text.

PRINCIPLE ① Design compelling, communicatively meaningful environments.

Drama grew out of community rituals and occasions, and is still an occasion for people to gather and celebrate. The classroom is also an environment for performance and sharing, and ideally a place where everyone feels safe and everyone has something to contribute. The sense of safety is enhanced by a focus on the process as much as on the final text or performance.

Perhaps you've avoided drama because you worry that some students may have stage fright or be unwilling to risk being ridiculed by their classmates. However, this is rarely a problem, as long as there are varied opportunities to present or perform. Many teachers have turned to process drama, unscripted dramatic response to a text, a situation, or a content area. Process drama is a great way for students to get up and do, rather than sit and listen (McCaslin 2000; Wilhelm & Edmiston 1998; also see a collection of lesson plans at www.childdrama.com/lessons.html). Start with group scenes, choral readings, or simple tableaus in which students freeze in place (perhaps with one line spoken as a caption). Later, small groups might rehearse and perform scenes for each other and use guided questions to focus assessment on the goals of the project.

Performing for an outside audience ups the ante. Students who are used to sharing their work inside the classroom are usually excited to perform for others. Especially for younger children, the broader school community is a significant audience. Influencing peers is important.

Using the School's PA System to Improve Fluency

Fluency is more than rapidly reading words or nonsense syllables from a page: Fluent readers read accurately, at an appropriate rate, and with effective emphasis, intonation, and inflection (National Institute of Child Health and Human Development 2000). An effective way to improve all aspects of fluency is to have students read a text a number of times, paying attention to meaning and expression (Ness 2009; Rasinski 2003). Preparing to read or perform for a group provides just that kind of practice, aids comprehension, and is more motivating than reading for a timed test.

Molly Ness (2009) has successfully used rereading and retelling jokes to improve expression in student reading. Kelly Nevison, a colleague of Dawn's, created an authentic audience for her third- and fourth-grade struggling readers. Her students chose and practiced reading jokes from joke books, and Kelly then recorded them on her laptop so they could hear themselves reading. Ultimately they took turns reading their jokes for the entire school during morning announcements, which other children thought was very cool.

The school becomes a more closely knit community when teachers and students work with and perform for other classes. Another class, perhaps of younger children, can be an audience in your classroom, or your students can perform outside of your classroom, as in Dawn Kennaugh's case. If classes in your school or district all read the same play, performing that play, either for students who have also read it or younger children, helps both performers and audience understand the relationship between play script and performance.

The most authentic purpose for dramatic genres is publication or performance outside the school. Students can write and perform plays for a variety of purposes and audiences, including convincing others (students at Cavanaugh Elementary performed a play for other schools on recycling) or providing information (your students can perform a historical play for others studying a time period or famous person or for a community celebration). Whatever the occasion, performing for a real audience focuses students' attention on every step of moving from the page to the stage, from text analysis to final dress rehearsal.

Live or Video?

Today's high-quality cameras and editing software have made video projects, in a variety of content areas and genres, including writing and performing scripts, a fast-growing phenomenon. Children can create public service announcements, soap operas, newscasts, and documentary films using this new technology, and there are numerous websites and publications to help them. However, this chapter focuses on live performances, because those can take place in any classroom or community.

Poetry and drama contests, for both writing and performing, are increasingly popular and another way to connect with real audiences. One of Samantha's earliest performances occurred in fifth grade, when she won first prize for an Arbor Day poem and read it at a community celebration. Communitywide contests are sponsored by county fairs, the local newspaper, unions, libraries, universities, and others. Find out about contests from your local professional organizations or the community calendar in your local paper.

PRINCIPLE ② Provide exposure and experience.

Students need to read and perform dramatic genres and view performances by others.

Introduce readers theater.

Readers theater—in which anywhere from two to dozens of students read a text aloud, from a script, but with expression and gestures, as a performance piece—is a bridge to play performance. Students practice oral interpretation, timing, and expression and, in some cases, perform characters using voice. It's a safe beginning, the script is always present, and you can start with choral readings (in unison). This early practice in projecting their voices and working with others will make the complex job of acting easier when they begin to work with voice, body, and space in developing a character. Readers theater also improves fluency, because it requires students to pay attention to rate, accuracy, and expression (Martinez, Roser & Strecker 1998/1999; Worthy 2005).

☰ *Where to Find Readers Theater Scripts*

http://www.teachingheart.net/readerstheater.htm

www.timelessteacherstuff.com/

Magazines published by Scholastic are another handy source for scripts for in-class performance. Storyworks, for grades 3–6, and Scope, for grades 6–12, offer play adaptations of stories, readers theater scripts, and other texts to read aloud.

Good Masters! Sweet Ladies! Voices from a Medieval Village *by L. A. Schlitz. Candlewick Press, 2008. (includes monologues to be performed by twenty-two students)*

Try these poems for two and four voices by Paul Fleischman:

Big Talk: Poems for Four Voices *by P. Fleischman. Candlewick Press, 2000.*

I Am Phoenix: Poems for Two Voices *by P. Fleischman. HarperCollins, 1985.*

Joyful Noise: Poems for Two Voices *by P. Fleischman. HarperCollins, 1988. (winner of the 1989 Newbery Award)*

Take students to see live theater.

Children already have many connections with drama through television and movies, and you can use this familiarity to help you teach character types, performance styles, and interpretation. However, nothing compares with taking students to live theater performances. Many cities have children's theater companies, and regular theater companies and university theaters often include a children's play as part of their season. Matinees for school groups often offer special pricing. Local arts groups may be willing to underwrite a trip to the theater for your class (or for individual students whose families can't afford the price of a ticket). Many performing companies provide workshops or talks with actors or directors before or after shows. Many also offer in-school workshops for classes attending their plays (see the websites for First Stage Milwaukee, www.firststage.org/inschooleducation/, or Theatre West's Storybook Theatre, www.theatrewest.org/education.html, for typical examples). These experiences help students understand the thinking and the work behind interpretation and performance.

Arrange a residency with a visiting artist.

Artists-in-residence provide a close-up look at the work of poets, actors, and playwrights. Start with people you know: a teacher or staff member at your school or someone in your community who acts in, writes, or directs plays. Or contact a university or college theater department: There is often a professor who specializes in theater for young people. Another great source of visiting artists is your state arts board, agency, or similar organization (find yours through the National

Assembly of State Arts Agencies, http://nasaa-arts.org); they often have directories of artists-in-residence—including poets, playwrights, and actors—who specialize in working in the schools. Many have had special training, and know how to relate what they do to students of any age and ability.

Make poetry an opportunity for dramatic performance.

Many of us have an image of the Romantic poet contemplating the world and expressing his or her deep thoughts in private writing. However, even Romantic poets got together with their friends and shared their poetry, with famous poets like Poe making money through public readings to enthusiastic crowds. Today's poets develop and revise their poetry at poetry readings and slams. Poets' authentic practices provide a great model for integrating the language arts.

A poetry slam is a mock Olympic-style poetry competition. After a poet performs his or her poetry, "judges" (sometimes established poets, other times people recruited from the audience) hold up numbered cards rating the quality of the writing, the significance of the content, and the performance (Jester 1997). Although this is done in fun, public evaluation is something teachers and students need to take into account.

Gina Coates and Liz Jorgenson (both names are pseudonyms), fourth- and fifth-grade teachers, presented a monthlong poetry unit with the help of our colleague Janine Certo and several visiting poets. Students began by reading poems and listening to poets perform their poetry and eventually held a poetry reading of their own for parents and friends.

Janine carefully chose poems from a variety of traditions as models for students' writing and reading aloud—classic and contemporary poetry, children's poetry, adult poetry, poems that matched children's particular interests, and poems centered on everyday life and ordinary objects. Students kept a poet's journal, talked with the visiting poets about writing and performing, and worked on their own poems in a writing workshop.

The students' writing ended with performing. Janine and her guest poets taught them how to read aloud and how to be good audience members:

- Hold your paper low.

- Speak clearly.

- Project your voice.

- Speak in a natural voice, following the language; don't overemphasize the meter.

- Be a good audience member: Listen quietly, and applaud at the end. (At a more traditional poetry reading, the audience may clap, or—as Gina and Liz's students adopted from a video shown in class—snap their fingers in response.)

Students' intense engagement in this project, and their willingness to find a larger audience for their poetry, was possible because Liz and Gina created a context in which poetry was both a personal expression and a valued adult activity (as undertaken by the visiting poets). Poetry became a way to explore language in new ways and use that language to speak to their world.

Janine's approach helped Gina and Liz avoid the two extremes of too much scaffolding and no scaffolding at all. They didn't use writing "frames" (templates with blanks for adjective, noun, etc.), which may prompt students to think about word choice but aren't necessary for writing age-appropriate poetry, and they also avoided the other extreme of providing too little assistance, which can result in poetry that, among other things, too closely resembles prose. Both Certo (2004) and Apol (2002) offer excellent articles about helping students read and write poetry.

As with dramatic performance, poetry writing and performance provide excellent vehicles for integrating all of the language arts, and more. Susan Kuchniki at El-Hajj Malik El-Shabazz Academy engaged her kindergarten class in reading, writing, speaking, listening, visual arts, music, motor skills, and socioemotional development through a project that centered on performing the poem "You're Wonderful" from Debbie Clement's book of the same name. They read and reread the book while listening to the accompanying CD,

Figure 5.3 Quilt constructed by Susan Kuchniki's class

Figure 5.4 Kyra shares her writing.

then learned the song and the sign language for "wonderful," "beautiful," and "dreams." Clement's book includes a quilt, and Susan's students made their own quilt squares out of five-by-seven-inch index cards, drawing colorful pictures of the wonderful things in their lives. The pictures were connected at the corners with yarn to make a vivid display, which they held up in front of the assembled guests to introduce the performance. As students sang along with the music, their hands waved in the signs for "wonderful" and "beautiful" and "dreams." They beamed during their peers' applause.

After the performance, students matched pictures of things that made them feel wonderful with captions expressing how they felt during the performance. Susan bound these pages into a book for their class library to commemorate the day, complete with a cover featuring a photo of the entire class holding up their quilt and smiling for the camera.

Use model or mentor texts.

High-quality drama for children can be difficult to find, although the rise of quality children's theater in the last thirty years has increased the supply of plays available. Children's theater websites often include links to current plays and popular playwrights. The American Alliance for Theatre and Education (AATE) has a Web page, http://usaplays4kids.drury.edu, which lists award-winning plays for children, along with their publishers. Anchorage Press and Dramatic Publishing are two companies that specialize in plays for children.

≡ *Sources of Plays for Children*

The Classic Fairy Tales: Retold for the Stage *by C. Wray. Aurora Metro Press, 2003.*

The Classic Fairy Tales 2: Retold for the Stage *by C. Wray. Aurora Metro Press, 2008.*

Cootie Shots: Theatrical Inoculations Against Bigotry for Kids, Parents,and Teachers *edited by N. Bowles. Theatre Communications Group, 2000.*

Multicultural Plays for Children. Volume I: Grades K–3 *by P. Gerke. Smith and Kraus, 1996.*

Multicultural Plays for Children. Volume 2: Grades 4–6 *by P. Gerke. Smith and Kraus, 1996.*

Plays for Youth Theatres and Large Casts *by N. Duffield. Aurora Metro Press, 2010.*

Shakespeare with Children: Six Scripts for Young Players *by E. Weinstein. Smith and Kraus, 2008.*

Theatre for Young Audiences: Twenty Great Plays for Children *by A. J. Coleman. St. Martin's, 2005.*

Links to websites

http://produceaplay.com/ (linked to www.youthplays.com)

www.youthplays.com (a collection of plays online—you can read them for free, and only pay when you decide to use one. Also has an annual contest for young playwrights)

http://www.playsforyoungaudiences.org/ (a partnership venture between Seattle Children's Theatre and the Children's Theatre Company in Minneapolis)

http://www.applays.com/ (Anchorage Press plays; they have been a leading publisher of children's plays for decades)

http://usaplays4kids.drury.edu/playwrights/bush/ (AATE's page for Max Bush, a Michigan playwright who writes plays for young audiences)

Use videos.

One of the best ways to help students understand the role of interpretation in creating a character is to have them view one or more filmed versions of a play they are reading. When an actor speaks a line in a way that catches students by surprise, or students distinctly disagree with the way a role is portrayed, they are beginning to understand that presenting a play is a matter of making choices and that a number of interpretations can be valid. It is much easier to find these resources for high school students than for younger ones. However, there are several film and television versions of William Gibson's *The Miracle Worker* (1959), an excellent play about Annie Sullivan's work with the young Helen Keller, that are appropriate for upper-elementary and middle school students. If you have students read a scene (and possibly perform it) in class, then show them two different interpretations [perhaps the 1962 film version with Patty Duke and Anne Bancroft (Coe & Penn 1962) and the 1979 made-for-TV version (Coe & Aaron 1979)], students will get a sense of how different actors use the clues in the play script to construct the same role.

You can also use various filmed versions of fairy tales to help students see different ways of portraying familiar events and personalities. Cinderella has been made into a Rogers and Hammerstein musical (several film versions are available), a Disney animated feature (Disney & Geronimi, Jackson & Luske 1950), and, more recently, as *Ever After* starring Drew Barrymore (Soria, Trench & Tennant 1998).

PRINCIPLE (3) Explicitly teach genre features.

What do I need to know about dramatic text characteristics?

Because play scripts are skeletal, their characteristics tend to be fairly straightforward. However, students read this genre less often than they do narratives or informational text, so they may need help seeing how this system of features works.

How do I teach dramatic text characteristics?

The annotated example in Figure 5.5 demonstrates how the characteristics of dramatic text facilitate oral reading. Developing a scene for performance is a great way to develop the ability to follow the code provided and enables readers to eventually stage a script in their heads when reading a play script. Writing a script, as Judy Jackson, Jill Mitchell, and Cheryl Sunday's seventh graders did, is another way to learn the characteristics of dramatic texts. The students move from reading and performing short plays (to become familiar with stage directions and formatting of character name with colon and line, scene, and act divisions) to using templates to write their plays (with spaces indicated for character names, dialogue, etc.).

It's helpful for students to be able to mark up a script for performance. Although we're all trying to save paper these days, every student needs his or her own copy of a scene or play on which to add stage directions, underline for emphasis, highlight his or her lines, and write in the margins. This is commonly done in the theater, television, and movies. Have students write in pencil, so they can change things. In early rehearsals, actors carry pencils for just that purpose. (If the class is reading a play in a trade book or anthology that will be passed along to next year's class, use sticky notes.)

Common Characteristics of Dramatic Text*

Elements

- **characters:** who the action involves

  - **protagonist:** the main character in the play: usually the character we are expected to empathize with or root for

  - **antagonist:** the character who opposes the protagonist in some way (can be the "bad guy," but does not have to be evil)

  - **foil character:** a character whose contrast with the main character makes the protagonist's characteristics particularly clear (e.g., the stepsisters in Cinderella)

- **setting:** the place and time (Setting is generally barely indicated in a play, but it is important to understanding character and action. Its impact often has to be inferred by the reader or director.)

- **plot:** what happens

  - **conflict:** usually comes from the opposition between the protagonist and antagonist (*person to person*), but not always: it can also be internal (*psychological*) or *situational*

    beginning conflict (aka instigating action)

    rising action (the conflict develops and becomes more complex)

    climax (the conflict reaches its peak)

    resolution (the conflict is resolved)

    falling action (loose ends are tied up)

- **narration:** A figure external to the story provides background information about characters and action

- **monologue or dialogue:** what character(s) say and do

  - sounds like spoken language, not like written language (may be written to indicate the dialect of the speaker)

  - background information about characters and action (known as *exposition*) may be woven into the dialogue—playwrights can also use *flashback* scenes to provide exposition

- **expository material:** material introducing setting and cast:

  - **when the play takes place:** identified at the beginning of the play ("The time is in the early 1920s. Act 1: A Monday afternoon in early spring") and often at the beginning of each scene ("It is now 8:00 at night. The table is cleared.")

  - **where the play takes place:** also usually identified at the beginning of the play and at the beginning of each act and scene, if there is a change

  - **cast list:** a list of all characters in the play, usually in order of appearance, with very brief identifiers, usually paired with the name of the actor who first performed that role—located at the front of the play, along with the place and time

 ©2012 by Nell K. Duke, Samantha Caughlan, Mary M. Juzwik, and Nicole M. Martin from *Reading and Writing Genre with Purpose in K–8 Classrooms*. Portsmouth, NH: Heinemann

- *acts*: major parts of the story
- *scenes*: parts of an act, usually marked by a change in location or time

Graphical characteristics

- *dialogue*, which takes up most of the page, in a regular font
- *stage directions*, where present, in italics
- *speaker designations* on the left-hand side, in italics or uppercase, followed by a colon
- *clues to expressive reading*, such as pauses indicated by punctuation (dashes or ellipses) or shouting indicated by dialogue in uppercase, possibly present

* *Any given dramatic text is unlikely to, and needn't, have all of these characteristics.*

Figure 5.5 Dramatic text features of excerpts from *Our Town* by Thornton Wilder (1938)

Plays are usually divided up into acts, and acts into scenes.

Note how character names are always capitalized and to the left: Actors can find their next line easily.

Material italicized in parentheses are stage directions, but optional: Mrs. Gibbs doesn't really have to drink coffee in this scene!

Placement of sound effect. This one's not optional, because Rebecca refers to it directly.

C., L., and R. refer to stage center, left, and right. That's left and right as you stand on stage, facing the audience.

This business, with the grouping of the kids and their exit up L., is a description of the staging of the first production, and so reflects the vision of the first director, Jed Harris, in 1938. Current productions are free to handle this exit any way that works for their situation.

Act I

. . . .

MRS. GIBBS: (*Crossing to R. of GEORGE to set down butter.*) I'll speak to your father about it when he's rested. Seems to me twenty-five cents a week's enough for a boy of your age. (*Crossing to stove to pour own coffee.*) I declare I don't know how you spend it all.

GEORGE: Aw, Ma,—I gotta lotta things to buy.

MRS. GIBBS: Strawberry phosphates—that's what you spend it on. (*Crosses to between CHILDREN with cup, sips.*)

GEORGE: I don't see how Rebecca comes to have so much money. She has more'n a dollar.

REBECCA: (*Spoon in mouth, dreamily, to the audience*) I've been saving it up gradual.

MRS. GIBBS: Well, dear, I think it's a good thing to spend some every now an' then.

REBECCA: Mama, do you know what I love most in the world, do you? Money.

MRS. GIBBS: Eat your breakfast. (*Crosses to set cup above stove.*)

(An old-fashioned SCHOOLBELL is heard in the distance, off L.)

REBECCA: (*Rising, running front of table to pick up her books*) There's the first bell. I gotta go.

(*All CHILDREN rise and rush for their books, then out to meet down C. REBECCA and WALLY lead out, followed by GEORGE and EMILY. On meeting, they ad lib greetings and, as they hurry up C. and off L., the GIRLS pair together, as do GEORGE and WALLY, chatting gaily.*)

(*STAGE MANAGER drifts off down R. as they pass up Main Street.*)

PRINCIPLE ④ Explicitly teach genre-specific or genre-sensitive strategies.

The strategies in this section apply mostly to reading and its corollary, production. We address writing more in Principle 5; however, because drama is a genre students are less familiar with, the work in this section is essential to prepare for writing.

Teach how to read a play script.

In contrast to the dense information in short stories and novels, exchanges in plays scripts are skeletal:

(Len's bedroom)

Bobby: So, what do you want to do today?

Len: I don't know, what do you want to do?

Are these fast friends bored because it's the last week of summer? Or are they new friends, tentatively feeling each other out? Friendly or hostile? And this bedroom, is it messy or neat? What posters are on the walls? Are there books? Toys?

The answers to these questions are in the circumstances set up by the playwright and in these characters' previous interactions. If this is the beginning of the play, we might have to withhold judgment regarding the topic and tone of this scene until we read further. Withholding judgment is a useful general reading strategy and one that can be practiced in play reading. Also, until we read further, it may be difficult to keep Len and Bobby straight in our mind, because we don't know what distinguishes one from the other. If this is the climax of the play, however unlikely, how would it be emphasized? What are the two boys doing? Plays raise more questions than they answer, but this provides great opportunities to infer meaning and action.

Thus students need to understand that many questions in a play remain unanswered. Readers of plays have to stage them in their minds. It is useful to teach students to ask themselves questions as they read (best initially practiced together with a short play or the first act of a play):

- What is happening? What do you think is going to happen?
- How are the characters related, and how do they feel about each other?
- What do we know about their past, their physical appearance, and their personalities from reading what they say?
- What do others say about them?
- What must their environment look like? Sound like?
- What do they wear?

And always, with all the above:

- How do you know?

You might have students write about these things or draw pictures of what they imagine is happening.

Stage directions can provide some guidance in interpretation of dramatic texts, but they are considered only aids to reading or suggestions (in most modern plays, the stage directions are a description of the first production's staging). That is why they are in parentheses and/or in italics. The reader will still need to do much of the interpretation and, as we have emphasized, various interpretations are possible. For example, many actors have played Willy Loman in *Death of a Salesman* (Miller 1949). The two most famous interpretations are probably those of Lee J. Cobb, the original Willy, and Dustin Hoffman, who played Willy in a later revival that was filmed in 1985 (Colesbury & Schlöndorff). Cobb's performance emphasized Willy's tiredness and sense of resignation, and Hoffman's highlighted Willy's anger and his contradictory nature. If you read the play, you can see all of those traits in the dialogue: Although quite different, both performances were true to the play.

Interpreting a play differs from interpreting a poem or short story in that the consequences of interpretation are playable action and production design. Typically, plays taught in schools were originally written for directors, actors, and designers to take the dialogue blueprint and read it closely to create a living staged experience. With drama, play production is the ultimate act of reading. Every detail of setting and performance has to be decided with the text in mind.

Head toward performance.

Putting on a play as a class is different from the drama club staging one as an extracurricular activity. To benefit from the instruction everyone in the class must have a role, everyone must have some voice in the proceedings. However, it's difficult to find plays with large casts of thirty or so meaningful parts, evenly split between boys and girls. Dawn Kennaugh dealt with the problem by choosing two shorter plays, one with ten characters, the other with twelve, each with several good roles.

Any number of books and other resources provide detailed instructions for putting on a community or school play. When doing so as part of the English language arts curriculum, the following guidelines will help you and your students get the most out of the experience:

- *The first read-through:* The students first encounter the characters and action. In this reading, students read for what happens, where, why, to whom, and how everyone is related to one another.

- *Second and third read-throughs:* Students gain a deeper understanding of character and theme. Teaching students to ask themselves a set of guiding questions can help them get deeper and deeper into the play (see Figure 5.6). These understandings will inform rehearsals by making the characters' motivations clear.

- *Casting:* You may want to make the casting decisions, but engage students in the casting process. Have students take different roles as you reread the plays, so they will understand your decisions. The more transparent and fair your process is, and the more you are able to take students' preferences into consideration, the better. Dawn Kennaugh asked her students to write down which play they wanted to be in and whether they wanted a major or a minor part. Most students were able to get something they asked for.

Exploring your play—to find out what you need to know for performance

In your small groups, read your script again, and then answer the questions below, going back to the play as often as you need to. These questions will help you make decisions about what we need to do to bring this play to life onstage.

Plot. What are the most important events?

Why are they important?

Character. On the reverse side of this sheet list the characters, and for each character, answer:

What does the character want?

How does he or she change over time? In what ways? (If there is no change, then this is a minor character.)

How character defines plot and action

What obstacles does each character face?

What does each do to overcome those obstacles and attempt to reach the goal? (Use other side if necessary)

How do different characters' goals conflict?

Setting. How does the setting of the play, or the time in which it is set, influence the action and characters?

Figure 5.6 Guiding questions for early read-throughs

- *Blocking and set design go together:* Blocking is placing and moving actors onstage. Blocking should satisfy the literal requirements of the events, help draw the audience's attention to what is most important, build the action toward the climax, and help actors express their characters. In the theater, the director usually makes these decisions, but in the classroom, students should have a major voice in deciding what happens onstage and why. During the second and third readings, have students begin plotting key scenes on paper templates containing an outline of the playing area. Alternatively, have actors improvise in rehearsal while students not onstage provide feedback and ideas for improvement. Blocking requires a set—an environment within which the characters move. What needs to be onstage for the actors to carry out their roles (a throne for a king, a pond for a frog)? What other elements make the environment more realistic (desks in a classroom, phones and computers in an office)? Some of this is decided through close readings of the play: Students responsible for set design and construction should be on the lookout for necessary scenery, furniture, and props as they read through the script.

- *On-book rehearsals:* Actors have their scripts in hand, although they should refer to them less and less frequently. They should nevertheless concentrate on bringing out the meaning through expression, gesture, gaze, and movement.

- *Off-book rehearsals* (no scripts, lines memorized): Whether or not you get to this point may depend on the age of your students. We've all been at performances where very young performers freeze. Students younger than third grade may only memorize very short or simple plays or those containing a lot of choral lines. However, Dawn's fourth graders learned their lines quickly and well and were completely off book a couple of weeks before performance. When students first put down their scripts, things feel as though they've moved backward, but the actors quickly get back on track; they can really work on their roles once the scripts are out of their hands. Actors should also practice with any props or costumes that take getting used to (long skirts, boots, sporting equipment, proclamation scrolls).

Figure 5.7 Once actors are off book, Maddie stands by as stage manager to feed them their lines as needed.

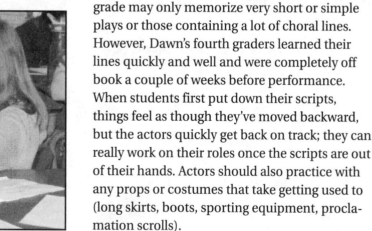

- *Concurrent work on sets, costumes, music, sound effects, and whatever else you intend to use to help express the action:* As much as possible, the setting should express the students' understanding of the play's genre (comedy? melodrama? detective story? drama?), the time period, and the characters' environment and personalities. Settings can be very spare if need be: A few blocks on which to sit and simple costume pieces may be sufficient, especially if you are performing in other classrooms. However, if your curricular objectives coincide with those of the art or music teacher, enlist their help if you can; the integration can be very powerful.

Figure 5.8 A program from a theater for young audiences production. Providing a variety of such models can help your students design a program for their own production.

- *Performance:* Who is your audience? Other classes at the same grade level who are reading the same play? Children in other schools? Parents? Is a spoken or written introduction necessary to help the audience understand how to approach the play? Do you need a program? The introduction and the program are additional genres students can produce.

If this sounds overwhelming, remember that a project like this is an accordion. If you have limited time and resources, or very young students, your plays will be shorter, perhaps less polished, and your setting simpler. However, if the play you are producing is central to your curriculum, if you can integrate it with other content and arts areas, or if yours is an arts magnet school, you may consider it worthwhile to spend a great deal of time on such a project.

≡ Dramatic Activities for the Classroom

These activities can help students develop a play for performance or open up a class reading. They can also motivate deeper reading and writing in response to any literature.

- **Writing as the character:** *Have each student write letters, diaries, or memos about the events in the play in the voice of one of the characters. These can be shared and used to deepen the understanding of characters in developing performance.*

- **Tea party:** *Have students take on character roles and chat at a tea party or some other event where they might meet socially. (Variation: Put labels with character names on the foreheads or backs of students and have them guess who they are by how others interact with them.)*

- **Prequels and sequels:** *Have students write scenes about important events before or after the time of the play. Actors get a sense that their characters come from somewhere, are real people with a history and future.*

- **Scene work:** *Divide the play into short scenes and monologues for students to rehearse and perform for the class. (Maybe gather some basic props and costume pieces.) Students could write a one-page description of what their character is thinking, feeling, and doing to achieve her or his goal in the scene. After each scene is played, have the actors share their decisions about how to play the scene.*

- **Design:** *Have students prepare drawings, paintings, or models of the settings or costumes. Tell them to include colors and objects that express some larger idea or get across the tone or mood of the play.*

PRINCIPLE ⑤ Offer ongoing coaching and feedback.

During rehearsals help students deepen their understanding of a text, become more fluent speakers and more confident performers, and become more genre-aware writers.

Help young playwrights make their script work for actors.

Let students who have written their own scripts hear the play being read aloud by their peers (real playwrights attend rehearsals of the first production for just this purpose). Just because students think something will sound good when they read it to themselves does not mean it will play well onstage. Playwrights often rewrite parts of their play until opening night. Rehearsal is the best road to revision (poets also "test-drive" their poetry at poetry readings).

Teach students to use their eyes and ears.

One of Samantha's favorite pieces of advice was given to her by an actress who had been an artist-in-residence in many schools: "Don't tell me what you think, tell me what you see." Telling "what you think" too often passes judgment in an unhelpful way, saying, in essence, "I think you should." The teacher or peer observer is applying their tastes and values rather than helping the poet or actor achieve their goals. When the actor hears, instead, "I saw," or "I heard," he or she is getting an audience member's view of how he or she is coming across. "I heard you being so loud at the beginning that you really sounded angry" is useful information whether the actor was trying to communicate anger and has been having trouble with projection or whether the goal was to sound excited and happy (in which case the portrayal needs some adjusting).

Model for students how to report on what they experience, what they do and do not understand in what they see or hear, and have students role-play giving feedback. Also give students rehearsal response sheets with guided questions that keep them on track with the class' objectives for the rehearsal. Objectives can range from hearing voices clearly to keeping track of pace and expression to creating characters through voice and movement that are different from the students' everyday lives.

> ### Guiding Questions for Responding to Actors as Audience Members
>
> - What do you think this character wants? Why do you think that?
>
> - How is this character different from the actor's everyday self? How does he or she talk differently? Move differently?
>
> - Has the actor used movement creatively to make the story understandable?
>
> - Have performers used their voices to reveal meaning and emotion?
>
> - How did the costume and props (if used) help communicate meaning and character?
>
> - What surprised you about this performance, if anything?

As you approach the culminating performance, step back, let students run through the entire show, and give notes on details that still need work. This allows everyone to get a sense of how the whole thing works together and make adjustments (alter blocking, pacing, and other aspects of a scene to make the climax more effective, for example). It also reminds them (and you!) that once they are performing for an audience, they cannot stop to correct mistakes and you can't call out reminders or do their work for them!

Don't be a puppet master.

The process should be as transparent as possible, and the students should participate as much as possible. Don't direct students without discussing why a change might be made; solicit suggestions from other audience members. Dawn Kennaugh kept rehearsals on track while allowing student input. She pointed out what worked in each scene and prompted students to work on areas that didn't. Her students came up with the best ideas for costumes and comic bits, deciding that the heralds should pick the sleeping king's pocket to find a coin to toss and finding a way to have snow blow in on March's entrance. These decisions came out of their understanding of what each play needed. Through her coaching and feedback, Dawn helped to conserve what worked in each scene, while prompting students to work on problem areas.

Get knowledgeable outsiders to view final polishing sessions.

Fresh eyes and ears are needed when you and the students can't see things any more. They also provide an authentic response when the people in the room are having trouble listening to one another. Having a "preview" audience gives students the confidence that they are ready for performance (and validates the things you have been saying for weeks!).

The Rewards of Putting on a Good Show

Your apprehension about staging dramatic genres will vanish after one successful performance in front of an authentic audience. As you watch students respond with pride to the applause, you'll reflect on the process that got them there: All they learned about the texts and themselves, their improved abilities to comprehend and infer what they read, their enhanced speaking and listening skills, and the knowledge of the human condition and the world that comes from deep immersion in literature, as interpreted in performance. Good show!

For Further Reading

All Aspects of Play Production

Break a Leg: The Kids' Guide to Acting and Stagecraft *by L. Friedman. New York: Workman Publishing, 2002.*

Kids Take the Stage: Helping Young People Discover the Creative Outlet of Theater *2nd ed. by L. Peterson & D. O'Connor. Backstage Books, 2006.*

Directing and the Rehearsal Process

Theater Games for the Classroom by V. Spolin. *Northwestern University Press, 1986.*

Theater Games for Rehearsal: A Director's Handbook *by V. Spolin. Northwestern University Press, 1985.*

Classroom Drama Resources

Drama for Learning *by D. Heathcote & G. Bolton. Heinemann, 1995.*

Drama Structures: A Practical Handbook for Teachers *by C. O'Neill & A. Lambert. Hutchinson, 1994.*

Dramatic Literacy: Using Drama and Literature to Teach Middle-Level Content *by J. L. Smith & J. D. Herring. Heinemann, 2001.*

Imagining to Learn: Inquiry, Ethics and Integration Through Drama *by B. Edmiston & J. Wilhelm. Heinemann, 1998.*

Reading/Watching Plays

www.firststage.org/inschooleducation/enrichmentguides.asp

Playwriting

Playmaking—Children Writing and Performing Their Own Plays *by D. J. Sklar. Teachers and Writers Collaborative, 1990.*

Theatre West's middle school playwriting program: www.theatrewest.org/educationPlaywrighting.html.

New Jersey Writers Project and Playwrights Theatre (www.ptnj.org/) cosponsors residencies in playwriting in districts around the state. Plays are produced locally and by Playwrights Theatre. Playwrights Theatre has been holding playwriting contests for writers as young as fourth grade for twenty-seven years (www.ptnj.org/pages/nj-young-playwrights).

Matt Buchanan, on his website www.childdrama.com/trail1.html, tells how he wrote a play with fourth graders, including the issues that arose.

On how to write scripts and format them so they're easy to use: www.playwriting101.com/.

Effecting Change:
Persuasive Genres

What Genre with Purpose Looks Like: The Caffeine Wars, Grade 5

As Samantha enters Niki's classroom, she hears some students murmur, "No coffee." Niki grins, and says, "They were wondering if you would have it."

"You gave up caffeine?" someone says hopefully.

Samantha says, "Let me tell you about my thought process as I read your letters, and then I'll tell you my decision." The students pay close attention as she lists the effects of caffeine they had raised in persuasive letters trying to convince her to quit or cut back: the stomachaches, interference with sleep—none of these had been surprising. But what Adam had said about caffeine's association with bone loss caught her attention, as her parents both had osteoporosis, and she went right to the Internet to confirm the facts. Caffeine has been shown to increase the calcium excreted from the body, and it interferes with the absorption of vitamin D. Because they had studied the body systems, the students knew what that means for healthy bones. As a result of the efforts of these fifth graders, Samantha had begun to cut back on her coffee drinking. She shares her plan for cutting back to one cup of coffee in the morning and a cup of tea at lunch.

After her successful body systems project (see Chapter 4), Niki McGuire was looking for other authentic ways to put that knowledge to use. "Every year students bug me about having caffeinated pop (Michigan-speak for soft drinks) at the end-of-school picnic," she said. "I don't think they need it, but I'll give them the chance to research its effect on body systems and try and convince me." However, what about those students who already shared Niki's point of view? Samantha Caughlan, caffeine addict, agreed to provide a target for the opposing side.

Designing compelling, communicatively meaningful environments To help frame the debate, Samantha came into Mrs. McGuire's caffeine-free room carrying a large, stainless-steel travel cup of coffee. She sipped from it as she explained how she had started drinking coffee over thirty years ago, and that, although she kept an eye on coffee studies as they came up in the news, she really had not seriously looked into the health effects. At the end of a discussion on caffeinated drinks, fourteen of the nineteen students intended to try to convince Mrs. McGuire to let them have caffeinated soda at the picnic, and five were taking up the challenge of getting Samantha to quit. The genre for addressing either Niki or Samantha would be a persuasive letter written by each student.

Explicitly teaching genre features To prepare her students for this assignment, Niki compared propaganda techniques advertisers use to persuade, such as the bandwagon effect ("All the cool kids are doing it!"), testimonials ("Now that I wear Noise-Be-Gone ear plugs, I fall right asleep every night!"), and traditional rhetorical appeals to an audience (see pages 153–154). Students evaluated several persuasive articles for their claims and use of evidence.

Explicitly teaching genre-specific strategies Once the class spent a period in the library and conducted an Internet search of the effects of caffeine on the body, they were much less excited about drinking caffeine: Now only five students were working to convince Mrs. McGuire; the rest were out to save Dr. Caughlan from her caffeine addiction (some independently came to the more nuanced idea that just getting Samantha to cut back would be a worthwhile goal). Niki used a persuasive essay graphic organizer to help them come up with their position and arguments for and against (similar to Figure 6.7, page 159).

Offering ongoing coaching and feedback As the students wrote their letters, Samantha and Niki circulated, listening to their beginning efforts at persuasion and providing on-the-spot feedback regarding the effectiveness of different claims. They encouraged the students to use what they knew about body systems to explain how caffeine affected the body (for example, Jordan described how coffee upsets the stomach): Good information is persuasive. Samantha also pointed out that they needed to be careful about their claims: The bold but unsupported claim from one caffeine supporter that consuming caffeine resulted in an 80 percent lower risk of cancer was hard to believe, although the more modest report from Brendan that moderate consumption of caffeine lowers the risk of colon cancer by 28 percent was more believable and interesting. The students worked hard to convince, and the results showed an attention to rhetorical impact and to editing for mechanical errors.

Postscript Samantha has drastically cut her caffeine consumption, and she sticks with it. In addition, Niki agreed to allow soft drinks with moderate amounts of caffeine at the end-of-school picnic.

Rethinking Popular Persuasive Assignments: Beyond the Persuasive Essay

When Samantha taught high school, the persuasive assignment of choice was the five-paragraph persuasive essay, still the dominant persuasive genre in grades 3 through 12. The five-paragraph persuasive essay generally includes an introduction with an attention-catching "hook," a preview of the argument, and a position statement; three body paragraphs, each containing one reason to support the position and evidence for each reason or claim; and a conclusion that tidily restates the argument. In more advanced versions, a rebuttal paragraph is included, which states one or more reasons someone might oppose the chosen position and then rebuts that counterargument.

Teachers who rely on the persuasive essay say that it provides structure, but this structure is often presented rigidly. The form is not adapted to a rhetorical purpose, a topic, potential arguments, or the author innovations. The requirement to write three body paragraphs explaining three reasons for an issue that might only have two good reasons or that might require four to make the point results in what Hillocks (2002) calls "blethering"—paragraphs written in order to fulfill a formula rather than to convince someone. This problem is intensified by even more specific models—those requiring that each body paragraph contain two pieces of evidence, each accompanied by two sentences of commentary, for example. This problem is made still worse by the fact that the persuasive essay normally lacks a real audience to persuade or a real forum in which to persuade (e.g., a newspaper letter to the editor, a blog post). Students' frequent struggles with the rebuttal paragraph highlight the problem of writing for a nonexistent audience. How are students supposed to know which of a number of possible opposing points would be most persuasive to some abstract person? The rigid templates of the persuasive essay are not necessary, or even helpful, when teaching students to research their positions on topics they care about and then craft persuasive texts that can actually influence events close to home or far away.

Purposes of Persuasive Texts

The projects showcased in this chapter share a concern with influencing the target audience's ideas or behavior. The audiences largely comprise people the students know: fellow students, family, community members, teachers. Students' need to persuade these real and important audiences motivates hard work. Some projects involve working with a variety of genres in secondary research, online and in print, conducting primary research in the community, and adhering to the conventions of whichever genre was chosen to communicate one's persuasive effort. Quite a contrast with the five-paragraph persuasive essay directed to the teacher or a fictitious audience!

Persuasive texts are everywhere—television commercials wanting us to buy something, editorials supporting a particular political position, blog postings urging us to think in a particular way, proposals for funding or policy change—a great variety of text types! Persuasive texts share many features with the other genres discussed in this book—and they illustrate how genres can sometimes be hard to categorize. Features in informational texts, such as graphs and bulleted lists of facts, convince us to follow one course of action rather than another. Dramatic reenactments are used to persuade others that particular ways of acting, thinking, or feeling will have particular consequences. A politician's life story is featured in a campaign ad or in an autobiographical narrative he or she writes. Even a procedural text can be used to persuade you to perform a task one way rather than another.

What are we calling persuasive texts for this chapter? A persuasive text has the *primary* purpose of convincing a particular audience to change their ideas or behavior. In the classrooms featured here, persuasive texts included formal letters designed to convince an individual to give up a habit, oral presentations designed to convince preschoolers that kindergarten was going to be a great experience and, described on the following page, a magazine designed to convince young people to make healthier choices.

"Hybrid" Texts

Sometimes when a text has more than one clear purpose, we call it a hybrid text. For example, this book about oil spills may be intended both to inform readers about oil spills and to persuade readers to use less oil or be more careful about the oil we do use. It is both an informational and a persuasive text. It is part of a series of informational science texts, most of which (the one on the changing seasons or the one on dinosaurs, for example) do not include attempts to persuade.

Figure 6.1 *Oil Spill* by Melvin Berger (1994) cover

What Genre with Purpose Looks Like:
The Write for Your Life Project, Healthy Teens, Healthy Choices Magazine, Grade 6

Sixth graders dressed in their best look out into the audience of parents, community members, and fellow students. Tonight is the publishing party for the latest edition of Healthy Teens, Healthy Choices, *a magazine their class has produced to distribute to fellow students, parents, and various outlets in the community. Tonight they are presenting the results of their research into issues that have consequences for the health of people who live in the community surrounding Detroit's Dewey Center for Urban Education. These students are carrying on a tradition: Earlier classes engaged in the Write for Your Life project presented at the National Service Learning Conference and were interviewed by WDET, the local NPR station. This edition of the magazine has sections for each of the five topics chosen by the class and researched in small groups: guns, gangs, and violence; abstinence and teen pregnancy; child abuse; HIV and drug abuse; and alcoholism. Inside are typical magazine genres: brief reports on each issue based on community-based research; tips for avoiding unhealthy behavior; fiction stories illustrating choices and their consequences; rap-style poems; cartoons and drawings. The chosen topics are more than abstractions for these young people who live in the Cass Corridor area of Detroit, which has the highest incidence of AIDS, prostitution, and drug abuse in the state. The serious yet optimistic tone of this magazine is in itself an accomplishment.*

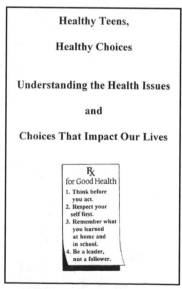

Figure 6.2 Scan of magazine cover: *Healthy Teens, Healthy Choices*

The Write for Your Life project began as a collaboration between university professors and public school teachers who wanted to address teen health issues while providing students with the English language arts skills they need to be successful (Swenson 2003). During each of the five years of the project, students read, discussed, and chose issues related to health outcomes in their communities. They produced a wide spectrum of genres aimed at real audiences in their communities: a teen magazine, a one-act play dealing with substance abuse, a video encouraging teens to recycle, a brochure on anorexia, and support groups for students who had lost family members to AIDS or experienced their parents' divorce.

Designing compelling, communicatively meaningful environments: This is what we do in sixth grade. Toby Kahn-Loftus, a sixth-grade teacher at the Dewey Center, was part of this project from its beginning. After the first edition of *Healthy Teens, Healthy Choices* was published, the magazine became an annual tradition, printed and distributed to Dewey students and the surrounding neighborhood through a grant from the Wayne County Regional Education Service Agency and service learning funds available through their principal. The purpose of the magazine was to convince community youth to make healthier choices through the presentation of solid information about the impact those choices would have on their community and through cautionary tales. This class chose their own topics and, in small groups, gathered data and crafted specific sections of the magazine. Their goal (from the introduction): "Our hope is that the students who read our magazine will think hard about the choices that they make in life."

Providing exposure and experience: Arguing from a strong knowledge base. While preparing *Healthy Teens, Healthy Choices*, students read and produced a wide variety of genres. Research included both secondary and primary sources. Toby's students distributed surveys on each issue to over 150 teens and adults in their community, graphed the responses, and juxtaposed the opinions and experiences of their local informants with what they learned from published sources. These studies anchored each section of the magazine.

Explicitly teaching genre-sensitive strategies: Bridging audience and text. Knowing their teen audience well, students realized that they would need to use several different strategies to be convincing. Each section opened with their research on community impact. Next were students' realistic fictional accounts of people their age whose lives were affected by having a child too early, by losing a family member to AIDS, or by peer pressure to join a gang. Each story was followed by an afterword spelling out the take-away message (e.g., "If anyone reading this story needs help, they should see our school counselor"). Each section also included tips for avoiding danger and staying healthy, as well as contact information for community groups that help young people deal with the issue.

How to Teach Persuasion with Purpose: Five Principles for Instruction

Our five principles can help teachers engage students in reading and writing to effect change.

PRINCIPLE (1) Design compelling, communicatively meaningful environments.

A classroom can so easily become a self-contained world. You and your students focus on your reading, your discussions, your interactions with one another, your writing. The first challenge in getting your students interested in the work needed to effect change is to turn their attention toward the school, community, and the world. This helps them find something that they agree needs changing. Topics also emerge from the curriculum: A science unit can finish with a conservation project; social studies lessons on local, state, and national issues can turn into lessons on civic participation as students contact elected officials to promote action on an issue.

Shira Epstein reports on a teacher she calls "Scott" (a pseudonym), working in an urban New York school, who encouraged his eighth graders to keep journals on events they observed in their neighborhood, focusing especially on social problems and on people who were working for change (Epstein 2010). At the same time, the class read and discussed texts about change makers through history and current social issues around the country. In individual and group projects, students studied and created writings and presentations about the local conditions they observed. In similar classrooms, students discuss issues and bring in concerns, stories, or news articles (Heffernan & Lewison 2000; Atwell 2011).

Once you and your class have identified a problem, find something your students can do to contribute to a solution. "Think globally, act locally" is a good rule of thumb for class projects. Children become concerned about the fate of endangered species or hungry children: This becomes a motivation for research and thinking about "What can we do here? Raise funds? Convince local authorities to change policy?" Change the World Kids (www.changetheworldkids.org/), a national organization with local chapters, encourages groups of young people to take action and provides them with help in implementing their ideas (Change the World Kids Juniors is for elementary-age children).

Smaller Worlds for Younger Citizens

Effecting change in the school community gives very young children a sense of engagement, purpose, and a real audience. Nell observed a first-grade class in which the students complained about the lack of ketchup in the cafeteria. Working with a large piece of chart paper, the teacher coordinated a group letter to the lunchroom supervisor advocating that ketchup be available at lunch. A small act—but the lesson that you can advocate for your interest is a powerful one.

Most projects like this involve reading, watching, and producing a variety of texts and media genres. In the world outside school, people use texts to solve problems. For example, childhood obesity is a national problem. Students can find out more about the problem and how to address it by researching websites, magazine articles, and materials in their health and science courses. Acting locally, students can create oral or written persuasive texts to convince their schoolmates to eat healthily and exercise (public service announcements for the school PA system, short plays, posters, brochures, PowerPoint presentations) or lobby the school board or administration to offer healthier alternatives in the lunchroom (through research reports, persuasive letters, and oral presentations at board meetings). They can make posters promoting events or better behavior to post in the halls and lunchroom (see Taylor 2008).

Project Ideas for Effecting Change

Within the School

- *Plan and carry out a letter-writing campaign to establish a peer mediation program or a tutoring program for younger readers and writers.*

- *Write letters or give presentations to get local businesses to donate bins and containers and start a recycling program.*

- *Make presentations, create videos, or write and perform plays for younger students about issues such as peer pressure, bullying, preventing the spread of illness, not smoking.*

- *Prepare and deliver speeches to lobby the principal, district administration, or the school board for programs students either want to begin or save from the budget ax: a drama club, an annual arts night, a book club, an intramural sports league, an outing club.*

In the Community

- *Organize an annual cleanup day for a local stream or park; write posters or flyers to convince others to participate.*

- *Read about and get involved in an effort to preserve a local landmark.*

- *Develop fund-raising brochures to raise money to buy more children's books for the local library.*

- *Write a play about a local issue—recycling, driving carefully in school zones, home fire prevention—and perform it for local groups or events.*

- *Distribute pamphlets or posters on health or safety issues to educate community members.*

In the Larger World

- *Petition state and national legislators and leaders to take action on significant social or environmental problems.*

- *When disaster strikes—the oil spill in the Gulf, flooding along the Mississippi, an earthquake in Pakistan—research it, find out who is helping, and involve your community in a substantial way.*

- *Consult material that advocacy groups prepare specifically for children and post on their education web pages. For example, the National Wildlife Federation has both lessons on environmental issues and suggestions for volunteer efforts (www.nwf.org/At-School.aspx).*

PRINCIPLE ② Provide exposure and experience.

Get students talking and writing.

Introduce students to texts and problems that will get them thinking about project ideas and how they can make a difference. Show them the wide variety of genres adults use to expose problems, discuss them, and take action.

Lee Heffernan's third graders in Childs Elementary School read about local issues, discuss them, and propose activities to address them. One year Lee began by sharing several books about people who had suffered injustices and fought to correct them (Heffernan & Lewison 2000). She read aloud the nonfiction book *From Slave Ship to Freedom Road* (Lester 1999), giving students time to look closely at the pictures and listening carefully to what they had to say about these past cruelties. To fuel classroom discussion, she had them write questions and comments about what surprised them about the book. Then they read and talked about Shange's *Whitewash* (1997), a tale of present-day harassment that brought home the message that racism is not just an unpleasant memory. With this exposure to issues, students mentioned the anti-hate-speech signs in their neighborhood, and they initiated the discussion of a news story about local opposition to distribution of anti-Semitic literature. In response, students drafted a petition against hate speech, collected the signatures of everyone in the school, and posted it prominently in the school's front hallway. Later that same year, they wrote essays for a community contest with the theme, "Where Does Hate Come From?" about how children can improve the atmosphere in their community.

Because Toby Kahn-Loftus (who developed the *Healthy Teens, Healthy Choices* magazine with her students) taught both language arts and social studies, she could explore a wide variety of texts with her students. They read news articles and *Junior Scholastic* pieces on a variety of social issues, acquiring background knowledge and seeing how authors used research and graphics to make a point. Fictional narrative authors such as Sandra Cisneros showed them how to communicate their life experiences in a compelling way. Although not all of these were persuasive texts, they all provided models of writing useful to them in creating their magazine for the community.

Show students they can effect change.

Most students have little experience trying to effect change in the adult world and few role models. Introduce them to stories about young people who have acted on great ideas. For example, Okemos, Michigan sixth-grader Veronica Mills talked five of her friends into joining her in not cutting their hair for a year and then donating it to Cuts for a Cause, an organization that provides wigs to cancer patients (www.wilx.com/news/headlines/94704459.html). You can find stories like this through your local news outlets. The story of Ryan and Jimmy and the Ryan's Well Foundation (see Chapter 1) is another good example of what children have accomplished.

Many advocacy organizations have education departments that provide ideas and guidance for student projects. Interest may be prompted by current community issues or grow out of your curriculum. Some are mentioned on pages 143 and 144. Others include:

HEALTH ORGANIZATIONS

- Students Taking Charge: www.studentstakingcharge.org/
- The American Cancer Society's Relay for Life and Making Strides Against Breast Cancer (these programs are open to all ages, and they also have state-specific campaigns): www.cancer.org/Involved/index

ANTIPOVERTY GROUPS

- Heifer International: www.heifer.org/site/c.edJRKQNiFiG/b.6134611/
- UNICEF: http://teachunicef.org/

CHILDREN'S RIGHTS GROUPS

- Artists Helping Children: www.artistshelpingchildren.org/links_childadvocacy.html
- United Nations Convention on the Rights of the Child: www.unicef.org/crc/

Sites and programs aimed at school children are bridges to learning and thinking about adult issues. Of course, students of different ages and maturity are able to comprehend complex issues and take substantive action to different extents. In the early grades, children's grasp of serious illness might be limited to empathizing with someone feeling very, very sick. However, the sixth graders in Toby Kahn-Loftus' class had close relatives who had died of AIDS or become pregnant too early—they had firsthand experience with health issues young people in other communities might only read about. This gave urgency to their efforts to effect change. They were also able to bring in people they knew from their neighborhood who could talk with them about programs developed to help their community.

Use model or mentor texts.

Genres used to effect change include petitions; letters to elected officials, public offices, and organizations; letters to the editor; brochures; posters; advertisements and public service announcements; proposals for new programs or targeted changes in established programs; grant proposals; PowerPoint presentations; and speeches. Use these texts as models.

Scott, introduced earlier, brought in various kinds of persuasive texts—letters, fliers, and zines (small-circulation magazines, usually written and published by one person or a small group)—and had his eighth-grade students examine them during a guided reading activity (Epstein 2010):

- Students read an example piece and independently answered questions such as, "Who wrote the letter? What is the letter regarding? Why was it written?"

- They looked up the meaning of unfamiliar words or determined new connotations for familiar words.

- They shared the answers to their questions in small groups.

- Then they shared the results of their examination of persuasive texts as a class.

Then Scott and his students used the texts to develop criteria for writing that promotes social justice effectively: clearly defined topics, good reasons for changing things, ways of involving the audience emotionally, and effective pictures. Later, students used these descriptors to peer-review one another's writing.

Nancie Atwell (1998) brings in editorials, columns, and articles from newspapers and magazines as models of writing that influences others and has her students identify and list effective techniques and conventions. (She never brings in a five-paragraph persuasive essay.)

Should I Teach the Five-Paragraph Essay for High-Stakes Testing?

Without an audience or a compelling need, the persuasive essay does not persuade anyone of anything. Does this mean you shouldn't teach the persuasive essay? Given that your students will be expected to produce them in high-stakes tests throughout their schooling, of course you should. Rubrics for evaluating high-stakes test essays reward sticking to this form (Hillocks 2002), and students who understand the real-world uses of persuasion easily learn how to convince an essay grader they understand the form. But don't make it the center of your writing program; it's one more genre serving a specific purpose. Teach it and move on.

Models for many persuasive genres are easily found, especially newspaper or magazine articles and editorials, advertisements, petitions, and brochures. Many others can be located on the Internet. Here are some hints for online searches:

- Speeches are collected on a variety of Internet sites, not just YouTube. An amazing site for adults and adolescents is www.ted.com/, which stands for "Technology, Education, Design" and gathers talks by innovative thinkers on a variety of topics (transcripts are also posted). See also the links to helpful sites for public speaking at www.surfnetkids.com/publicspeaking.htm.

- Niki McGuire used advertisements—which are omnipresent and rely heavily on visuals, graphic layout, movement, and music—as vehicles for teaching students about persuasive appeals and techniques. Good teaching resources include:

  - ReadWriteThink, sponsored by the National Council of Teachers of English and the International Reading Association, provides lessons for various grade levels on teaching about advertising: www.readwritethink.org/

  - The Center for Media Literacy offers a very good handbook for questioning all kinds of media texts: www.medialit.org/cml-framework.

  - Media Literacy has a page on advertising and consumerism in the media: www.medialiteracy.com/advertising_consumerism_media.htm

- Models for grant applications can also be found online, for example on the grant-writing websites listed below. Writing grant applications is an ever-more important skill in this age of shrinking state and municipal budgets.

Grant and Grant Writing Websites

- *Teacher Tap (sources for grants and advice on writing grants): www.eduscapes.com/tap/topic94.htm*

- *About.com's page for teachers on how to locate and apply for grants: http://712educators.about.com/od/grantwriting/Grant_Writing.htm*

- *The Northland Foundation of Duluth, Minnesota (a useful grant-writing checklist): www.northlandfdn.org/KidsPlus/GrantwritingChecklist.shtml*

- *The Grantwrangler Bulletin (current information about organizations and upcoming grants for students, parents, and schools): http://grantwrangler.com/*

- *Sheryl Abshire, chief technology officer for a Louisiana school district, has amassed this collection of Web pages for finding grants and learning how to write grants:.www.cpsb.org/scripts/abshire/grants.asp*

- *SchoolGrants.org was last updated in 2008 but provides directories of granting agencies and organizations and a wide variety of examples of successful grants: www.k12grants.org/*
- *Grantproposal.com, developed by Elizabeth Brunner (a grant writer and consultant), is oriented toward nonprofit organizations seeking larger grants but is quite comprehensive: www.grantproposal.com/*

These national sites do not replace becoming acquainted with funding sources in your district and community. Local sources tend to be somewhat less competitive and they're in business to help you. An example of the sorts of small, local grants available for classroom projects can be found at the Lansing, Michigan, Capital Region Community Foundation's Youth Action Committee website (http://crcfoundation.org/content/youth-action-committee).

Just about any kind of writing can be used to change minds and move people toward action. Toby's students wrote realistic fiction and poems to illustrate the consequences of particular choices. The students at Cavanaugh Elementary performed a play to promote recycling. Email messages can alert large numbers of people to a problem or promote an upcoming event. Web pages can educate, entertain, and convince. If you and your students keep your eyes open, you'll find models everywhere you go.

PRINCIPLE ③ Explicitly teach genre features.

What do I need to know about persuasive text characteristics?

The purpose of any persuasive text is to change people's minds or move them to action. Over time, human beings have developed many effective means of persuading. Because there are so many different persuasive genres (a television commercial, a speech, a Web page advocating action), no one persuasive text will have all characteristics listed on pages 149–150. However, you need to have them at your fingertips as you choose texts or activities and help students achieve their goals.

A helpful way to determine the characteristics necessary in any particular instance of persuasion is to evaluate the *type of question* in dispute. Is it a *question of fact* (convincing the audience that something is true or not true: that global warming is caused by human action); a *question of value* (convincing the audience that something is of value or not, is morally right or wrong: that it would be wrong to let global warming continue unchecked because of the impact on future generations); or a *question of policy* (convincing the audience that action should be taken: that we should all take steps to conserve energy in our homes in order to combat global warming)? A question of fact is most likely to require information on both sides of an issue, and a question of policy is most likely to state solutions to problems and steps for achieving them (Lucas 2008).

Common Characteristics of Persuasive Texts*

Content Characteristics

- *claim:* any argument makes a claim—a statement that is supported by data and evidence (Hillocks 2010) ("Caffeine is bad for you.")

- *evidence:* everything that supports the claim (e.g., reasons, anecdotes, examples, expert testimonials, facts, and/or statistics)

- *warrants:* how the evidence is linked to the claim (De La Paz 2005; Hillocks 2010; Toulmin 1958) (In general, if something interferes with your health functioning, we say it's bad for you.)

- *appeals:* tools used to get a particular audience on your side (*All* persuasion makes an appeal; which kind depends on audience and purpose.)

  - *appeals to the writer or speaker's credibility* (The kindergartners had credibility in talking about the attractions of kindergarten.)

  - *appeals to the audience's needs or desires* (Toby Kahn-Loftus' students appealed to their audience's desire to avoid harm and live a good life.)

  - *appeals to reason and evidence* (Jordan explained how caffeine injures the stomach lining.)

Special Characteristics Necessary for Arguing Questions of Policy (Lucas 2008)

- *clear definition and description of problems* ("Our schoolwide survey shows most students have access to alcohol, and most have tried it.")

- *essential background information* ("Alcohol is of particular danger to teen health because . . .")

- *clear explication of solution, with links to causes of the problem* ("Ten things you can do if you are tempted to try alcohol are . . .")

Structural Characteristics

- *compelling opening* (can include prose, graphics, or music)

- *explication of context* ("You preschoolers will be kindergartners next year—are you nervous?")

- *counterarguments or rebuttals:* acknowledgments of possible protests or doubts regarding the claim that might be expressed, usually presented in order to be refuted (Ferretti, MacArthur & Dowdy 2000) ("It is true that caffeine improves concentration and alertness.")

- *refutations or countered rebuttals:* reasons or explanations why the protest or doubt is inaccurate, insufficient, or inapplicable (De La Paz 2005; Ferretti et al. 2000) ("However, caffeine also wears off, causing you to crash and lose concentration.")

- ***qualifications or constraints:*** limits to the conditions under which the argument holds true (De La Paz 2005: Toulmin 1958) ("Caffeine can help you lose weight, so it can be good for some people's health.")
- ***conclusion:*** a final summary of the author's strongest evidence or a discussion of implications

Language Characteristics

- ***direct address*** (e.g., *you, your*)
- ***questions for the reader/listener*** ("Have you ever smelled the too-sweet, rotten odor coming from that factory?")
- ***periodic restatement of the claim***
- ***attempts to establish solidarity with the audience*** (e.g., *we, us, our*)
- ***attempts to establish distance from the opposition*** (e.g., *they, them, those*)
- ***transitions that signal opposition*** (e.g., *but, however, instead, on the contrary*)
- ***logical links*** (e.g., *because*)
- ***qualifiers*** (e.g., *often, usually, sometimes*)

Graphical Features

These are not always found, but can add to the power of the message.

- ***pictures or realistic photographs*** designed to evoke an emotional response
- ***devices such as diagrams, charts, maps, tables, and graphs*** that exemplify or support the author's reasoning

* *Any given persuasive text needn't have all of these characteristics.*

The Web page in Figure 6.3 illustrates the use of many of these genre features.

This advocacy website argues a question of policy: it attempts to move its readers to act. In order to do so, it has to establish a problem (orangutans are threatened), the cause of that problem (rainforest destruction for palm oil plantations), and a solution (see box below left). The claim: you can do something to save the orangutans. The evidence: the list of simple actions linked to reducing palm oil use.

Figure 6.3 Persuasive text features of website developed by Girl Scouts Madison Vorva and Rhiannon Tomtishen when they were 12.

This closeup of the orangutan's face and the invitation to "just look into their eyes" are meant to appeal to people's sympathies, and motivate them to take action.

This quotation is an appeal to our need to feel efficacious and powerful enough to take on invisible forces far away to help the sympathetic orangutan. The individual reader of the website is encouraged: "Yes, you can make a difference. Join us."

By including all of these facts about both orangutans and how rainforests are threatened by our use of palm oil, Madison and Rhiannon use the appeal of logos to make a case that action is necessary.

Only twelve years old themselves when they researched, wrote, and posted this website, Madison and Rhiannon understand that their readers need to be given goals that are achievable by young people with few resources themselves. This list is composed of easy steps that anyone can follow. It is also evidence for their claim that we can do something to save the orangutans.

Help students think about arguments, warrants, and appeals.

In order to convince an audience, a persuasive text has to make an argument in a way that will appeal to its audience. Students can be taught to look for and produce arguments and appeals at an age-appropriate level.

Arguments

All arguments make a claim and support that claim with evidence and reasoning. The claim can be implicit (e.g., soft drink commercials that say nothing about the qualities of the drink advertised but use images of happy, dancing, healthy young people that imply the drink is delicious and life enhancing) or explicit.

Amy Houts' *Let's Exercise!* (2008) is a simple argument (see Figure 6.4). It is clear what she wants young readers to do: exercise! The claim is stated right away ("It is good to exercise"). The evidence includes statements on health, some of which are also claims ("Exercise makes your heart beat faster. . . . Your heart will get stronger"). She also claims social benefits ("When you exercise, you can make friends"—two teammates pose with a soccer ball and their arms around each other). You may have noticed that these claims could be supported by evidence. The heart rate claim is supported by a chart next to it.

Even the most concise argument has a claim and evidence. For most student projects, the argument must be explicit, with the evidence clearly supporting the claim. In the earlier grades, this may mean stating clearly one or two reasons something should happen, with some background on the nature of the problem. In the later grades, this becomes more developed. For example, the letters to Samantha about caffeine included not only what they wanted Samantha to do (give up caffeine or reduce her intake) and some of the health effects but also, in some instances, lists of alternative beverages or references to the (few and insignificant) health benefits of caffeine.

Figure 6.4 Pages from *Let's Exercise!* by Amy Houts (2008a)

Warrants: Looking deeper into argument

The *warrant* is the link between a claim and its evidence. It is a general rule that the audience will recognize as valid and that can be supported by *backing*, or underlying ideas. In *Let's Exercise!*, the claim "When you exercise, you can make friends" is supported by a picture of two girls wearing the same soccer uniform. We generally agree that you are likely to make friends with your teammates, so we buy the claim, especially because it's qualified—you "can" make friends, not definitely *will* make friends. However, such a warrant is implicit, and most warrants are not explicitly stated. Warrants are hard for many adults to pick out, and difficult for even older students to state and use effectively—although George Hillocks (2011) has used an inquiry-driven approach to teach seventh graders to identify warrants. Even if you don't teach students to identify warrants, it helps to know as a teacher what warrants are so you can talk with students about the assumptions that underlie arguments they encounter or why certain claims may be stronger than others.

Yeh (1998) describes a tool called a *bridge* that he has used successfully with struggling middle school writers. A bridge can consist of substantiating facts, if-then propositions, or values that can link parts of an argument through exposing the underlying assumptions.

You should not drink coffee because it can contribute to bone density loss.

- *Substantiating fact:* Caffeine does interfere with the absorption of vitamin D.

- *If-then statement:* If your body does not absorb enough vitamin D, you can't absorb calcium and use it to keep your bones strong.

- *Value:* When something you don't really need causes you a specific health problem, it is foolish to continue consuming it.

Students using such heuristics in Yeh's study wrote better-developed arguments and used a more mature voice in writing than those who did not.

Appeals

All the teachers referenced in this chapter help students identify ways to appeal to their particular audience:

- Appeals to the speaker's credibility (*ethos*): What special knowledge, experience, or qualities of character makes this audience want to listen to or believe this person on this topic?

- Appeals to the audience's desires and needs (*pathos*): What do they want? To get rich? To feel smart? To appear important? To feel virtuous?

- Appeals to reasoning and evidence (*logos*): What facts are convincing? Does this match how the world works? Is the argument sound, full of holes, or circular?

These technical terms have been used since Aristotle coined them thousands of years ago. Which appeals are chosen depends on the writer or speaker's knowledge of who the audience might find credible, what the audience wants, and what the audience may or may not know. The three forms of appeal can be considered at any grade level without explicitly using the terms. For example, to promote the good time the preschoolers can have in their school's kindergarten, Hattie Dornbush's students use their own status as kindergartners (*ethos*), the preschoolers' desires to attain that status and to have fun (*pathos*), and all the fun things they get to do once they are big kindergartners (*logos*)—see What Genre with Purpose Looks Like, below).

PRINCIPLE ④ Explicitly teach genre-specific or genre-sensitive strategies.

Children of any age use persuasion—and they can learn to become more deliberate and strategic in their use of appeals. Even kindergartners can learn strategies to make a difference.

GENRE PROJECT

What Genre with Purpose Looks Like:
Kindergarten Testimonials

The preschoolers file into the kindergarten classroom and sit cross-legged on the rug around the author's chair. One by one, each kindergartner sits in the chair, reads a piece about what she or he likes best about kindergarten (often too quietly—an amplification system would be helpful!), and holds up a hand-drawn illustration. The preschoolers applaud. After everyone has taken a turn, one of her students asks Mrs. Dornbush, "What is your favorite thing about kindergarten?" She thinks for a few seconds and says, "I guess it would have to be that you all come in knowing just a little and you go out knowing everything! And I like our treasures and celebrations and that I have twenty-five best friends!"

Figure 6.5 The audience applauds Dai Shanay's reading

Designing compelling, communicatively meaningful environments: Address a real need in the community. Five-year-olds spend as much energy as anyone else trying to get what they want from others: parents, teachers, playmates. In the play areas, negotiation is continuous. But what academic genres are appropriate for them? Hattie Dornbush's class at El-Hajj Malik El-Shabazz Academy took on the job of promoting their kindergarten program to preschoolers. Many preschoolers are understandably nervous about the move to kindergarten (the "big kids" class), so these kindergartners were addressing a true need while also addressing their writing objectives: linking pictures and writing, sticking to a topic, and reading their work from the author's chair.

Explicitly teaching genre-sensitive strategies: Think and learn about the audience you want to convince. Hattie prompted her students to reflect on the progress they had made over the year. She seated them around her on the rug and read Natasha Wing and Julie Durrell's *The Night Before Kindergarten* (2011), the book she had shared with them on the first day of school. "Do you remember the night before you started kindergarten? How did you feel?" As they listed their apprehensions, she pointed out how much fun and "unscary" kindergarten had turned out to be.

Next, she engaged children in thinking about how this year's preschoolers might be feeling about kindergarten. She pointed out that they could help change this nervousness to anticipation: "You are almost in first grade, and the pre-Ks are almost in kindergarten. What is your favorite thing about kindergarten? Think of something fun that would make the pre-Ks feel excited about coming back here next year." Everyone came up with an example: playing on the swings at recess, calendar time, math (especially addition!), learning sight words. Hattie made sure everyone had a specific topic before sending them to their tables to write.

Offering ongoing coaching and feedback: Helping beginning writers. The writing the students produced looked like any day's writing: A picture took up the top third of the page, and an explanation followed on the lined section beneath the picture. But today they were trying to convince someone of something. They were sharing this with an invited audience, and they worked particularly hard, as their teacher, the classroom aide, and Samantha circulated and provided scaffolding. The writing reflected a range of abilities. Some children made ample use of the high-frequency words on the word wall and worked with their grown-up helpers on spelling out words they did not know. Others were only able to sound out the first letter of each word, so their sentence marched in individual letters along the page. Some practiced reading their writing out loud to prepare for the presentation.

Figure 6.6 Amaria writes: "We go to the calendar because I like calendar."

When writing persuasive text, students often have trouble reading an audience and taking different perspectives on an issue, aligning evidence with reasoning in an argument, and they often lack the background knowledge needed to decide what is true or false, significant or insignificant. The following are strategies to build arguments that your students can take up as they read, write, and discuss to make a difference in the world.

Explore audience considerations.

The appeals your students use, the evidence they choose to include, and the form of the genre they use to promote their cause all depend on their understanding of audience. The following steps can help students keep audience considerations front and center.

- *Define your target audience first.* Who are you attempting to convince? Is this a local, a regional, a national, or an international issue? Are you addressing it at a local level (raising money during lunch to help hurricane victims) or at a distance (petitioning your senator to support humanitarian relief for the victims)?

- *Gather information about your audience.* Toby Kahn-Loftus' students constructed and distributed written surveys about health issues in their community to fellow students, teachers, and adults in the community. These surveys not only provided background information on the local issue, but allowed them to gauge how much their audience knew about the target issue, their attitudes toward it, and their degree of experience with it. An added bonus: The graphs of responses in their research reports added to the impression of scientific objectivity to support their claims and anchored their investigations in community experience.

- *Consider the appeal of pathos.* What does your audience want? How do they feel about your issue? Generate ideas for using facts, visual images, and ways of representing your perspective that would appeal to this audience.

- *Consider the appeal of ethos.* You must position yourself as credible. What do you know, and how do you know it? You might list your accomplishments, skillfully marshal your evidence, or tell a compelling story from your experience. Who else might your audience listen to? Is your audience more likely to listen to a doctor or a celebrity on a health-related issue? Are they likely to be more impressed by government statistics or a compelling story?

- *Consider the means usually used to address this audience about this kind of issue.* What genres are likely to be effective? A graphic poster displayed where people congregate? A brochure available at the local grocery store? A magazine for teens? A presentation to an elected body? A letter to the editor? A blog posting?

Book Reviews: One of Our Favorite Genres

One of our favorite genres to involve in K–8 classrooms is the book review. Why? First, book reviews (not "book reports") are a real genre used outside of schools in publications ranging from the New York Times Review of Books to amazon.com to the Spaghetti Book Club (www.spaghettibookclub.org). Second, book reviews focus on one of our favorite topics—books! Third, book reviews engage students in two key things we want them to be able to do—to summarize a book (informational or descriptive writing) and to make an argument about the book (persuasive writing). Is this book worth reading? Does it compare favorably to other work by this same author? Does it convey information effectively (for informational text)? Does it convey experience effectively (for narrative text)? Through book reviews students can build arguments around these and other questions.

Book reviews shouldn't be written just to turn in to the teacher for a check mark or a grade. Students can post book reviews in the classroom, in school hallways, or on any number of websites. They can send them to their pen pals, to same-aged family and friends, or to publishing houses. They can swap reviews with a partner classroom within or beyond the school. You may find the reviews become like trading cards—students may vie for the review of the latest Clementine book or a book about shark attacks. This is a great way to generate greater interest in books.

Good models of book reviews can be found at http://worldreading.org/ and http://teacher.scholastic.com/activities/swyar/.

It is most challenging for younger students to learn to take different audience perspectives—it can be a significant challenge even for adults—but with your help, they can do it. Once Hattie Dornbush primed her kindergartners with reminiscences of what it was like to look forward to kindergarten, they were able to project their feelings—a little excited, a little scared—onto their audience. The fifth graders in Niki's class used a variety of tools to convince Samantha that their evidence was sound. They borrowed different ways of convincing her from persuasive articles Niki provided, including *explaining why* caffeine has the effect it does (Stefani: "Caffeine is not good for your body. It affects your central nervous system by closing blood vessels."), *using statistics* (Breana: "People who buy these drinks every day spend at least $1,095 a year! You could buy a laptop with that money!"), and *asking rhetorical questions* ("Did you know that . . . ?").

Craft an argument.

The appeal of logos also relies on reading your audience, in order to use what you know about the issue and about your audience to craft an argument. There are whole books about appealing to evidence and reasoning, but here are some things to consider teaching students to do:

- Be clear about your purpose. You want your town to keep your playground in good condition. Your want your lunchroom to serve more fruit and fewer sugary desserts. You want to convince others that it is never right to bully another student.

- Choose several strong reasons for your position. Strong reasons are those you have good evidence to support and that are likely to appeal to your audience.

- Make sure that your evidence supports your reason (that your reason is warranted). Sometimes you find an amazing story or devastating statistic not directly related to your point. Focus on the best reasons for your position and then on the most convincing evidence. (Organizers like the one in Figure 6.7 can be helpful.) George Hillocks (2010) models this very well in his description of teaching a class of seventh graders how to argue a murder case while making their warrants explicit. Using a drawing of a fictional crime scene and a short text, he has students take on the roles of detectives who have to make a watertight case to their chief inspector by clearly stating the rules that support their conclusions (or claims) about the evidence presented in the picture and the text.

Teach students to strengthen their arguments through information.

An important strategy students need to use in building and evaluating arguments is to bring considerable information to bear. Students need to develop their knowledge base when it is clear they don't know enough about the context of the problem, its cause, and how others view it to take an informed stance. For example, if a student encounters the widely held opinion that a heavy snowfall during the winter is evidence negating the theory of global warming, they need to build their knowledge about the relationship between local weather and climate to respond appropriately. Niki McGuire's students had to weigh caffeine's positive and negative effects on the body and decide whether the evidence warranted giving up caffeine. In that case, the whole class was working on the same issue, so they were able to share and discuss the same set of texts. However, if your students are working on different projects, then finding background information for different problems will be a time-consuming challenge. Teach students to enlist the help of librarians and other resources.

Solid information provides evidence for students' claims. Finding the right kind of evidence to support one's reasoning is key to making a convincing argument for change. The techniques suggested in Chapter 4 for evaluating sources of information are essential. Evidence is often found in a library or Internet search, but if students are arguing for change within their community, they also need to

Argument Organizer

Audience:
_____

Claim:
_____

Evidence to suport claim:
_____
_____
_____
_____
_____

Evidence to suport claim:
_____
_____
_____
_____
_____

Possible opposing claim and evidence against it:
_____
_____
_____
_____
_____

Strategies to make the argument more convincing to this audience:
_____
_____
_____
_____
_____
_____
_____

Figure 6.7 Argument organizer

use the strategy of gathering local evidence. The seventh graders Elizabeth Moje worked with interviewed local experts. Elizabeth and their teacher taught the interview genre, modeled how to conduct an interview by interviewing each other in front of the class, and taught students how to transcribe and write up the results of their interviews (Moje 1999).

Consider opposing points of view on your issue.

Read about and discuss differing perspectives, and think about what others have written and why.

Reading in Preparation for Writing: Comparing Points of View

Susan De La Paz (2005) had middle school students read, discuss, and take notes on readings from differing points of view in preparation to writing argumentative essays on historical events. Students who were taught this method for reading conflicting documents and a method for writing persuasive essays wrote longer and more persuasive essays than those in a control group. Her historical reasoning strategy for considering conflicting sources can be adapted for a range of projects.

1. Determine author or speaker.	Describe his or her argument.	• **What was his or her purpose?** • **Do the reasons make sense?** • **Do you find evidence of bias?** (Word choice? Only one view?)
2. Compare details.	Look for conflicting views.	• **Is an author inconsistent?** • **Are people or events described differently in different sources?** • **What is missing from an author's argument?** • **What can you infer from looking across sources?**
3. Make notes on each source.	Consider author/speaker and details from each source as you make notes.	• **What is the best way to organize and display your notes?** • **Cornell notes?** • **Graphic organizer?**

Adapted from De La Paz (2005)

Craft and deliver your message.

Your students have decided on an issue that is important enough to act on. They have carefully researched and considered their audience, decided on the genre most appropriate for reaching their audience, and developed the argument most likely to convince their audience. There are still a few things you need to teach them to do.

- Weigh your evidence. Information is often thought of as not specific to an audience. Facts are facts, right? But people do differ in the facts they attend to. For example, there are many reasons not to smoke. However, harming your unborn child is unlikely to persuade a senior citizen, even if it is a fact, and eventual lung cancer might not influence a teenager wanting to look cool, as it seems remote. For this reason, the American Cancer Society's "Smoking Is Very Glamorous" campaign focused on horrendous images of smoker's teeth, reddened eyes, etc., to convince students not to start smoking.

- Consider including a good story. Your argument may be more likely to resonate with your audience, and appeal to their values, their well-being, or their feelings if you include a compelling story related to your issue.

- Carefully consider language, visuals, and other composition and design elements. Some audiences will disregard anything other than Standard English; some adolescent audiences find dialect more credible. Images of disaster attract attention, but if they're too graphic, some will turn away. Humor can be engaging, but it can also cause some to take your opinion less seriously.

- Make arrangements for your message to be delivered. Broadcast it on the local radio station as a public service announcement; promptly mail it to the legislator or the newspaper; reserve the auditorium for a special assembly; deliver magazines, put up posters, hand out fliers.

The adult world takes note when students make a solid argument and skillfully use the proper register. This is a major way students can establish ethos. As a bonus, students feel very smart and capable. And that is a feeling they will want to have again.

PRINCIPLE ⑤ Offer ongoing coaching and feedback.

Sometimes an attempt to effect change can seem pretty overwhelming. The stakes might be high, either because students care deeply about the outcome or are aware they are addressing a possibly critical audience. Through coaching and feedback, you can help them find ways to organize their work, provide support during reading and writing, and use evaluation tools to focus their efforts.

You can provide coaching and feedback to the whole class, small groups, and individual students. In the ketchup example (page 143), the class worked on their letter to the lunch supervisor together. Niki McGuire provided model persuasive articles and guided her students through a series of questions as they prepared to write their own letters to her and Samantha. Students often have little exposure to persuasive texts and little experience in writing to convince someone, so providing lots of feedback and sharing your response to their texts as a reader is important.

Students can provide ongoing coaching and feedback to one another, as well. Toby Kahn-Loftus' students worked on their health issues in small groups. Each group chose its topic, designed a community survey together, distributed and analyzed the results, and divided up the writing among individuals and pairs. The seventh-graders Elizabeth Moje observed also researched their issues in groups. To research something well takes time and effort. Having several people looking for material, evaluating its merits, and discussing conclusions makes it less likely that important points will be missed. Much of the work of questioning a source, pointing a student to a likely interpretation, and clearing up misconceptions can be done by other students, leaving you free to provide support where a group's reach exceeds its immediate grasp.

When working individually, students can use guiding questions or heuristics to make sure they examine their work from a variety of angles. A *heuristic* is simply a device that helps students apply concepts and strategies they've learned to a new problem. It helps them focus but does not confine them within a rigid formula. One example is the planning graphic for argument that follows on pages 163–164. Graphics can help make concepts more visible to students new at working with them (Yeh 1998). This example (based on the caffeine project), is designed to help students keep track of the different elements we have talked about in this chapter. It can be adapted for different grades and project goals.

Effecting Change in the World Through Literacy

Students of all ages find the possibility of making a difference in the world a compelling reason to engage in challenging literate activity. Students of different ages and abilities have different approximations to an adult standard of persuasion, but all students can learn to work toward making the world a better place. If you make your classroom an environment in which students are used to bringing up and discussing what is going on in the world, if you listen carefully to their reasoning and help them understand their own and others' perspectives, and if you offer them chances to read and compose texts in an effort to influence a variety of audiences, your students will have greater knowledge of the world outside the classroom and of themselves as effective actors in it.

Revision Check: Are You Convincing Your Audience?

Name _____

Answer each of the questions below before redrafting your piece. Then return to your draft and make any changes or improvements you think of.

1. What is the main goal here? What do you want your audience to think or do?

2. Who is the audience?

3. What do you know about your audience that you have to pay attention to in order to be convincing?

4. What have you done in your project to take what you know about your audience into consideration?

5. What is the best argument you have for your case?

6. What is the best evidence you have?

7. Why is that good evidence for your argument (make the bridge)?

8. What do most people who don't agree with you think?

9. How do you answer their points? You don't want to get blindsided by an opposing argument.

10. What sort of language are you using to address your audience?

Okay, now go back to your piece.

Have you done everything you can to be convincing and credible?

Is this likely to convince this particular audience?

When you feel sure you can answer yes to these questions, then please type and print out a final copy.

If you find yourself comparing teaching to pulling teeth or declaring that you feel like pulling your hair out, then stop pulling. . . . Teaching, as does learning, needs to be joyful.

—SHARON TABERSKI (2001, 27)

Perhaps one of the best reasons to teach genre with purpose is that it is joyful. Students enjoy the challenge and reward of reading and writing for real purposes, and teachers take pleasure from watching and helping students succeed in real-world activities.

As explained in Chapter 1, genres often appear as systems or sets (Bazerman 2004; DeVitt 1991; Prior 2009). People rarely use isolated genres in everyday life but typically conduct activities within, or through, or with the mediation of systems or sets of genres. Consider a simple trip to the movies. You marshal a wide range of genres—a marquee, posters of current and coming attractions, perhaps a coupon, a ticket, maybe a credit card receipt, the refreshments menu, and so on.

All the projects featured in this book involve several genres, though most highlight one particular genre above others. We hope that eventually some of your projects will address a number of genres so substantially that they can't be associated with a single category. To be clear, we are not referring to using several genres within a single text, often called multigenre writing (e.g., Romano 2000; Youngs & Barone 2007), although there is value in doing so when combining genres best serves the particular purpose and audience (when a memoir by a cook includes recipes, for example, or a historical account incorporates letters and official documents). Rather, we are referring to using several genres within a larger project. The multigenre research paper includes different ways of showing the teacher what has been learned in a project, but in a genre-with-purpose project, students read and write a set of genres during the life of the project.

Here's an example:

GENRE PROJECT

What Genre with Purpose Looks Like:
The Boulder Book Project, Grades 6–8

Mary developed the Boulder Book Project in 1998 for her multi-aged middle school students in Boulder, Colorado. The six-week project had three goals:

1. to help students become more connected to the community and natural world in which they lived

2. to give students the opportunity to act as experts

3. to teach students research skills

The end product was a book that shared information and stories about places in the community (for more detail about the project, see Juzwik 1999).

The Boulder book project highlights important considerations when you are using a number of genres within a larger project.

Incorporate many genres that address the project's purpose

Close to Denver and home to a university, Boulder is a popular destination for visitors. Mary and her students wanted to create a tour guide for children and adolescents who visit their community. Within this broad purpose, Mary and her students learned about and worked with a wide range of genres: telephone books (to identify and set up interviews with experts about the places they were writing about), websites, newspaper articles, field notes, narratives, face-to-face interviews, published interviews, informational brochures, dramatic performances (Hannah went to see a play at the Boulder Dinner Theatre as part of her research), thank-you notes, and many others. Even the ultimate "product" of the project included different kinds of text. Although all the students wrote narratives about the places to include in the book, they innovated with different genres appropriate to their interests and interpretations of their places, such as historical fiction (e.g., Erik's story about going back in time to Chautauqua 100 years ago [Juzwik 1999]) and narrative nonfiction (e.g., a budding actress writing about the Boulder Dinner Theatre). Some students incorporated elements of informational text into their narratives (e.g., the piece about the local guitar shop, written by a guitarist). An airplane enthusiast extolling the virtues of the Boulder Airport wrote a piece that was more description than narration. The students also published their interviews with experts in the book—yet another genre. Mary encouraged this range of genres, especially hybrid texts that flexibly incorporated elements of two or more genres.

Develop student expertise about content whenever applicable

Whether one is writing nonfiction narrative or informational text, deep content knowledge is important. Outside school, one does not write a nonfiction narrative without knowing quite a lot about the events that unfolded; one does not write an informational text without considerable knowledge of the topic. Therefore, the projects in this book emphasize research.

Mary's students undertook many forms of research to build expertise. They conducted and transcribed audiotaped interviews with experts. They conducted archival research at the historical library branch in Boulder (many found themselves especially drawn to the historical photographs of places they were learning and writing about). They consulted websites as well as print-based sources. They observed and wrote field notes (like anthropologists). They collected or created photos and drawings of the place to illustrate their contributions.

Develop student expertise about text but teach students that text characteristics are more than a checklist Mary taught students about a number of text characteristics, such as elements of narrative (see Chapter 2, page 36) and elements of published interviews. However, she never treated these characteristics as a checklist each student should blindly follow in developing his or her writing. She repeatedly drew students' attention to their particular topics and purposes, asking which characteristics would help them achieve their goals. This is the great balance to strike in teaching genre with purpose. You cannot, on the one hand, get so wrapped up in the excitement of the project that you forget to teach textual details. You cannot, on the other hand, become so concerned with teaching content, structural, language, and navigational features that you lose sight of the larger purpose and context the texts are supposed to serve.

Encourage innovation One of the great frustrations, and fears, about genre instruction is that it all too often seems to stifle innovation. Teachers and students become overly focused on making texts typical of the genre and lose the voice, options, and innovations that could make the text more effective and engaging. Mary resisted this tendency. She provided model texts that were themselves innovative (e.g., an artful and educative tour guide she had picked up on a trip to Germany). She encouraged students to try out a range of writing techniques in their drafts. And she reminded students to use language to communicate their intended tone.

Value coaching and feedback Coaching and feedback may be last in our list of principles, but this is definitely a case of last but not least! As we point out in Chapter 1, highly effective teachers tend to engage in more coaching than less effective teachers. In the Boulder Book Project, as her students' expertise and enthusiasm grew, Mary increasingly coached on the sidelines (Juzwik 1999, p. 47). She offered individualized feedback on both research and writing tailored to the particular interests and genres students were working with (see pages 47–49).

Follow through When you teach genre with purpose, you set up a contract with your students. Make sure the project accomplishes the purposes and reaches the audience you have identified. Just one failure to follow through may cause students to become jaded and no longer embrace—or even trust—the purposes and audiences you (and subsequent teachers) establish for them.

Mary and her students never lost sight of their collective goal: making a guidebook for and about the community for youth visiting Boulder. The feedback Mary provided constantly invoked the larger goal to justify questions and comments. With Mary's help, the students continually evaluated whether their composing and revising decisions were orienting adolescent visitors to the local community. Whenever their decisions did not contribute to their goal, students made changes until Mary or the other students agreed that the texts were aligned with the purpose and audience. In the end, Mary and her students produced durable hardbound guidebooks describing their community in ways an adolescent visitor would most appreciate.

Purpose-driven activities like the Boulder Book Project can help teachers at all grade levels (we've seen projects that employ sets of genres used successfully with children as young as pre-K!) move past the artificial assignments so common in schools and still address—in fact, better address—external expectations for student learning. And we believe this experience will help reinvigorate, perhaps even bring a joyfulness, to your teaching. We invite you to send your best projects to proposals@heinemann.com, and include "Genre with Purpose" in the subject line. We are especially eager to hear about projects that meaningfully incorporate genre sets in K–8 classrooms. Your examples of what teaching genre with purpose looks like will inspire teachers like you, teachers who are willing to try something new because they want to nurture students to become literate, critical, innovative, and reflective adults.

Appendices

Sharing and Making Meaning of Experience (Narrative Genres)

Teacher(s) _____ Date _____

Project Title _____

Communicatively Meaningful Context (e.g., histories or places to study and share; captivating past experience(s) that would be instructive or entertaining for a particular audience; collective memories that a group of students would like to learn more about [e.g., 9/11]):

Genres This Context Gives Rise To (What do students need to know? What inquiries do students need to conduct to learn the details of the past? What genres might they encounter in pursuing such inquiries?):

(If one of the genres is narrative text)
Narrative Text Context Check:

For reading and listening:

- Do students want or need to learn about or vicariously experience the past?
- Does the written or oral narrative evoke relevant past experiences of others?

For writing and speaking:

- Is there an audience interested in learning about and/or vicariously experiencing others' past and present experiences?
- Do students have relevant experiences to share?

Objectives and Assessment (What do you want students to be able to do with each genre by the end of the project?):

Learning How and Teaching Others (Procedural Genres)

Teacher(s) _____ Date _____

Project Title _____

Communicatively Meaningful Context (e.g., need or problem; solution that involves learning how and/or teaching others how; use of text to achieve solution):

Genres This Context Gives Rise To:

(If one of the genres is procedural text)
Procedural Text Context Check:

For reading and listening:
- Do students want or need to know how to do something?
- Do students not already know how to do it?
- Could a written or oral procedural text help students learn how to do that thing?

For writing and speaking:
- Is there an audience that wants or needs to know how to do something (that they don't already know how to do)?
- Do students know (or can they learn) how to do that thing?
- Could a written or oral procedural text help the audience learn how to do that thing?

Objectives and Assessment (What do you want students to be able to do with each genre by the end of the project?):

Developing and Communicating Expertise
(Informational Genres)

Teacher(s) _____ Date _____

Project Title _____

Communicatively Meaningful Context (e.g., a situation that involves a want or need to develop expertise or share expertise with others):

Genres This Context Gives Rise To:

(If one of the genres is informational text)
Informational Text Context Check:

For reading and listening:

- Do students want or need information?
- Do students not already know that information?
- Does a written or oral informational text convey that information?

For writing and speaking:

- Is there an audience that wants or needs to know information?
- Do students have that information/expertise?
- Could a written or oral informational text help the audience get that information?

Objectives and Assessment (What do you want students to be able to do with each genre by the end of the project?):

Exploring Meaning Through Performance (Dramatic Genres)

Teacher(s) _____ Date _____

Project Title _____

Communicatively Meaningful Context (e.g., need or opportunity for people to gather and share through performance; use of text to enable gathering and sharing through performance):

Genres This Context Gives Rise To:

(If one of the genres is dramatic text)
Dramatic Text Context Check:

For reading and listening:
- Is there a conflict in the story that students will find compelling?
- Is there room for students to develop a multifaceted interpretation?
- Are there characters students can develop and empathize with?
- Are there opportunities for all students to practice and improve fluency?

For writing and speaking:
- Is there an audience that would find a play interesting or enlightening?
- Is the play within the powers of the acting troupe?
- Are there opportunities for everyone in the class to have an onstage or off-stage role?
- Are there other performers or readers to write for? If so, what grade/age level are these readers/performers?

Objectives and Assessment (What do you want students to be able to do with each genre by the end of the project?):

Effecting Change (Persuasive Genres)

Teacher(s) _____ Date _____

Project Title _____

Communicatively Meaningful Context (e.g., need or problem; solution that involves changing others' opinions or actions; use of text to achieve solution):

Genres This Context Gives Rise To (What do students need to know? How will they encounter different perspectives and arguments? What can they write or produce to influence the situation?):

(If one of the genres is persuasive text)
Persuasive Text Context Check:

For reading and listening:

- Does the text constitute a real-world attempt to persuade?
- Does the text add to the perspectives and knowledge students already possess about the problem?
- Are your students part of the audience for this text, or does this text address an audience your students are interested in addressing?

For writing and speaking:

- Is there an audience that wants or needs to be convinced of something? Can student writing reach this audience?
- Do students have enough background knowledge to address this issue?
- Do students have sound reasons and sufficient evidence to make a potentially convincing argument to their audience?

Objectives and Assessment (What do you want students to be able to do with each genre by the end of the project?):

Project Steps	Principle Addressed					Lesson Summary and Target Date(s)
Describe each step and check off the instructional principle(s) addressed.	Design Compelling, Communicatively Meaningful Environments	Provide Exposure and Experience	Provide Explicit Teaching of Text Features	Teach Genre-Specific or Genre-Sensitive Strategies	Provide Ongoing Coaching and Feedback	Briefly describe each lesson and when it will be presented.

This book is intended to get you started on what we hope is a long journey of exploration with your students. As you create your own projects to develop your students' proficiency in working with a variety of genres, you may find yourself wanting to dig deeper into certain aspects of teaching with genre or genre theory and research. We know that continuing professional reading provides us with new insights and helps us develop our ideas. We suggest that you go first to your favorite chapters, as each already includes many references to authors, studies, and teaching stories that have influenced our work. In addition, the following list provides a few carefully chosen pieces on genre theory and research that did not make it into the body of the book. Happy reading!

- Bawarshi, A. (2003). *Genre and the invention of the writer: Reconsidering the place of invention in composition.* Logan, UT: Utah State University Press.

- Bazerman, C. (1988). *Shaping written knowledge: The genre and activity of the experimental article in science.* Madison, WI: University of Wisconsin Press.

- Bhatia, V. K. (2004). *Worlds of written discourse: A genre-based view.* New York: Continuum.

- Biber, D. (1988). *Variation across speech and writing.* New York: Cambridge University Press.

- Coe, R., Lingard, L., & Teslenko, T. (Eds.). (2002). *The rhetoric and ideology of genre.* Cresskill, NJ: Hampton Press.

- Cope, B., & Kalantzis, M. (1993). *The powers of literacy: A genre approach to teaching writing.* Pittsburgh, PA: University of Pittsburgh Press.

- Crowhurst, M. (1991). Interrelationships between reading and writing persuasive discourse. *Research in the Teaching of English, 25*(3), 314–338.

- Donovan, C. A., & Smolkin, L. B. (2006). Children's understanding of genre and writing development. In C. A. MacArthur, S. Graham, & J. Fitzgerald (Eds.), *Handbook of writing research* (pp. 131–143). New York: Guilford.

- Hade, D. (1988). Children, stories, and narrative transformations. *Research in the Teaching of English, 22*(3), 310–322.

- Halliday, M. A. K., & Hasan, R. (1976). *Cohesion in English.* London: Longman.

- Hartley, J., & McWilliam, K. (Eds.) (2009). *Story circle: Digital storytelling around the world.* Malden, MA: Wiley-Blackwell.

- Rose, D. (2009). Writing as linguistic mastery: The development of genre-based literacy pedagogy. In R. Beard, J. Riley, D. Myhill, & M. Nystrand (Eds.) *Sage handbook of writing development* (pp. 151–166). Thousand Oaks, CA: Sage.

- Russell, D. R. (1997). Rethinking genre in school and society: An activity theory analysis. *Written Communication, 14*(4), 504–554.

- Swales, J. (1990). *Genre analysis.* New York: Cambridge University Press.

References

A Note from the Authors: No royalties are received for the sale of any educational products cited within.

Angelillo, J. (2005). *Writing to the prompt: When students don't have a choice.* Portsmouth, NH: Heinemann.

Apol, L. (2002). "What do we do if we don't do haiku?" Seven suggestions for writers and teachers. *The English Journal, 91,* 89–97.

Applebee, A. N. (1986). Problems in process approaches: Toward a reconceptualization of process instruction. In A. R. Petrosky & D. Bartholomae (Eds.), *The teaching of writing: 85th Yearbook of the National Society for the Study of Education* (pp. 95–113). Chicago: University of Chicago Press.

Arafeh, S., & Levin, D. (2003). The digital disconnect: The widening gap between Internet-savvy students and their schools. In C. Crawford et al. (Eds.), *Proceedings of Society for Information Technology and Teacher Education International Conference 2003* (pp. 1002–1007). Chesapeake, VA: AACE.

Asaro-Saddler, K., & Saddler, B. (2010). Planning instruction and self-regulation training: Effects on writers with autism spectrum disorders. *Exceptional Children, 77,* 107–124.

Atwell, N. (1998). *In the middle: Writing, reading, and learning with adolescents* (2nd ed.) Portsmouth, NH: Boynton/Cook.

Bakhtin, M. M. (1981). *The dialogic imagination: Four essays.* (M. Holquist, Ed.; C. Emerson & M. Holquist, Trans.). Austin: University of Texas Press.

Bakhtin, M. M. (1986). *Speech genres and other late essays.* (V. W. McGee, Trans.). Austin: University of Texas Press.

Baumann, J. F., & Bergeron, B. S. (1993). Story map instruction using children's literature: Effects on first graders' comprehension of central narrative elements. *Journal of Reading Behavior, 25,* 407–437.

Bazerman, C. (2004). Intertextuality: How texts rely on other texts. In C. Bazerman & P. Prior (Eds.), *What writing does and how it does it* (pp. 83–96). Mahwah, NJ: Lawrence Erlbaum.

Beck, I. L., & McKeown, M. G. (2006). *Improving comprehension with questioning the author: A fresh and expanded view of a powerful approach.* New York: Scholastic.

Beck, I. L., McKeown, M. G., Sandora, C., Kucan, L., & Worthy, J. (1996). Questioning the author: A yearlong classroom implementation to engage students with text. *Elementary School Journal, 96,* 385–414.

Berger, M. (1994). *Oil spill!* New York: HarperCollins.

Berger, M. (1995). *Germs make me sick!* New York: HarperCollins.

Berger, M., & Berger, G. (2004). *You're tall in the morning but shorter at night and other amazing facts about the human body.* New York: Scholastic.

Berkenkotter, C., & Huckin, T. N. (1995). *Genre knowledge in disciplinary communication: Cognition culture power.* Hillsdale, NJ: Lawrence Erlbaum.

Best, R. M., Floyd, R. G., & McNamara, D. S. (2004, April). *Understanding the fourth-grade slump: Comprehension difficulties as a function of reader aptitudes and text genre.* Paper presented at the 85th Annual Meeting of the American Educational Research Association, San Diego, CA.

Boiko, C. (n.d.) Punctuation proclamation. *Plays magazine: Scripts for young readers.* Retrieved August 28, 2001, from www.playsmagazine.com.

Castle, K. (2006). *My first ballet book.* London: Kingfisher.

Caswell, L. J., & Duke, N. K. (1998). Non-narrative as a catalyst for literacy development. *Language Arts, 75,* 108–117.

Certes, J. L. (2004). Cold plums and the old men in the water: Let children read and write great poetry. *The Reading Teacher, 58,* 266–271

Cervetti, G. N., Bravo, M. A., Hiebert, E. H., Pearson, P. D., & Jaynes, C. A. (2009). Text genre and science content: Ease of reading, comprehension, and reader preference. *Reading Psychology, 30,* 487–511.

Clarke, P. (2006). *Unicorns.* London: Usborne Publishing, Ltd.

Clement, D. (1997). *You're wonderful.* Columbus, OH: Rainbows Within Reach.

Clyne, M., & Griffiths, R. (2005). *Let's make music.* Parsippany, NJ: Pearson Education.

Coe, F., & Aaron, P. (Director). (1979). *The miracle worker* [Motion picture]. United States: Half-pint Productions.

Coe, F. (Producer), & Penn, A. (Director). (1962). *The miracle worker* [Motion picture]. United States: MGM.

Coiro, J. L. (2003). Rethinking comprehension strategies to better prepare students for critically evaluating content on the Internet. *The NERA Journal, 39,* 29–34.

Cole, M. (1996). *Cultural psychology: A once and future discipline.* Cambridge, MA: Harvard University Press.

Colesbury, R. F. (Producer) & Schlöndorff, V. (Director). (1985). *Death of a salesman* [Motion picture]. United States: H. M. Television Company.

Collins, J. L., Lee, J., Fox, J., & Madigan, T. (2011). *Bringing together reading and writing: An experimental study of writing intensive reading comprehension (WIRC) in low-performing urban elementary schools.* Manuscript submitted for publication.

Common Core State Standards Initiative (2010a). *Common Core State Standards for the English Language Arts & Literacy in History/Social Studies, Science, and Technical Subjects.* Retrieved August 28, 2011, from www.corestandards.org.

Common Core State Standards Initiative (2010b). *Mission statement.* Retrieved from www.corestandards.org/.

Cooper, H., Nye, B., Charlton, K., Lindsay, J., & Greathouse, S. (1996). The effects of summer vacation on achievement test scores: A narrative and meta-analytic review. *Review of Educational Research, 66,* 227–268.

Corden, R. (2007). Developing reading-writing connections: The impact of explicit instruction of literary devices on the quality of children's narrative writing. *Journal of Research in Childhood Education, 21,* 269–289.

Daiute, C. (2004). Creative uses of cultural genres. In C. Daiute & C. Lightfoot (Eds.), *Narrative analysis: Studying the development of individuals in society* (pp. 111–133). Thousand Oaks, CA: Sage Press.

Daiute, C. (2010). *Human development and political violence.* New York: Cambridge University Press.

Davies, N. (2009). *What's eating you? Parasites—the inside story.* Cambridge, MA: Candlewick Press.

Dean, D. (2008). *Genre theory: Teaching, writing, and being.* Urbana, IL: NCTE.

Deedy, C. A. (with Naiyomah, W. K.). (2009). *14 cows for America.* Illustrated by T. Gonzalez. Atlanta, GA: Peachtree Publishers.

De La Paz, S. (2005). Effects of historical reasoning instruction and writing strategy mastery in culturally and academically diverse middle school classrooms. *Journal of Educational Psychology, 97,* 139–156.

Delpit, L. (1995). *Other people's children: Cultural conflict in the classroom.* New York: The New Press.

DeVitt, A. (1991). Intertextuality in tax accounting: Generic, referential, and functional. In C. Bazerman & J. Paradis (Eds.), *Textual dynamics of the professions: Historical and contemporary studies of writing in professional communities* (pp. 336–357). Madison: University of Wisconsin Press.

Disney. W. (Producer), Geronimi, C., Jackson, W. & Luske, H. (Directors). (1950). *Cinderella* [Motion picture]. United States: Walt Disney Productions.

Donovan, C. A., & Smolkin, L. B. (2001). Genre and others factors influencing teachers' book selections for science instruction. *Reading Research Quarterly, 36,* 412–440.

Dressel, J. (1990). The effects of listening to and discussing different qualities of children's literature on the narrative writing of fifth graders. *Research in the Teaching of English, 24,* 397–414.

Dubrow, H. (1982). *Genre.* New York: Methuen.

Duke, N. K. (2000). 3.6 minutes per day: The scarcity of informational text in first grade. *Reading Research Quarterly, 35,* 202–224.

Duke, N. K. (2008, May). *The impact of a project-based approach to building informational literacy (PABIL) on first graders' informational reading and writing.* Poster session presented at the meeting of the International Reading Association, Atlanta, GA.

Duke, N. K., & Kays, J. (1998). "Can I say 'Once upon a time'?": Kindergarten children developing knowledge of information book language. *Early Childhood Research Quarterly, 13,* 295–318.

Duke, N. K., Pearson, P. D., Strachan, S. L., & Billman, A. K. (2011). Essential elements of fostering and teaching reading comprehension. In S. J. Samuels & A. E. Farstrup (Eds.), *What research has to say about reading instruction* (4th ed., pp. 51–93). Newark, DE: International Reading Association.

Duke, N. K., & Purcell-Gates, V. (2003). Genres at home and at school: Bridging the known to the new. *The Reading Teacher, 57,* 30–37.

Duke, N. K., Purcell-Gates, V., Hall, L. A., & Tower, C. (2006/2007). Authentic literacy activities for developing comprehension and writing. *The Reading Teacher, 60,* 344–355.

Duke, N. K., & Roberts, K. M. (2010). The genre-specific nature of reading comprehension. In D. Wyse, R. Andrews, & J. Hoffman (Eds.), *The Routledge international handbook of English, language and literacy teaching* (pp. 74–86). London: Routledge.

Eagleton, M. B., & Dobler, E. (2007). *Reading the Web: Strategies for Internet inquiry.* New York: Guilford Press.

Englert, C., Raphael, T., & Anderson, L. (1992). Socially mediated instruction: Improving students' knowledge and talk about writing. *Elementary School Journal, 92,* 411–449.

Epstein, S. E. (2010). Activists and writers: Student expression in a social action literacy project. *Language Arts, 87,* 363–372.

Ferretti, R. P., MacArthur, C. A., & Dowdy, N. S. (2000). The effects of an elaborated goal on the persuasive writing of students with learning disabilities and their normally achieving peers. *Journal of Educational Psychology, 92,* 694–702.

Fitzgerald, J., & Markham, L. R. (1987). Teaching children about revision in writing. *Cognition and Instruction, 4,* 3–24.

Fleischer, C., & Andrew-Vaughan, S. (2009). *Writing outside your comfort zone: Helping students navigate unfamiliar genres.* Portsmouth, NH: Heinemann.

Fleming, S. (2000). *Make a paper hat.* Cambridge, UK: Cambridge University Press.

Freedman, A., & Medway, P. (1994). Locating genre studies: Antecedents and prospects. In A. Freedman & P. Medway (Eds.), *Genre and the new rhetoric* (pp. 1–22). New York: Taylor & Francis.

Gajria, M., Jitendra, A. K., Sood, S., & Sacks, G. (2007). Improving comprehension of expository text in students with LD: A research synthesis. *Journal of Learning Disabilities, 40,* 210–255.

Gere, A. R., Christenbury, L., & Sassi, K. (2005). *Writing on demand: Best practices and strategies for success.* Portsmouth, NH: Heinemann.

Gersten, R., Fuchs, L. S., Williams, J. P., & Baker, S. (2001). Teaching reading comprehension strategies to students with learning disabilities: A review of research. *Review of Educational Research, 71,* 279–320.

Gibson, W. (1959). *The miracle worker.* New York: Samuel French.

Graham, S., & Harris, K. R. (2005). *Writing better: Effective strategies for teaching with learning difficulties.* Baltimore, MD: Paul H. Brookes.

Graham, S., Harris, K. R., & Mason, L. (2005). Improving the writing performance, knowledge, and self-efficacy of struggling young writers: The effects of self-regulated strategy development. *Contemporary Educational Psychology, 30,* 207–241.

Graham, S., & Perin, D. (2007). *Writing next: Effective strategies to improve writing of adolescents in middle and high schools—A report to Carnegie Corporation of New York.* Washington, DC: Alliance for Excellent Education.

Guthrie, J. T., Anderson, E., Alao, S., & Rinehart, J. (1999). Influences of Concept-Oriented Reading Instruction on strategy use and conceptual learning from text. *The Elementary School Journal, 99,* 344–366.

Guthrie, J. T., McRae, A., & Klauda, S. L. (2007). Contributions of Concept-Oriented Reading Instruction to knowledge about interventions for motivations in reading. *Educational Psychologist, 42,* 237–250.

Guthrie, J. T., Meter, P. V., Hancock, G. R., Solomon, A., Anderson, E., & McCann, A. (1998). Does Concept-Oriented Reading Instruction increase strategy use and conceptual learning from text? *Journal of Educational Psychology, 90,* 261–278.

Guthrie, J. T., Wigfield, A., & Perencevich, K. C. (Eds.). (2004a). *Motivating reading comprehension: Concept-Oriented Reading Instruction.* Mahwah, NJ: Lawrence Erlbaum.

Guthrie, J. T., Wigfield, A., & Perencevich, K. C. (2004b). Scaffolding for motivation and engagement in reading. In J. T. Guthrie, A. Wigfield, & K. C. Perecevich (Eds.), *Motivating reading comprehension: Concept-Oriented Reading Instruction* (pp. 55–86). Mahwah, NJ: Lawrence Erlbaum.

Guthrie, J. T., Wigfield, A., & VonSecker, C. (2000). Effects of integrated instruction on motivation and strategy use in reading. *Journal of Educational Psychology, 92,* 331–341.

Halliday, M. A. K., & Hasan, R. (1985). *Language, context and text: Aspects of language in social-semiotic perspective.* Geelong, VIC, Australia: Deakin University Press.

Hanks, W. F. (1996). *Language and communicative practices.* Boulder, CO: Westview Press.

Harris, K. R., Graham, S., & Mason, L. (2006). Improving the writing, knowledge, and motivation of struggling young writers: Effects of self-regulated strategy development with and without peer support. *American Educational Research Journal, 43,* 295–340.

Harste, J. C., Woodward, V. A., & Burke, C. L. (1984). *Language stories and literacy lessons.* Portsmouth, NH: Heinemann.

Hart-Davidson, W. (2009, November). An introduction to technical writing for middle grades and secondary ELA students. In C. Thralls (Chair), Technical communication and 21st century literacies: A roundtable for the secondary English education community. Roundtable conducted at the annual meeting of the National Council of Teachers of English, Philadelphia, PA.

Hasan, R. (1985). *Linguistics, language and verbal art.* Geelong VIC, Australia: Deakin University Press.

Heath, S. B. (1982). What no bedtime story means: Narrative skills at home and at school. *Language in Society, 11,* 49–76.

Heath, S. B. (1983). *Ways with words: Language, life, and work in communities and classrooms.* Cambridge, UK: Cambridge University Press.

Heath, S. B. (1998). Working through language. In S. Hoyle & C. T. Adger (Eds.), *Kids talk: Strategic language use in later childhood* (pp. 217–240). New York: Oxford University Press.

Heffernan, L., & Lewison, M. (2000). Making real-world issues our business: Critical literacy in a third-grade classroom. *Primary Voices K–6, 9*(2), 15–22.

Henry, L. A. (2007). *Exploring new literacies pedagogy and online reading comprehension among middle school students and teachers: Issues of social equity or social exclusion?* Unpublished doctoral dissertation, University of Connecticut, Storrs.

Hicks, D. (2001). *Reading lives: Working-class children and literacy learning.* New York: Teachers College Press.

Hillocks, G. (1986). *Research on written composition: New directions for teaching.* Urbana, IL: National Conference on Research in English and Educational Resources Information Center.

Hillocks, G. (1996). *Teaching writing as reflective practice.* New York: Teachers College Press.

Hillocks, G. (2006). *Narrative writing: Learning a new model for teaching.* Portsmouth, NH: Heinemann.

Hillocks, G., Jr. (2002). *The testing trap.* New York: Teachers College Press.

Hillocks, G., Jr. (2010). Teaching argument for critical thinking and writing: An introduction. *English Journal, 99*(6), 24–32.

Hillocks, G., Jr. (2011). *Teaching argument writing, grades 6–12: Supporting claims with relevant evidence and clear reasoning.* Portsmouth, NH: Heinemann.

Hodgkins, F. (2007). *How people learned to fly.* New York: HarperCollins.

Hollingsworth, P. M., & Reutzel, D. R. (1990). Prior knowledge, content-related attitude, reading comprehension: Testing Mathewson's affective model of reading. *The Journal of Educational Research, 83,* 194–199.

Holyoke, N. (2006). *A smart girl's guide to money: How to make it, save it, and spend it.* Middleton, WI: Pleasant Company Publications.

Houts, A. (2008a). *Let's exercise!* Parsippany, NJ: Celebration Press.

Houst, A. (2008b). *Pattern fun.* Parsippany, NJ: Celebration Press.

Jeong, J., Gaffney, J. S., & Choi, J-O. (2010). Availability and use of informational texts in second-, third-, and fourth-grade classrooms. *Research in the Teaching of English, 44,* 435–456.

Jester, J. (1997). Audience and revision: Middle schoolers "slam" poetry. *Voices from the Middle, 4*(1), 43–46.

Jetton, T. (1994). Information-driven versus story-driven: What children remember when they are read informational stories. *Reading Psychology: An International Quarterly, 15,* 10–130.

Jiménez, L., & Duke, N. K. (2011). *Interest matters: Fourth-graders reading multiple high- and low-interest texts.* Unpublished manuscript, Michigan State University.

Juzwik, M. (1999). A vision of the possible: How adolescents built a rhetoric about place. *Ohio Journal of the English Language Arts, 40*(1), 46–58.

Juzwik, M. M. (2004). The dialogization of genres in teaching narrative: Toward a theory of hybridity in the study of classroom discourse. *Across the disciplines: A journal of language, learning, and academic writing, 1.* Retrieved August 28, 2011, from http://wac.colostate.edu/atd.

Juzwik, M. M. (2009). *The rhetoric of teaching: Understanding the dynamics of Holocaust narratives in an English classroom.* Cresskill, NJ: Hampton.

Kamberelis, G. (1999). Genre development and learning: Children writing stories, science reports and poems. *Research in the Teaching of English, 33,* 403–460.

Keene, E. O. (2008). *To understand: New horizons in reading comprehension.* Portsmouth, NH: Heinemann.

Kinloch, V. (2009). Literacy, community, and youth acts of place-making. *English Education, 41,* 316–336.

Klingner, J. K., Vaughn, S., Arguelles, M. E., Hughes, M. T., & Leftwich, S. A. (2004). Collaborative strategic reading: "Real-world" lessons from classroom teachers. *Remedial and Special Education, 25,* 291–302.

Klingner, J. K., Vaughn, S., Dimino, J., Schumm, J. S., & Bryant, D. (2001). *From clunk to click: Collaborative strategic reading.* Longmont, CO: Sopris West.

Klingner, J. K., Vaughn, S., & Schumm, J. S. (1998). Collaborative strategic reading during social studies in heterogeneous fourth-grade classrooms. *The Elementary School Journal, 99,* 3–22.

Kucan, L., & Beck, I. L. (1997). Thinking aloud and reading comprehension research. *Review of Educational Research, 67,* 271–299.

Kuhn, K. (2011). *How to make a wind vane: A procedural text.* Washington, DC: National Geographic School Publishing.

Labov, W. (1972). The transformation of experience in narrative syntax. In *Language in the inner city* (pp. 354–396). Philadelphia: University of Pennsylvania Press.

Lamott, A. (1994). *Bird by bird.* New York: Pantheon.

Langer, J. A. (1995). *Envisioning literature: Literary understanding and literature instruction.* New York: Teachers College Press.

Langer, J. A. (2001). Beating the odds: Teaching middle and high school students to read and write well. *American Educational Research Journal, 38,* 837–880.

Lester, Julius. (1999). *From slave ship to freedom road.* New York: Puffin.

Lucas, S.E. (2008). *The art of public speaking* (10th ed.). Columbus, OH: McGraw-Hill.

Mahiri, J. (1998). *Shooting for excellence: African American and youth culture in new century schools.* New York: Teachers College Press and Urbana, IL: National Council of Teachers of English.

Marshall, J. (1989). *The three little pigs.* New York: Dial.

Martin, J. R., Christie, F., & Rothery, J. (1987). Social processes in education: A reply to Sawyer and Watson (and others). In I. Reid (Ed.), *The place of genre in learning: Current debates* (pp. 58–82). Geelong, VIC, Australia: Deakin University, Centre for Studies in Literary Education.

Martin, N. M., & Duke, N. K. (2011). Interventions to enhance informational text comprehension. In R. Allington & A. McGill-Franzen (Eds.), *Handbook of reading disabilities research* (pp. 345–361). London: Routledge.

Martinez, M., Roser, N. L., & Strecker, S. (1998/1999). "I never thought I could be a star": A readers theater ticket to fluency. *The Reading Teacher, 52,* 326–334.

McCaslin, N. (2000). *Creative drama in the classroom and beyond.* New York: Longman.

McCullough, D. (2006). *1776.* New York: Simon & Schuster.

McKeown, M. G., Beck, I. L., & Blake, R. K. (2009). Rethinking reading comprehension instruction: A comparison of instruction for strategies and content approaches. *Reading Research Quarterly, 44,* 218–253.

Meyer, B. J. F., & Rice, G. E. (1984). The structure of text. In P. D. Pearson (Ed.), *Handbook of reading research* (Vol. 1, pp. 319–352). New York: Longman.

Michael J. Perkins School. (2007). *Why do we celebrate evacuation day?* (3rd ed.). Boston: Author.

Miller, A. (1949). *Death of a salesman.* New York: Viking Press.

Miller, C. (1984). Genre as social action. *Quarterly Journal of Speech, 70,* 151–167.

Mitchell, K. (1995). A Juneau school district literacy "dig": Students explore the ways of reading and writing. *Bread Loaf Rural Teacher Network Magazine* (Spring/Summer), 30.

Moffett, J. (1987). *Teaching the universe of discourse.* New Portsmouth, NH: Boynton Cook. (Original work published 1968.)

Mohr, K. A. J. (2006). Children's choices for recreational reading: A three-part investigation of selection preferences, rationales, and processes. *Journal of Literacy Research, 38,* 81–104.

Moje, E. B. (1999). From expression to dialogue: A study of social action literacy projects in an urban school setting. *The Urban Review, 31,* 305–330.

Moll, L., Amanti, C., Neff, D., & Gonzalez, N. (2001). Funds of knowledge for teaching: Using a qualitative approach to connect homes and classrooms. *Theory into Practice, 31,* 132–141.

Morrow, L. M. (1985). Retelling stories: A strategy for improving young children's comprehension, concept of story structure, and oral language complexity. *The Elementary School Journal, 85,* 646–661.

National Assessment Governing Board. (2008). *Reading framework for the 2009 National Assessment of Educational Progress.* Retrieved August 28, 2011, from www.nagb.org/publications/frameworks/reading09.pdf.

National Institute of Child Health and Human Development. (2000). *Report of the National Reading Panel. Teaching children to read: An evidence-based assessment of the scientific research literature on reading and its implications for reading instruction* (NIH Publication No. 00-4769). Washington, DC: U.S. Government Printing Office. Retrieved August 28, 2011, from www.nationalreadingpanel.org/Publications/publications.htm.

Ness, M. (2009). Laughing through rereadings: Using joke books to build fluency. *The Reading Teacher, 62,* 691–694.

Pappas, C. C. (2006). The information book genre: Its role in integrated science literacy research and practice. *Reading Research Quarterly, 41,* 226–250.

Paré, A., & Smart, G. (1994). Observing genres in action: Towards a research methodology. In A. Freedman & P. Medway (Eds.), *Genre and the new rhetoric* (pp. 146–154). London: Taylor and Francis.

Park, Y. (2008). *Patterns in and predictors of elementary students' reading performance: Evidence from the data of the Progress in International Reading Literacy Study 2006.* (Unpublished doctoral dissertation). Michigan State University, East Lansing, MI.

Pearson, P. D., & Gallagher, M. C. (1983). The instruction of reading comprehension. *Contemporary Educational Psychology, 8*, 317–344.

Pellegrini, A. D., Perlmutter, J. C., Galda, L., & Brody, G. H. (1990). Joint reading between Black Head Start children and their mothers. *Child Development, 61*, 443–453.

Polacco, P. (1988). *The keeping quilt.* New York: Simon and Schuster.

Polanyi, L. (1985). *Telling the American story: A structural and cultural analysis of conversational storytelling.* Norwood, NJ: Ablex.

Poveda, D. (2003). Literature socialization in a kindergarten classroom. *Journal of Folklore Research, 40*, 233–272.

Pressley, M., & Afflerbach, P. (1995). *Verbal protocols of reading: The nature of constructively responsive reading.* Hillsdale, NJ: Lawrence Erlbaum.

Prior, P. (2009). From speech genres to mediated multimodal genre systems: Bakhtin, Voloshinov, and the question of writing. In C. Bazerman, A. Bonini, & D. Figueredo (Eds.) *Genre in a changing world* (pp. 17–34). Fort Collins, CO: WAC Clearinghouse and Parlour Press. Retrieved August 28, 2011, from http://wac.colostate.edu/books/genre.

Priore, F. V. (n.d.). Seasonal . . . whether. *Plays Magazine: Scripts for young readers.* Retrieved August 28, 2011, from www.playsmagazine.com.

Pritchard, R. (1990). The effects of cultural schemata on reading processing strategies. *Reading Research Quarterly, 25*, 273–295.

Purcell-Gates, V. (2011) *Real-life literacy instruction, K–3: A handbook for teachers.* Vancouver, BC: University of British Columbia. Retrieved August 4, 2011, from www.authenticliteracyinstruction.com/img/HandbookK3.pdf.

Purcell-Gates, V., Duke, N. K., & Martineau, J. A. (2007). Learning to read and write genre-specific text: Roles of authentic experience and explicit teaching. *Reading Research Quarterly, 42*, 8–45.

Rasinski, T. V. (2003). *The fluent reader: Oral reading strategies for building word recognition, fluency and comprehension.* New York: Scholastic.

Reid, M. E. (1996). *Let's find out about ice cream.* Photographs by J. Williams. New York: Scholastic.

Reutzel, D. R., Smith, J. A., & Fawson, P. C. (2005). An evaluation of two approaches for teaching reading comprehension strategies in the primary years using science information texts. *Early Childhood Research Quarterly, 20*, 276–305.

Riddle Buly, M., & Valencia, S. W. (2002). Below the bar: Profiles of students who fail state reading tests. *Educational Evaluation and Policy Analysis, 24*, 219–239.

Robb, L. (2004). *Nonfiction writing from the inside out: Writing lessons inspired by conversations with leading authors.* New York: Scholastic.

Roberts, K. L., Norman, R. R., Morsink, P. M., Duke, N. K., Martin, N. M. & Night, J. A. (2011). *Moving beyond "they're pictures" and "they're for looking at": Developing young children's comprehension of graphical devices in informational text.* Unpublished manuscript, Michigan State University.

Roberts, K., & Wibbens, E. (2010). Writing first: What research says about writing instruction in the primary grades. In G. Troia, R. Shankland, & A. Heintz (Eds.), *Writing research in classroom practice: Applications for teacher professional development* (pp. 179–205). New York: Guilford.

Romain, T. (1997). *How to do homework without throwing up*. Minneapolis, MN: Free Spirit Publishing.

Romano, T. (2000). *Blending genre, altering style: Writing multigenre papers*. Portsmouth, NH: Heinemann.

Routman, R. (2008). *Teaching essentials: Expecting the most and getting the best from every learner, K–8*. Portsmouth, NH: Heinemann.

Sawyer, R. J., Graham, S., & Harris, K. R. (1992). Direct teaching, strategy instruction, and strategy instruction with explicit self-regulation: Effects on the composition skills and self-efficacy of students with learning disabilities. *Journal of Educational Psychology, 84*, 340–352.

Schwartz, A. (1999). *How to catch an elephant*. New York: DK Publishing.

Shanahan, T., Callison, K., Carriere, C., Duke, N. K., Pearson, P. D., Schatschneider, C., & Torgesen, J. (2010). *Improving reading comprehension in kindergarten through 3rd grade: A practice guide* (NCEE 2010-4038). Washington, DC: National Center for Education Evaluation and Regional Assistance, Institute of Education Sciences, U.S. Department of Education. Retrieved August 28, 2011, from http://ies.ed.gov/ncee/wwc/publications/practiceguides.

Shange, N. (1997). *Whitewash*. New York: Walker & Company.

Shea, P. D. (1996). *The whispering cloth: A refugee's story*. Honesdale, PA: Boyds Mills Press.

Shoveller, H. (2005). *Ryan and Jimmy and the well in Africa that brought them together*. Toronto: Kids Can Press.

Smith, M. W., & Wilhelm, J. D. (2002). *"Reading don't fix no Chevys": Literacy in the lives of young men*. Portsmouth, NH: Heinemann.

Soria, M. & Trench, T. (Producers), & Tennant, A. (Director). (1998) *Ever After*. [Motion picture]. United States: Twentieth-Century Fox Film Corporation.

Spiegelman, A. (1996). *The complete MAUS: A survivor's tale*. New York: Pantheon.

Stone, J. (2005). Textual borderlands: Students' recontextualizations in writing children's books. *Language Arts, 83*(1), 42-51.

Stone, J. C. (2007). Popular websites in adolescents' outside-of-school lives: Critical lessons on literacy among others. In M. Knobel & C. Lankshear (Eds.), *A new literacies sampler*. London: Peter Lang.

Sturm, J. M., & Rankin-Erickson, J. L. (2002), Effects of hand-drawn and computer-generated concept mapping on the expository writing of middle school students with learning disabilities. *Learning Disabilities Research & Practice, 17*, 124–139.

Swenson, J. (2003). Transformative teacher networks, on-line professional development, and the Write for Your Life project. *English Education, 35*(4), 262–321.

Symons, S., MacLatchy-Gaudet, H., Stone, T. D., & Reynolds, P. (2001). Strategy instruction for elementary students searching informational text. *Scientific Studies of Reading, 5*, 1–33.

Taberski, S. (2000). *On solid ground: Strategies for teaching reading, K–3*. Portsmouth, NH: Heinemann.

Taberski, S. (2011). *Comprehension from the ground up: Simplified, sensible instruction for the K–3 reading workshop*. Portsmouth, NH: Heinemann.

Tatchell, J. (2005). *Dragons*. Illustrated by P. Scott. London: Usborne.

Taylor, B. M., Pearson, P. D., Clark, K., & Walpole, S. (2000). Effective schools and accomplished teachers: Lessons about primary grade reading instruction in low-income schools. *The Elementary School Journal, 101*, 121–165.

Taylor, S. P. (2008). *A quick guide to teaching persuasive writing, K–2*. [Part of the Workshop Help Desk Series. (Calkins, Ed.)]. Portsmouth, NH: Heinemann.

Toulmin, S.E. (1958). *The uses of argument*. Cambridge, UK: Cambridge University Press.

Wallace, R. M., Kupperman, J., Krajcik, J., & Soloway, E. (2000). Science on the Web: Students on-line in a sixth-grade classroom. *Journal of the Learning Sciences, 9*, 75–104.

Widener, S. (2008). *The world of soccer*. Parsippany, NJ: Celebration Press.

Wiesner, D. (2001). *The three little pigs*. New York: Clarion.

Wilder, T. (1938). *Our town*. New York: Samuel French.

Wilhelm, J., & Edmiston, B. (1998). *Imagining to learn: Inquiry, ethics, and integration through drama*. Portsmouth, NH: Heinemann.

Williams, J., Brown, L. G., Silverstein, A. K., & deCani, J. S. (1994). An instructional program in comprehension of narrative themes for adolescents with learning disabilities. *Learning Disabilities Quarterly, 17*, 205–221.

Williams, J. P., Hall, K. M., Lauer, K. D., & Lord, K. M. (2001). Helping elementary school children understand story themes. *Teaching Exceptional Children, 33*, 75–77.

Wing, N. (2001). *The night before kindergarten*. New York: Grosset & Dunlap.

Wolf, S. (2004). *Interpreting literature with children*. Mahwah, NJ: Lawrence Erlbaum.

Worthy, J. (2005). *Readers theater for building fluency*. New York: Scholastic.

Xu, H. (1999, April). *Continuities and discontinuities: Lessons from ESL children's school and home literacy experiences*. Paper presented at the annual meeting of the American Educational Research Association, Montreal, Canada.

Yeh, S. (1998). Empowering education: Teaching argumentative writing to cultural minority middle-school students. *Research in the Teaching of English, 33*, 49–83.

Youngs, S., & Barone, D. (2007). *Writing without boundaries: What's possible when students combine genres*. Portsmouth, NH: Heinemann.

Zhang, S., & Duke, N. K. (2011). The impact of instruction in the WWWDOT Framework on students' disposition and ability to evaluate websites as sources of information. *The Elementary School Journal, 112*, 132–154.

Zhang, S., & Duke, N. K. (in press). The WWWDOT approach to improving students' critical evaluation of websites. *The Reading Teacher*.

Index